WHAT WILL
IT TAKE
TO MAKE A
WOMAN
PRESIDENT?

WHAT WILL
IT TAKE
TO MAKE A
WOMAN
PRESIDENT?

Conversations About Women, Leadership and Power

MARIANNE SCHNALL

SEAL PRESS

What Will It Take to Make a Woman President?
Copyright © 2013 Marianne Schnall

Published by
Seal Press
A Member of the Perseus Books Group
1700 Fourth Street
Berkeley, California
www.sealpress.com

All quotes and material included in this book are from Marianne Schnall's exclusive interviews, most of which were conducted specifically for this book. Some individual quotes were excerpted from interviews that originally appeared in publications including CNN.com, Feminist.com, *The Huffington Post*, Omega Women's Leadership Center, and Women's Media Center; some also appeared in *Daring to Be Ourselves: Influential Women Share Insights on Courage, Happiness, and Finding Your Own Voice*. Portions of the Maya Angelou and Kirsten Gillibrand interviews also appeared at *The Huffington Post* and Feminist.com. Portions of the Marianne Williamson interview also appeared at *The Huffington Post*.

ISBN: 978-1-58005-496-6

Library of Congress Cataloging-in-Publication Data

Schnall, Marianne.
What will it take to make a woman president? / by Marianne Schnall.
p. cm.
1. Women—United States—Interviews. 2. Women political activists—United States. 3. Women presidential candidates—United States. 4. Politicians—United States—Attitudes. 5. Women—United States—Attitudes. I. Title.
HQ1161.S378 2013
305.4092—dc23
[B]
2013031218

Cover design by Faceout Studio, Kara Davison
Interior design by meganjonesdesign.com

Printed in the United States of America
Distributed by Publishers Group West

*To my incredible daughters, Jazmin and Lotus, and all
the other extraordinary girls and women around the world*

*May your sense of self-worth, abilities, dreams,
and opportunities be limitless*

CONTENTS

INTRODUCTION

THIS BOOK STARTED with a question. When Barack Obama was first elected, my family and I were talking about how wonderful it was to have our first African American president. My then-eight-year-old daughter, Lotus, looked at me through starry eyes and deadpanned this seemingly simple, obvious question: "Why haven't we ever had a woman president?" It was a really good question, one that, despite having spent two decades running the women's nonprofit website Feminist.com and writing about women's issues, I found difficult to answer. But it is these types of questions, often out of the mouths of babes, that can wake us up out of a trance. Many inequities have become such a seamless part of our history and culture that we may subliminally begin to accept them as "just how it is" and not question the "why" or explore the possibility that circumstances could be different.

It does seem a bit crazy when you think of it: When so many other nations have women presidents, why doesn't the United States? Margaret Thatcher was elected prime minister of Great Britain three times. Argentina, Iceland, the Philippines, Nicaragua, Ecuador, Finland, Ireland, Liberia, Chile, and South Korea have elected female heads of state. Yet the United States, presumably one of the most progressive countries in the world, lags dismally behind. We have finally elected an African American president; when will we celebrate that same milestone for women?

The closest we have come to having a woman president was Hillary Clinton's nearly successful primary campaign against Barack Obama in

2008. In Obama, she had a formidable opponent, one who also broke through important barriers. Though it was a tight, fascinating, and at times contentious race, Obama prevailed. As Hillary observed in her powerful concession speech, "Although we weren't able to shatter that highest, hardest glass ceiling this time, thanks to you, it's got about eighteen million cracks in it." She added, speaking to the emotional crowd gathered at Washington's National Building Museum, "And the light is shining through like never before, filling us all with the hope and the sure knowledge that the path will be a little easier next time. That has always been the path of progress in America."

Fast-forward a few years later to the 2011 primary season, when I was talking to an editor at CNN's In America division about writing a piece for them. I was about to cover the Women's Media Center awards, where I would be interviewing people like Gloria Steinem, Jane Fonda, Sheryl Sandberg, Arianna Huffington, and others, so I asked CNN if there were any questions in particular they wanted me to ask. They said they were interested in the attendees' impressions of why women have gained such little momentum in Washington just four years after having a near presidential contender, and what we can do to get more women into the pipeline of political leadership. Taking that one step further, I decided to add a question related to my daughter's query by asking, "What will it take to make a woman president?" That article wound up on the CNN home page and received hundreds of comments, both positive and negative. The popularity of the article made me realize how important and timely this topic really was, and that it was worth exploring even further.

So here it is: my journey to get answers to some of these questions through speaking to some of the most influential journalists, activists, politicians, and thought leaders of today. Why haven't we had a woman president? What will it take? And why is it important? While I use a woman president as a symbol, this book is also about the broader goal of encouraging women and girls as leaders and change agents in their lives, their communities, and the larger world. It also explores the many changing paradigms occurring in politics and in our culture, which the recent election seems to confirm. I hope to spotlight these positive shifts, as well as identify where the remaining obstacles and challenges are, in hopes that by looking at these themes from so many sides and perspectives, we can move closer to meaningful and effective solutions.

Certainly, we need to imagine not only a world where a woman can be president, but one in which women are equally represented in Congress and many other positions of leadership and influence in our society. While it was history-making to have elected twenty women to the Senate in 2012, 20 percent is still far from parity. Women are 50 percent of the population, yet they occupy just a fraction of that in elected office. The United States currently ranks seventy-seventh on an international list of women's participation in national government. And the numbers are not much better in the corporate world: a meager twenty-one of the Fortune 500 CEOs are women, and women hold about 14 percent of executive-officer positions and 16 percent of board seats. Women are in only about 5 percent of executive positions in the media. Across the board, women are rarely adequately represented at the tables where important decisions are being made.

Yet everywhere I look today, very promising campaigns and projects are emerging to help women attain positions of influence and leadership. A few years ago, I wrote an article about then–Secretary of State Hillary Clinton's Women in Public Service Project, whose ambitious goal is global, political, and civic leadership of at least 50 percent women by 2050. I also interviewed Senator Kirsten Gillibrand about her Off the Sidelines Project, which is "a nationwide call to action to get more women engaged . . . to enter political life and be heard on political issues." And Facebook COO Sheryl Sandberg's book, *Lean In,* has certainly helped to spark a nationwide conversation and movement and an important debate over the factors impacting women's leadership and advancement in the workplace.

When I first set out to create this book, I estimated that I might do twenty interviews. As it turns out, I more than doubled that number. And since these important topics of women, leadership, and power have come up frequently in so many of my past interviews with high profile figures, I decided to also include some of their insightful quotes on spreads interspersed throughout the book. Writing this book has indeed been a fascinating journey and adventure in and of itself, and has almost had a life of its own. I was so heartened and felt so supported by the many incredible people who not only granted me an interview for this book but also suggested others I should talk to, often giving me contact information or making introductions for me. From this response, I realized that this is a topic that is on everyone's mind right now, and, as many of the people I interviewed—from Donna Brazile to Pat Mitchell—seemed to indicate, "now is the time."

These are issues that I think benefit from a hashing-out of multiple perspectives: men's, women's, Republicans', Democrats', racial, and generational. I tried as best I could within the limited time, capacity, and access I had to include and reach out for that diversity, but, of course, I do recognize that this is but a small sampling of outlooks. My hope is that this book will be enlightening, educational, thought-provoking, and entertaining, as well as a call to action.

While it does not necessarily offer any easy, quick, or complete solutions to the complex, multifaceted questions of how we can help women move into more positions of influence and leadership, my hope is that it will help to identify some of the obstacles so that we can at least be aware of them—and be woken up, as my daughter's question did for me, to being proactive, rather than simply accepting the current state of affairs as "just how it is." It will take long, engaged, thoughtful conversation and effort, from both men and women, to move our systems and culture along.

I thank all of the remarkable people in this book for being a part of this literary roundtable and for the meaningful work they do on the many prongs of these issues. And, since I would still like to include so many viewpoints and ongoing resources, a portion of the proceeds of this book will go toward continuing the conversation and community around women's leadership at the eighteen-year-old women's website and nonprofit I run, Feminist.com. I hope you will join me in supporting this movement, and I hope by the time my daughter has her own children (if that is her choice!), we will live in a world where having a woman president seems not like an unachievable and daunting milestone, but instead like one that girls everywhere can aspire to and reach, if that is their destiny and calling.

MELISSA HARRIS-PERRY

"I am constantly telling the women in my classes that they should consider running for office, mostly because what we know is that when men are talented and when men are smart and when men show some leadership, it's hard for them to even get to college without someone, at some point, asking them, 'Hey, have you ever thought about running for office? Man, you would be a great president.' Even as little tiny boys, right? It turns out that we don't have those same kinds of standard messages for girls. So if a woman is very talented and can remember people's names and she shows a lot of interest in politics, we tend to say things like 'Good job' or 'Here's an A on your paper,' but we don't tend to say, 'Hey, have you ever thought about running for office?"

MELISSA V. HARRIS-PERRY is host of MSNBC's *Melissa Harris-Perry*. She is also professor of political science at Tulane University, where she is founding director of the Anna Julia Cooper Project on Gender, Race, and Politics in the South. She previously served on the faculties of the University of Chicago and Princeton University.

Harris-Perry is author of the well received new book, *Sister Citizen: Shame, Stereotypes, and Black Women in America*, which argues that persistent harmful stereotypes—invisible to many but painfully familiar to black women—profoundly shape black women's politics, contribute to policies that treat them unfairly, and make it difficult for black women to assert their rights in the political arena. Her first book, *Barbershops, Bibles, and BET: Everyday Talk and Black Political Thought,* won the 2005 W. E. B. Du Bois Book Award from the National Conference of Black Political Scientists and the 2005 Best Book Award from the Race and Ethnic Politics Section of the American Political Science Association.

Harris-Perry is a columnist for *The Nation* magazine, where she writes a monthly column also titled Sister Citizen. In addition to hosting her own show on MSNBC, she provides expert commentary on U.S. elections, racial issues, religious questions, and gender concerns for *Politics Nation with Reverend Al Sharpton, The Rachel Maddow Show, The Last Word with Lawrence O'Donnell,* and other MSNBC shows. She is a regular commentator on *Keeping it Real Radio* with Reverend Al Sharpton and for many print and radio sources in the U.S. and abroad.

MARIANNE SCHNALL: Why do you think we've not yet had a woman president, and what do you think it will take to make that happen?

MELISSA HARRIS-PERRY: I think we haven't had a woman president because we live in a country that systematically disenfranchised women for its first 100 and some years. I mean, we've had fewer than 100 years of women as full citizens in this country, and so I think that's obviously part of it. You can't expect women to be in leadership when they don't even have an opportunity to choose who their elected leaders are. And so part of it is not only couldn't women vote, but in many places couldn't run for office, couldn't hold office, couldn't have credit in their own names—any of the things that would make having public life possible for women. I mean, I guess there were states that still had coverture laws as late as the 1950s and 1960s, right? So even if you imagine that with the end of those coverture laws, with the opening of the ballot to women and with the opportunity for women to run for office, that then you would end up with a pipeline situation. Even if at that moment all barriers dropped away, and I don't think they did, but even if they did, then you would still have to begin the process of women entering into a field where they had previously been shut out. And then you would have to grow that pipeline until you got to the level of presidency.

I don't think it's a small thing that the first woman to get very near to her party's nomination for the U.S. presidency actually came through the private sphere. She first came to the public knowledge, national public knowledge, as the *wife* of the president. Of course she had her own political career and ultimately became senator and all of that, but the first way that we got to know the name of Hillary Clinton was through her husband. That strikes me as kind of indicative of precisely how narrow that pathway has been—that women are still in the situation of coming to office under the terms of patriarchy and a coverture in that way.

I think it is fundamentally a different question than what are we going to do about it, like how do we end up with a woman president? I'm back and forth on this. I still believe that the first woman president is highly likely to be a Republican, and because of that, I guess I'm a little less enthusiastic for the first woman president [*laughs*]. On the one hand I really do [believe] that we must break this, and even if we break it with a woman Republican, then there will be a part of me that celebrates that. But I do think we have to be careful . . . from the very beginning of the suffrage question in this country, there's been this assumption that women will bring something specific to the public sphere, as a result of their womanhood, and I don't think that's quite right. I'm not sure that we can say that there is a way that women govern, and, in fact, the women who are most likely to rise to the top of governing tend to govern an awful lot like men.

MS: You're not the first one to have said that, but I'm curious about your reasons. Why do you think the first woman president could possibly be a Republican?

MHP: Well, just because we elect three different kinds of people as president in this country. We elect vice presidents, governors, and senators. And right now the most recent person to almost to be vice president, who was a woman, was a Republican. The majority of women governors are Republicans, and although there are Democratic women senators, I look at them and I don't see—at least at this moment—I don't see kind of a clear contender. So as much as I know people talk about Hillary, the fact is that we don't really elect Secretaries of State as president; we mostly elect governors and vice presidents—every once in a while, a senator—and right now those pipelines are dominated by Republican women.

MS: I agree with you that there aren't magic qualities that women would automatically inject, but at the same time, why is it important that we have more women's voices—not necessarily just in the presidency, but represented more in Washington and in leadership positions generally?

MHP: I think there are basically two categories of reasons. One is descriptive representation and the other is substantive. So let's take the substantive off the table for a moment. Let's say that women don't govern any differently than men, that women will pass exactly the same kinds of laws and use the same basic procedures for governing and that really it would make no difference to elect a woman than to elect her husband or her brother—that they're just precisely the same. Nonetheless, there would still be a descriptive representation claim for having as close to 50 percent representation of women in legislature and in the executive positions—and that's because part of how we think about what constitutes a democracy is that all members, of all groups, or any member from a group, should have an equal opportunity for governing, based solely on merit and not on identity. So in order for democracy to be constituted as healthy and as fully democratic, with a little "d," it simply needs to be true that your barrier to entry is primarily about your qualification, and not about your identity. So let's just take it as the socially and politically relevant demographic groups—by race, by ethnic identity, by gender. Even if women are no different, you still need to have 50 percent women, or upwards of it, in order to be able to say that you have a completely fair democracy.

But then I think there *is* reason to think that there are some substantive differences in how women govern, both stylistically and in terms of the policy output. And again, that's just the empirical work of women in politics—scholars who show us that, in fact, when you have more women in a state legislature, for example, you're more likely to have real bipartisan bills passed, that women tend to introduce more legislation on issues of the environment and education than their male colleagues. So there do, in fact, seem to be substantive reasons for having women, but even if there weren't, the descriptive ones, I think, are pretty strong.

MS: You were talking about ideally achieving 50 percent. Sometimes we forget, even with all of the strides we made in this last election, that twenty senators is still really far from parity—and even when you look at the low numbers of female Fortune 500 CEOs or just in general the corporate world. Do you have a sense of what's going on there? Why we are lagging behind? There's been a lot of discussion right now that some of this may be self-imposed, that women aren't pursuing these positions, or do you think more that it's these other structural obstacles holding women back?

MHP: Most of these things don't have to be mutually exclusive—both that women may be making a choice more frequently not to pursue and that

that is because of the institutional barriers they face. It's one thing to run a marathon; it's another thing to run a marathon with one leg. There will be one-legged people who will run marathons and they're kind of extraordinary, but when you have that barrier to overcome, too, more people are going to opt out of that. So I suppose what I would say is that the first piece of evidence we have is simply the reality of the incumbency advantage, so because women were shut out for most of the history of the country, when women tended to run, they were running against incumbents. And incumbents tend to win. That's just kind of a political truism. The single best advantage you can have for office is already holding that office. Women tend to do as well as their male counterparts in open-seat races. So if you hold all things constant—so you have Man A, Woman B, and they have basically the same kind of résumé—in an open-seat race, women are just as likely to win as men are. But the fact is that we mostly aren't facing open-seat races. You mostly have to win these national races, especially in the House of Representatives, by beating somebody who's already there. It's really tough for challengers, and women are going to be more likely to be the challengers. So that's part of it.

The second thing is, clearly the expense of running for office deters all kinds of newcomers and all kinds of people who have fewer institutional resources, and women continue to be poor in this country, on average and in general, more than men are. They have less access to capital, less access to the opportunities to raise the highest levels of capital, and so because it is almost unthinkably expensive to run . . . even our recent School Board race here in New Orleans was upward of like $250,000 [laughs]. I was just like, Who has that kind of money to run for office? Who has that kind of money to be on the school board? Add to that, then, what it takes to run for much higher levels of office. So part of it is that money tends to discourage newcomers and newcomers are, again, going to be more likely to be women.

Then, of course, we have all the institutional barriers that start from early school on. I am constantly telling the women in my classes that they should consider running for office, mostly because what we know is that when men are talented and when men are smart and when men show some leadership, it's hard for them to even get to college without someone, at some point, asking them, "Hey, have you ever thought about running for office? Man, you would be a great president." Even as little tiny boys, right? "Oh man, you're good at this. I bet you'll be president someday." It turns out that we don't have those same kinds of standard messages for girls. So if a woman is very talented and can remember people's names and she shows a lot of interest in politics, we tend to say things like "Good job" or "Here's an A on your paper," but we don't tend to say, "Hey, have you ever thought about running for office?" Some of it is just the very basics of being recruited. And then I think at least one of the things that Jennifer Lawless and some other folks have shown in their research is that women are perhaps more discouraged by the ugliness of running than are their male counterparts, that just because of how we tend to socialize women to have a very strong desire to please people, they are less comfortable with the level of ugliness that occurs in modern campaigning.

MS: You wrote this really important book, *Sister Citizen,* and I'm hoping with my own book that it conveys two things: that it's not just about women, it's about having greater diversity in general, and also about the fact there are many ways to participate in our government, not just being president or an elected official, but also being an empowered citizen. How do you see what you wrote about in your book as connected to this conversation?

MHP: Yes, I appreciate your saying that, because we've been talking about elected office, we've been talking about a woman president, which requires running for office at various stages. That's an important point: I can't imagine what would happen for me to run for office, but I certainly see myself as engaged politically. And not just because of the show, but I write to my representative, my mother is one of those retired ladies who goes up to the State House and protests. So I always have and I hope always will be engaged in the political world. It's something that I've tried to pass on to my own daughter, as part of what you need to know in the world—in addition to math and science and English—is to know how your government works, know who represents you, and put pressure on them toward the ends and goals that you see as important.

You know, *Sister Citizen* is meant to be more analytic than prescriptive. It's not so much how to fix this, as it is to try to say: here is at least one story about how African American women end up constrained in the way that they engage the political world, and they're constrained by all these very old, very deep stereotypes, and it can create actual emotional and psychological residue that makes it hard to do the work of politics. And yes, I certainly am talking about African American women, but although I would never compare myself to Toni Morrison, I do take from Toni Morrison the lesson that when we tell a specific story, it's actually for the purpose of telling the universal. Right? We go narrow in order to illuminate something larger. So even though I'm talking about black women, it's with the goal of saying that when we enter into the political world, all of us, we don't just come in as our political selves, we bring our whole selves, all of our expectations about what a woman is supposed to be, what an African American is supposed to be, what an American is supposed to be—and those expectations that are racialized and gendered and classed can really impact the way that we engage politically.

MS: Now that we have also elected Barack Obama twice—and certainly in this last election there was, it seemed, a move toward greater diversity—do you feel hopeful? Do you see any new paradigms emerging? Are you optimistic?

MHP: I am, but I'm always optimistic. I was optimistic halfway through the George W. Bush presidency [*laughs*]. I'm just not a person who believes that we are in the worst time, that this is the decline of the American project, or that there was some better, nostalgic time in the fifties. No! Maybe for white folks there was some time that was better, but for black girls, nope, never a better time than this. However bad this is, it's always the very best time that there has ever been. And so I guess maybe it's not that I think that progress is inevitable or that it's easy or that we just kind of march forward without struggle, but I'm not nervous about the fact that it takes struggle to make progress. That does, in fact, seem right, and it seems like in many ways exactly what our founders expected. Democracy is supposed to be hard. Totalitarianism is easy; you don't have to be part of it.

MS: The media has such a big impact and that is a place where there has not been such great diversity either. There's a report from the Women's Media Center that actually said it is at crisis levels. One of the things that has made me optimistic is, for example, your having your own show, where you are basically getting to talk about all the things that you would want to talk about that aren't really being represented in many other places. Are you aware of the milestone of your show? And also, how do you feel about the role of diversity in media in general, because that is where people's political consciousness starts and their understanding of the issues and what needs to be done?

MHP: Yeah, I mean, I can't believe I have a TV show [*laughs*]. I am sure at some point that someone is going to come and take it away, because we do crazy things every week. I constantly am thinking to myself, *We just put that on television!* I was saying I wouldn't want to run for office; I also really would not want to have a prime-time show, for example, because part of the freedom that I have in my show is because we air in the middle of the day on the weekends, so we are not in a time when it is absolutely necessary to sell the most expensive commercials to the most important sponsors or whatever. For me, that's the freedom of being able to create the content that we want, even if it may have a smaller initial audience. But it can have a very engaged, small audience that is getting something useful from us. That's an easy trade-off for me. I definitely prefer the autonomy and the engagement over just the scope. I mean, I assume that, for example, Soledad O'Brien anchoring [*Starting Point*] at CNN just had broader scope than I ever have. And so even though Soledad is not really as ideological as I am, she's not pushing her own viewpoint as much—although I think she's really an incredibly good journalist because what she does seem really attached to is the truth, and trying to muckrake and all of that, but I saw that as critically important intervention in that kind of diversity question. Her being there in that space, where there are a lot of eyes. But when you have a lot of eyes, she can't necessarily do all the fun things and quirky things and transgressive things that we're able to do. I can have a uterus on set, or have a whole panel of transgender people, or have a spoken word artist at the end of my show, because I'm not on CNN at eight o'clock in the morning. And that just gives us more freedom.

But yeah, there is no doubt that there are moments on Sunday morning while I'm sitting on my set and I can look up and the whole newsroom has all of the different channels and everything that's on, and almost all of the other shows, *Face the Nation, Meet the Press,* all of them—we're the only set that doesn't have three or four white guys of advanced age all sitting around talking about politics. I think that matters. Again, no matter what the ideological perspective or the partisan viewpoint, it matters demographically. You have to have the descriptive representation of bodies in order to show that everybody is a citizen, that everybody gets a say in this process.

MS: I have two daughters, and I see that young girls are up against so many disempowering messages these days. What words of wisdom or what message would you most want to instill in girls and young women today?

MHP: I don't know; my kid is pretty funny. We actually just did an interview together for the July *Essence Magazine,* which is their body issue, and I did an interview with Parker about being an adolescent and going through puberty. I was expecting all of these horrible things and that she would say all this bad stuff about her body, but she was like, "I am great! I am beautiful! I am so sexy!" I was like, wow, this is fascinating. So I guess . . . I don't know; I hate advice. You know what, even though I hate advice, here's the one thing that I worry about: I worry that girls in particular, but just in general, that we're not willing to make mistakes. That we're very nervous about making a wrong move and we worry that if we make the wrong move, then the consequences will mean that you kind of never recover from them. And I guess what I try to instill in Parker, more than any other thing, is how okay it is—in fact, it's better than okay—to make mistakes, really big mistakes sometimes. One of our responsibilities as adults in a society is to make the world safe for young people to make mistakes, because that's how they learn. So I would want to say to young women, "Hey, run for office, even if you think you're going to lose. Take a hard class, even if you're going to get a C in it. Go ahead and follow love, even if it doesn't work out." Just a little bit of courage to make mistakes . . . because that strikes me as where all the good stuff happens.

WHAT ADVICE OR ENCOURAGEMENT WOULD YOU OFFER WOMEN WHO ARE CONSIDERING GETTING INVOLVED IN POLITICS?

Do it. Run. These campaigns, they are tough business, but they're not impossible. And the good, I swear, outweighs the bad. You meet the most amazing people on the campaign trail, you get support from people that you didn't even imagine. And when you get there, I know you watch television and it feels like they get nothing done, but the truth is you really do make so much difference for so many people, every day—whether you're in Congress, you're in the Senate, you're in the state House, you're in the City Council—every day you make a difference for somebody, and that's a pretty important piece of what our democracy is about. It's well worth it to take it on. . . . Democracy is not something you just sit on the sidelines of—you actually have to get involved, roll up your sleeves, and help out your sisters in doing this. And we can make this happen.

— STEPHANIE SCHRIOCK, PRESIDENT OF EMILY'S LIST

Focus on issues you care about, and know you can make a change. Don't listen to naysayers or victim-mongers.

— MARY MATALIN, REPUBLICAN POLITICAL CONSULTANT
AND TV/RADIO HOST

Voters don't like it either, so run and change it. Run and pass Campaign Finance Reform. You don't like raising the money? Voters don't like the way the money's being raised either. Run and change it. You don't like the personal attacks on your family? Say from the get-go, "No personal attacks. I will not tolerate anyone attacking my opponent personally. We're going to have a fight on the issues where there are big differences, but my family and his family are off-limits." Run and change it. You can't change it from the sidelines.

— CELINDA LAKE, POLLSTER AND DEMOCRATIC
POLITICAL STRATEGIST

I don't know that it would be all that different from what I say to people in general—that you are a possibly magnificent agent for change for everybody. My message really is that your work needs to be for everybody. . . . I think women should rise up, not just because our rights are being violated, but because when our rights are recognized and supported and upheld, everybody's are.

—JODY WILLIAMS, NOBEL PEACE LAUREATE

My mission in life is to promote and tell women in every way I can, "Be the woman you want to be." And that's it. That's my message.

—DIANE VON FURSTENBERG

Even though I think the political system is so corrupt and I believe in publicly financed elections and the media climate is terrible—all of these things—I still think there are women who totally have what it takes. And they need to do it, and we need them to do it. We need to support them in any way we can. So I don't think we can wait until the political system feels more comfortable to those of us who don't have a high tolerance for that kind of stuff, because we will just be waiting forever. We've got to just jump in. So those who have that capacity, I think we really need them to take the risk and jump in, and the rest of us need to get behind them like crazy and make sure they feel supported.

—COURTNEY E. MARTIN, AUTHOR, BLOGGER, AND SPEAKER

Even under the best of circumstances, politics is definitely a contact sport and you can get hurt in the process. But, to me, the reward of being able to implement policies that you know make life better for people outweighs the risks. And I think we need to teach young women to take risks, to understand that losing a race is not losing, really. It's just your next step on the way to winning. That's how men look at that.

—GLORIA FELDT, AUTHOR AND FORMER PRESIDENT OF
PLANNED PARENTHOOD

Share your voice. We live in a moment where communication is so, so important and so, so accessible. You have something to say and you should say it. We're all listening.

—DONNA KARAN

JENNIFER SIEBEL NEWSOM

"Having a daughter and a son, and another daughter on the way, I want so badly to shift this and create a healthier culture where we just raise the boys to be true to who they really are—these authentic, beautiful, emotional beings. But we as parents and as teachers and as educators in all forms . . . we're so stuck in what we've accepted as normal. This is what it is to be a man. This is what it is to be a woman. And it's increasingly then been pushed to extremes vis à vis media, which perpetuate it, and capitalism, which is all about sell, sell, sell. It's much easier, for them at least, to market that way. We're creating a very painful and lonely existence for both our men and our women."

JENNIFER SIEBEL NEWSOM is a filmmaker, speaker, actress, and advocate for women, girls, and their families. Newsom wrote, directed, and produced the 2011 award-winning documentary *Miss Representation,* which explores how the media's inaccurate portrayals of women contribute to the under-representation of women in positions of power and influence. Newsom is the founder and CEO of MissRepresentation.org, a call-to-action organization that provides women and girls the tools to realize their full potential. She is an executive producer of the Academy Award–nominated documentary *The Invisible War,* which exposes the rape epidemic in the U.S. military. Her next film series, *The Mask You Live In,* which explores "America's bifurcation of gender and the extremes of masculinity imposed on our boys and men," is currently in pre-production.

As an actress, Newsom has appeared in films and television shows including *In the Valley of Elah, Something's Gotta Give,* NBC's *Life,* and *Mad Men.* Newsom currently serves as a board member of PBS's Northern California affiliate KQED and a Global Advisory Board member of the Dove Self Esteem Project. Previously, she was a member of the Girl Scouts Healthy MEdia: Commission for Positive Images of Women and Girls and an honorary board member of the International Museum of Women. Newsom graduated with honors from both Stanford University and Stanford's Graduate School of Business. Newsom resides in the San Francisco Bay Area with her husband, California Lieutenant Governor Gavin Newsom, and their two young children. She is pregnant with their third.

MARIANNE SCHNALL: Why do you think we have not yet had a woman president?

JENNIFER SIEBEL NEWSOM: Before I directly address that, can I share one story with you that you might appreciate, that's kind of tragic? I'll start with the good: my daughter, Montana, is three and a half. A few months ago, when her teacher picked up a book on princesses to read to the class, my daughter went up to the teacher and said, "I'm sorry, but my mommy and I don't like princesses. I think we should read this book on puppies instead" [*laughs*]. So that's the good; that was sort of endearing and lovely. But then recently we were all lying around, just hanging out one day, and Gavin asked, "Montana, do you want to be president someday?" or something like that. And she looked at him and she said, "No, only boys can be president!"

MS: How old was she?

JSN: She's three and a half—this was literally two weeks ago. And she loves Obama. She sees him on television and she gets excited, so obviously that's all she knows, right? But it was so interesting that from seeing him she decides that only boys can be president. I just wanted to share that because it was really eye-opening. Here I am working so hard to transform this landscape . . . and yet, "Only boys can be presidents, Mommy." She was so sure of that! It was really interesting. It's scary. She was so ada-mant. I was like, whoa! [*laughs*] Where did this come from? How is this possible?

MS: That's why I think the work that you are doing is so important. It does start in girlhood with the images and stereotypes girls absorb. How is this connected to the conversation around empowering women's leadership? And what is the role of media in connection to the conversation of groom-ing women into leaders?

JSN: So, the media have been more damaging, to a certain extent, than good. They can be good, yet it feels like it's taking too long, in a sense, to recognize how critical it is that the media celebrate the diversity of women—what diverse women look like, what they sound like, how they behave, their occupations, their statuses, et cetera. So what we've seen, obviously, is this proliferation of hyper-sexualization and self-objectification that's encouraged by the media, celebrated by the media. And it's so overwhelming and so all-consuming. It takes videos like the recent Dove campaign piece; it takes that kind of stuff just to remind people of their true value, beyond youth or beauty or sexuality. But even then, the focus is still on beauty, right? And I think we're in a rut in our country; I feel like we're stuck. We give so much power to beauty and not enough to talent and brains and leadership when it comes to women. And that's been disappointing. Sure, we'll celebrate one woman in leadership—but then we're so quick to find flaws with her and want to pull her apart. And we're also quick to assume that if we have one woman at the top who's being celebrated in the media, that's all we need. So we're very narrow-minded in our perception of women. And there's that double standard that has been very harmful to many women, especially women seeking leadership, whether in the political or business arena, whereby they're expected to not only be intelligent and at the top of their game, but also to look like, to a certain extent, a Victoria's Secret model [*laughs*], which requires a lot of time, energy, plastic surgery, or whatever—Botox, all those sorts of injectables. And it's not natural—it's harmful, it's distracting, it's binding—and at the end of the day, then, it's so much harder to listen to their policy positions, because the media has made their appearance that much more important.

MS: I remember you documented in *Miss Representation* this negative depiction of strong women leaders—for example during Hillary's campaign or the coverage of Nancy Pelosi. Likewise, in Sheryl Sandberg's book she talks about this likability correlation, that the more successful women are, the less they are liked, whereas it's the reverse for men.

JSN: Right. There's a "bitch factor." And I hate to say this, but in some cases, the dumber and sexier and more under the radar they are, the more likable they are. But the more they put their ideas and thoughts and values out there, the media—I am going to be really extreme by using the word "witch hunt"—the media go after them and, in some sense, try to destroy them. I mean, for example, we like Hillary Clinton now because she's not threatening, but when she was aspiring toward leadership, she was threatening, and therefore it was as if it was our right, especially the media's right, to tear her apart. That's the other thing: I think part of the problem with having so few women and not having reached the tipping point for women in leadership in the public eye, is we're so quick to tear them down and hold them to these ridiculous standards. And no man is perfect; every man in leadership is flawed. Oh my God, I'm horrified by it. I'm horrified by many of our representatives. We are so tough on women. We are, period.

MS: One of the things that I'm hoping to also do with this book is to think about what the solutions are to so many of these problems, especially when it comes to media, because it's easy to just be a passive consumer. Where do you see the biggest entry points for change? Is it on the consumer? Is it on the media to get things to change?

JSN: I think it's conscious consumption across the board, so it's calling out sexism and bad behavior and demeaning and limiting behavior in the media vis à vis social media, and even on the ground activities and [petitions] and pledges and what have you. And all the work we're doing at Miss Representation, with other organizations like Ultraviolet, the Women's Media Center, you name it—I think that is critical and necessary. Similarly, men in leadership, the ones running these companies, have got to start taking responsibility. The women in leadership need to recognize that they bought into a masculine, patriarchal world by perpetuating these norms, and so both the men and women in leadership really have to stand up, be conscious, recognize the effect that their products or media are leaving on our society and how it's impacting culture in such unhealthy ways, and start shifting what they put out there into the world. I think that's us holding them accountable. It's a real transformation that's required that we're working on in our own next film series, *The Mask You Live In,* with our boys and men, in terms of raising men, authentic men of consciousness whose hearts aren't disconnected from their heads, who are the empathetic beings they were born to be, where empathy, care and collaboration aren't socialized out of them, where leaving the world a better place is a value that's given top priority. So all that, and I think it takes time, but I think it does start with conscious consumption. I think it also starts with recognizing our power as citizens, to stand up and speak out and really hold our representatives accountable, whether they are representatives in government or, to a certain extent, corporate representatives—really demanding more, expecting more and writing letters to those who are contributing to a culture that's so demeaning and disrespectful toward women. And just not being afraid. So many people are afraid to speak out; they're afraid to ruffle feathers. And we have to. We're in this together; there's no way around it. It's not okay to just go on living our lives and pretend like everything is okay and that we don't need background checks on automatic weapons and that it's okay that women make 77 cents on the man's dollar, African American women 63, Latina 57—that's not okay. So we've really got to start holding people more accountable.

MS: You mentioned men, and I do think that is the next frontier of this conversation—what you were saying about these destructive gender stereotypes perpetuated by the media aimed at boys and men. There are unhealthy paradigms of power and leadership that affect men, as well. That's partially why we can't view a woman doing it, because it's been such a hyper-masculine way of leading, but it's also—and *Miss Representation* did a great job of showing this—how these sexualized images of women affect men and boys, what they look at and what they notice when they see a woman, what they value.

JSN: Exactly. And that's become normalized for them, so women are objects for the male gaze. Women can be violated and that's okay, and we can laugh about it and those guys who raped a woman can get off and we'll come to their defense. I mean, it's so skewed. I was on *The Jeff Probst Show* yesterday, down in L.A., Jeff Probst from *Survivor*. He's raising a son and daughter, but in raising his son, *Miss Representation* totally opened up his eyes and now he sees the world in such a different way, which I love. I love hearing that, especially when men take the time to see the film. And he said, "It's my responsibility to raise my son to—obviously sexual urges, those are natural—but to respect women as he respects his sister and to see women as so much more than just an object, than just a thing, than just something for his own gain. And to really give them the dignity and respect that they deserve." And so to your point, we have to take into account now, more than ever, how this hyper-sexualized world, this normalized attitude toward women in our male population, so demeans and limits women and women's potential.

MS: There was a psychologist who talked about a study that there was a certain age at which both boys and girls say they want to be president, and then just a few years later, the girls stop saying that. Do you remember that stat?

JSN: At the age of seven, like 30 percent across the board, boys and girls want to be president. And then at the age of thirteen, the numbers completely skew. You have one girl for every nine guys that want to be president.

MS: So how do you explain that age drop off? What happens in those years, do you think?

JSN: At ages ten to twelve, girls learn patriarchy. They learn their place in the world. They learn that there isn't a seat for them at the table, that they aren't the natural born leaders. I mean, that's what they're taught. That's not truthful, but that's what our society has constructed, so to speak. Boys at four and five are learning patriarchy, they're learning hierarchy, the alpha male, the top dog. If you don't conform as a young boy, you're increasingly pushed out of that sort of club, so to speak. And they move along, and when boys are about ten to twelve, they start to devalue and dissassociate from the feminine more and more . . . that's oftentimes when they start to pull away from their mothers. Then you reach the later high school years . . . and by the way, so many boys are resisting and they're so unhappy in this period, but you don't see real depression in these boys as they enter their later high school years, because they recognize that in America—and it's not just in America, but our country is very unique in this regard—to become a man at the age of seventeen or eighteen is to be stoic, is to be independent, is to be empowered, is to be in control; to not preserve those relationships and those friendships that literally grounded them at their childhood years. And it's quite lonely because what we're learning, which is so beautiful to me, is that boys have this innate, natural empathy and a need for relationships. All their play is relationship based, so they need and crave and want their male friends. Unfortunately, through what they learn about being a man, they have to push those relationships away . . . because we feminize relationships, we feminize intimacy and care and love and empathy to a certain extent.

So you start to really see a period that's increasingly lonely and painful and isolating for young boys. And there obviously are the boys that resist it, and some resist it successfully, but oftentimes the ones that resist are made fun of and criticized and further subjected to ridicule and abuse. Having a daughter and a son and another daughter on the way, I want so badly to shift this and create a healthier culture where we just raise the boys to be true to who they really are—these authentic beautiful, emotional beings. But, gosh, we as parents and as teachers and as educators in all forms—coaches, after-school, grandparents, whatever—we're so stuck in what we've accepted as normal. This is what it is to be a man. This is what it is to be a woman. And it's increasingly then been pushed to extremes vis à vis media, which perpetuate it, and capitalism, which is all about sell, sell, sell. It's much easier, for them at least, to market that way. We're creating a very painful and lonely existence for both our men and our women.

MS: One of the things I keep hearing in my interviews about politics today is the role of money—everybody keeps bringing up how money is corrupting politics, but I also know *Miss Representation* addressed how money is also corrupting the media. Can you talk a little bit about the role that that plays?

JSN: We now have media conglomerates whose goal and mission is 100 percent the bottom line. It's all about eyeballs, and how do they attract eyeballs? They sexualize and they push extremes, whether they be violent extremes or verbal extremes, pitting people against each other—just any kind of tension, any kind of drama, any kind of opportunity to get people to pay attention. And it's horrific. It's a race to the bottom line. It's literally a race to the lowest common denominator of what it is to be an American. So in fact, with the news media, and the entertainment media . . . it's interesting, my husband was saying the other day, "The thing I love about MSNBC is that all of the hosts and personalities are really smart, they're just real intellectuals." He's like, "The thing I don't love is they're so smart that they're oftentimes really above the heads of your average American." And he wonders if they're losing the average American, just because they're almost too smart [*laughs*] and too thoughtful, as compared to—obviously I'm sounding partisan here—but compared to, like, Fox, who are all about fear mongering and also sexualizing their female news anchors and their guests. I was on [Fox News] and I had like an inch of pancake makeup and eyelashes and the whole thing, and I was just going, "Are you freaking kidding me? I look like a clown!" But that's what they push, that's how they think they're going to attract eyeballs and attract viewers and ultimately up their numbers. And by saying extreme things, by saying completely crazy things, but people buy into it—people who are afraid, people who are small minded—the more they see it, the more they view, the more they buy into that belief system, and then that closes them off to the reality in the rest of the world. We're not reporting the news anymore, right? It's entertainment.

MS: Part of this is about women feeling their own power and developing their own sense of being a leader or a change maker. For you, was that something that you had to purposely develop? You seem very comfortable speaking your mind. Where did that come from in you?

JSN: I was always the girl that raised my hand first in class and I was always the team captain pushing my teammates to help us win. So I was always, I don't know if the word "bossy" is correct, but I was always the, "Let's go, let's go, come on, come on,"—that girl. And I think I maybe just translated that to my role now in terms of trying to wake up people's consciousness and speak what I see as the truth in the hopes that they'll be able to see it through the lens that we've created. I was talking with Nicole Brown yesterday, and Nicole said to me, "Jennifer, I felt like when I watched *Miss Representation* that you were literally thinking my thoughts; you were in my head, because everything you said is everything I think about, all the time." And it was really cool. I thought, *That's awesome.* At the end of the day, I want *Miss Rep* to be not only a platform to enable other's voices to be heard, but to amplify—I really wanted to be a champion for and a voice for and an amplification of all the voices that are out there that are saying "enough." So I guess I do have conviction. I am fearless, although I do have thin skin. But I do feel like it's our responsibility and I feel like I've been given this opportunity through making this film and then being married to my husband and having this strong conviction to keep fighting the fight. As long as I'm allowed to and enabled to, I will.

In terms of further leadership, every once in a while—because I have such admiration for Senator Feinstein and Jackie Speier and Pelosi and Senator Kirsten Gillibrand—I think to myself, *Would I ever do that?* But right now I feel like I can have the most impact where I am, and I honestly admire them so much. I think I just want to be there with them, because I'm so annoyed with the pathetic, spineless leadership that we have across the country, that is not putting our country first and not putting our citizens first and our women and our kids and our immigrants and all the people that are elderly—that those in leadership in our country aren't thinking about our most vulnerable citizens. So there's a part of me that thinks that right now this is the most effective way: to keep making movies and producing content and getting out there and championing what so many people feel are the causes and the way forward that is necessary. And I love getting behind women who are fearless . . . and men who have consciousness. Let's not exclude them, because I guess my husband and I came together for a reason, and I'm so proud of him. I want more people to speak out the way he does and to use their positions and platforms to do good for the world. And so I'll continue to champion him, as I will continue to champion women, and other men who do that. We just need more of them.

MS: Coming back to the first question that I was going to ask—why do you think we've not had a woman president, and what do you think it will take to make it happen? Do you feel like we're ready for that?

JSN: Good question. So why have we not had a woman president? Because leadership has been masculinized. Interestingly with Hillary Clinton, I think to a certain extent she distanced herself from being a woman per some of her campaign leaders' instincts. I think it was a disservice, because all of a sudden women looked at her and they were like, "No, no, but wait, wait—you're one of us!" So there was that tension and conflict.

But are we ready? We are ready, and I think Hillary Clinton has to be our next president. And I'm obviously biased. I think it's going to get ugly when people start holding her to a real double-standard when it comes to the way she looks, because she's aging. We have a real ageism problem in our country at this time. But she's proved herself and I think there are enough women in our country—and men, for that matter—who would like to see her as president. She's smarter than any other potential candidates that I know of on the other side. She so deserves to be there. She's so capable. So at the end of the day I think she could be our next president.

MS: What advice or what message would you most want to give to young girls on valuing their voices and seeing themselves as leaders?

JSN: If you can see it, you can be it. But you don't even have to see it at this point. You are it. Your voice matters, most importantly. Every voice counts. Every voice matters and that voice needs to be heard. And by not using your voice, you're doing a disservice, not only to yourself, but to the community and to the world at large. So I actually like to approach it from, "It's your responsibility, girls. Get over your looks. Get over your insecurities. You have a responsibility to all of us. We need your help." I think girls and women are our heroes and they need to start seeing themselves as our heroes and to come help us out of the mess that we're in.

PAT MITCHELL

"What women don't know enough is that when women run, they win as often as men do. In spite of the obstacles . . . when they do decide, 'I'm going to do this because it's important,' they do win as often. What can we do about that? As consumers we can do one big thing: we can insist that the press cover a woman's campaign in the same way as a man. And when they don't . . . we can insist, 'I'm not reading that paper anymore, I'm not going to that website, I'm not going to listen to that newscast until you give that woman candidate the same kind of fair and accurate coverage.'"

P AT MITCHELL'S DIVERSE background in media includes work as a journalist and producer and executive. She has worked in front of the camera and behind, anchoring the news and reporting for broadcast networks, producing award winning documentaries as president of CNN Productions, becoming the first woman president and CEO of PBS, and currently is the president and CEO of the Paley Center for Media, whose mission is to convene media professionals and media consumers for programs that explore the role of media in society. Mitchell was the first woman to launch, produce, and host her own nationally syndicated program *Woman to Woman,* and continues to be active in breaking new ground for women across the media landscape, including a current series of initiatives and programs called Women@Paley, which includes producing

an annual TEDWomen conference in partnership with the TED organization. Her many awards include multiple Emmy Awards, five Peabodys,
and two Academy Award nominations. *The Huffington Post* named Pat
one of the Powerful Women over 50. She also recently was named one of
the 21 Leaders for the 21st Century and *Newsweek*'s 150 Women Who
Shake the World. The Women's Media Center has honored Mitchell with
the Pat Mitchell Lifetime Achievement Award, an award that will be given
annually in her name.

MARIANNE SCHNALL: Why do you think we have not had a woman
president?

PAT MITCHELL: Because we, as women, haven't decided that it's time to
have one and that we are going to make it happen. Truly, I don't know
where we can look outside ourselves. It is within our power to have elected
a woman president.

MS: You think so?

PM: Absolutely within our power! We have the numbers, and we have had
the numbers since we got the right to vote. And we have even more of them
now, so there's no question that if we decided, "This year we are going to
have a woman president," and we identified a candidate, got behind her,
and built her campaign and made it happen and went to the polls and
voted, there would be one! I just don't look any further than ourselves to
answer that question. I mean, look, there are all kinds of cultural reasons,
we know all of those, but Barack Obama didn't stop and look at it statisti-
cally or . . . he didn't look at this historical legacy. He just said, "I'm going

to be the one." So you need a candidate who's willing to say, "I'm going to be the one. I'm going to break this barrier." And then you need the women of this country to decide that it's time, and do it.

MS: Do you think now is the time?

PM: I thought now is the time a long time ago! [*laughs*] I do think we haven't had the right mix of candidate, will, and timing. But timing is the least of those in my opinion. Of those three factors, you have to take into consideration the most important two are the candidate, obviously, and then women uniting behind a woman candidate. We have the candidate with Hillary, but we didn't unite, if you remember.

MS: Do you think men are ready to have a woman president?

PM: Marianne, I think men have been ready longer than women have been ready in a funny way. There are enough men who have seen or experienced the leadership of women to believe that it is absolutely within our province and that women can do it just as well, if not better, than men. There's enough evidence now. I don't think we're proving the case to men. I think we're just getting behind it ourselves in a united way.

MS: Now, in terms of the last election, we had these record numbers of twenty women in the Senate, but that's far from parity. Considering everything you are saying, how do you explain that? Why do you think that we're still so underrepresented?

PM: Well, there are many explanations, and some people have the data more readily at hand than I do, but part of it is that we just don't run as often. There simply aren't as many women running, choosing to do this, and we know all the reasons why. It's a really hard thing to do and it's not a very attractive thing to do in this country, because of the way the press treats women candidates, number one. Number two, what it does to a woman's family, and number three, the sacrifices that are required for a woman to choose a life in public service. But what I am loving now about this new number of women, particularly in the Senate, where there is enough that you can observe it in a new way . . . I mean, seeing that front page *New York Times* story that said that twenty women in the Senate *are* making a difference, and then to give case-by-case examples of women crossing the aisle, women collaborating, women cooperating, women initiating, and therefore making things happen. So that twenty women out of one hundred starts to be less of a daunting figure if the case you're making is that women, whether they are Democrat or Republican, will unite their actions on the issues that matter to women. So . . . my hope is that we're going to come out of this Senate, out of this congressional period, with some new evidence that, yes, in fact, women can and do create a different kind of legislative activity, a different kind of effectiveness, as a congressional body. And I'm hoping that those twenty women in the Senate, they have the real opportunity to be more than trailblazers of just being there. It's nice that they're there, but it won't make any difference to the legacy and the history of women in this country unless they do something *differently* because they're there. And I do believe, if what they had done when they started out is any indication, then I think we're on our path to that number doubling. Because really what voters want, anywhere, above all, is effectiveness.

MS: One of the things we're saying is that women may not run enough, which is an observation I keep running into—there are a lot of studies that say that. And on the heels of Sheryl Sandberg's book, do you think that in addition to the structural obstacles that there may be, that it is true that women tend not to naturally want to pursue leadership positions, because of psychological obstacles?

PM: No, I don't think it's a natural inclination for women not to want to lead or to go for leadership positions. I know very few women who will say, "I'm not naturally inclined to want to be a leader." Some women might say, "I don't want to be CEO. I don't want that kind of job, that's not where my values are," I totally get that. But certainly the women I know, you show them that they can make a difference, and generally they'll step up to that in some way or the other. But not all of us are going to be the ones who need to run. Some of us are going to be the ones who need to run the campaigns and run the media and make sure that there's a fair and open pathway to success. But what women don't know enough is that when women run, they win as often as men do. In spite of the obstacles—the structural obstacles that you referred to, and they are there—when they do decide, "I'm going to do this because it's important," they do win as often. What can we do about that? As consumers we can do one big thing: we can insist that the press cover a woman's campaign in the same way as a man. And when they don't, and we know they don't—because there's a new report out that's just appalling, the difference in the way in which the campaigns are reported—we can insist, "I'm not reading that paper anymore, I'm not going to that website, I'm not going to listen to that newscast until you give that woman candidate the same kind of fair and accurate coverage." So that's one thing we can do. The second thing is to vote.

MS: It is very true, though, that it's a brutal thing to run these days, and you also brought up how the media can cover a woman candidate. When I interviewed Sheryl Sandberg, she talked about this whole likability correlation—that the more successful a woman leader is, the less she is liked. On the one side, you can't be perceived as too soft or too emotional, but if you come across as too strong, too tough, too confident or powerful, you get criticized as well. What do you think about that conundrum?

PM: Well, that is a conundrum, and I think at the core of that conundrum is that we haven't worked out yet the very basic relationship between men and women and how men—really at a deep, deep emotional level—feel about strong and powerful women. I think you have to start with men, because they are really conflicted about this. There's something about strong and powerful women that many men still find fearful. And it probably goes back to their mothers [*laughs*], so we've got some cultural things to unwind and unpack, there's no question, and one of them really is that. The second thing on this likability factor—as media consumers with more power than we've ever had because we are actually controlling what we consume as media, in a different way—if we start to just push the bar, "lean in" as it were, and start to demand a more fair representation of, "Okay, is she bossy or is she just doing her job just like the guy standing next to her is doing?" I mean, poor Nancy Pelosi. When she led that healthcare reform . . . Now, why am I saying 'poor Nancy Pelosi'? She's hardly one to be pitied. She's one of the strongest, most powerful, and most effective women leaders that I've ever had the experience of observing, and yet when she did exactly what she was voted into office to do, got legislation passed, she was attacked from every possible point of view. And generally, if you read through it, they were attacking her on a likability issue: She's this. She's that. She's ballsy. She's too tough. She's too . . . all these "too" things that, as you say, if they had been applied to a man, would have been all compliments. But what I like about Leader Pelosi is that she just didn't let any of that deter her. She understood that was part of the trade-off. Now I would love to find a day when she doesn't have to accept it as part of a trade-off, because enough of us who were reading that and seeing that and hearing that are objecting to it. That the reporters who are reporting it that way would stop and think, *Oh, wait a minute. Right now, is that really what I think?* and examine the basis on which they are reporting that observation. I don't think it happens voluntarily, though. I don't think it happens immediately, but I do think it happens through a kind of process, and we have a role in that process. We can't just say it's up to the editors, especially not now when we are making the decisions really on an individual basis, what we are consuming.

MS: Now, you have the distinction of being a lot of firsts. You were the first female president of PBS and you've had a lot of high-level positions like that, where you've been a pioneer in so many ways. What is your perspective on being a first, and also being a female leader in an industry where there hasn't already been a female at the top?

PM: I don't believe I ever walked into an office or a job and thought, *Hmm, now how am I going to do this as a woman? What about this am I going to get to do differently, as a woman?* I don't remember having that conscious thought on a daily basis, but I had it as a subconscious thought . . . because the one thing you do know if you're the first, in particular, is that you're modeling something. Whatever you do or don't do, it is the way women lead in that particular moment, so there would be times when I would think to myself, *Well, they're going to look at me and go, "Well, of course . . . she's doing that because she's a woman."* I decided a long, long time ago when I was one of the first women in television, that while in the beginning I went along with that—avoiding at all costs anything that brought attention to the fact that I was a woman—very quickly I learned that didn't feel good to me, and also I thought it was really letting myself down. The other way to go on that was to just make a point: "No, this is what I want to do, as a woman." So as a woman leader, you can't make every decision from that point of view, but my experience is as a mother, as a grandmother, a wife, a sister, a daughter, all those things. I tried to keep them in mind, because I know they're a part of me, so if I'm not bringing them to the table as the CEO or the executive producer or the host or whatever it may be, then I'm denying part of who I am and that means I'm not going to be as good as I could be. I've been challenged on it, though, at PBS, in particular. I was challenged by the board after my first five or six hires were all women. I was challenged by a board member who said, "Looks to me like you're running an affirmative-action program for women," and I remember thinking, *Oh, my gosh, is he right? Have I been?* Fortunately I was able to say back, "I think I'm running an affirmative-action program for the very best candidates, but I'll keep that in mind," because you don't want to ignore it completely. But here's the thing that I did differently. It was probably the first time that a CEO of PBS had ever said to a search executive, "Don't bring me any list unless there are women and minorities on that list." That's the difference. In fact, the search executive said to me, "Are you serious?" And I said, "I'm dead serious. I don't care what the job is, I want to interview the very best women and minorities you can find." So if you start there, then it's quite likely that you're going to end up with more hires that are women and minorities.

MS: I think about how they always put women on these "most powerful lists"—I know you've been on more than a few of those. What does being powerful mean to you, and how do you think—not just for women, for men, too—this whole power paradigm needs to change?

PM: Well, everything about it needs to change, because it's been defined by one gender. I mean, one gender throughout most of our history has had power, so there's little wonder that when we think of power, we think about it in one-gender terms. So we need to change that, and we can only change that by changing the people who have power. So we know that, number one. A new power paradigm emerges when a different gender holds it, has it, and then uses it differently. I mean, if women get power only to be just like the guys who had it before them, then that's not progress. I'm not for women getting power just so they can prove they can be as whatever—whatever the adjectives may be that follow. And then the second thing is to really think about power from the point of view of community and what we're building. We know that no one in history—not many anyway, I guess the Pope just did—but very few people ever give up power voluntarily. So why is that? And yet women give it away all the time because it is a way in which women approach power: sharing it. Well, of course that's a great way to look at power, but how do we get that to be the power paradigm, as it were, the prevailing power? By getting power and using it that way, using it in a way that shares it, that redefines it, that gives it other adjectives, other than the ones we attach to it now. There's little wonder that young women, particularly in the generation who came up right behind the pioneers—I guess that would be me and Gloria and all the rest—that generation did move away from power because they didn't like the way it looked. And still today, the reason forty-something percent of the women in corporate America are jumping off and taking the exit ramp before they get to CEO jobs is they look up there and they don't like the way that looks. They don't want that kind of power. But why don't we stay on the road up, taking a few sisters along the way, so that when we get up there we can change it? And it does take numbers. You can't do it one at a time. One woman at a time is just not enough to change the power paradigm. It takes more.

MS: Speaking of numbers, even in other industries, for example the media, I think the statistic is that women hold only 3 percent of clout positions in the media industry, and the numbers that you hear from organizations like the Women's Media Center are shockingly low in terms of overall representation of women in all forms of media. How do you also explain the disparity of women in the media and is that something that you think is important?

PM: I wish I could explain why it is that the overwhelming numbers of consumers of media are women [*laughs*] and the underwhelming numbers of people who are leading and making and creating media are not. The explanation again is that we haven't done enough for each other, those who are inside media. And then I think there is the very real cultural fact that there are just not that many women who are kind of sticking it out to make it to the top positions. Part of it may be that we haven't built the networks. And then the other part may be simply that we need to make some conscious noise [*laughs*], protest. I look at the Women's Media Center numbers—those seem to be reasons to be in the streets! Reasons to be saying to the networks, "Unacceptable, guys, unacceptable," especially since they'll be the first to tell you that 60 percent of the consumers that matter to them are women, so it's unacceptable. Because really it does have to do with the two things we've heard a lot about recently—since Women's Media Center and Miss Representation and others took on these issues—that representation matters. It matters, the images that we see of women and girls on television and on the Internet. So we can't be passive again. When are we going to start to take the power that we have as consumers of media and demand that it be different?

And then the underrepresentation is just as significant a problem. If women were in charge or making the decisions about prime-time shows, were the primary writers and producers of most or at least half of the programs . . . would it look different? I think it would.

MS: I think of all the programs that you make about women, for women—starting with your pioneering series *Woman to Woman,* and now with

She's Making Media, She's Making News—it seems like this is something that you've been consciously doing your whole life.

PM: Yeah, because that was the decision I made early on, that I talked about before. They said, "Don't do women's stories; stay as far away from it as you can." And when I looked around, that was the big missing thing. There were no women's stories. And every meeting we would have about programming, every single meeting would start with, "We've got to do programming that appeals to women." Well? So where are the women's programs? So that was my interest, that was what I cared about, and so I've always fought for it. But many times throughout my career, if you look at the decisions I had to make, many times I had to leave the networks to do that kind of programming. I didn't win a lot of the battles inside. And it does take battles. So an easier route is not to fight that way—the path of least resistance is not the one I took.

MS: There are so many problems right now, not just here, but globally, with everything from global warming to violence against women. What I'm hoping to present in the book is larger than just looking at the case for women's leadership, which I think sometimes gets misinterpreted like it's a competition or just about equality. Why *is* it important that women are in greater positions of leadership and influence in the world? What is the bigger picture?

PM: The bigger picture is that all those problems you mentioned, and all the ones we haven't mentioned, are just too complex to expect men to figure it out all by themselves. That's less than half of the population. Why would we go into *anything* as complicated and difficult as those issues you just named—climate change, violence against women—without the whole world engaged in solving the problem? So it's just a very practical thing.

We need every good mind we can possibly engage and every good leader we can possibly engage. It's like looking at half a room and saying, "Okay, we don't need you guys on the problem over here, we can do it without these minds." We can't! We can't. And the fact is that at their very best, at their fullest realization, women bring a different perspective to each and every conversation because we have a different set of experiences. That doesn't mean we can't respond exactly as the guy sitting next to us does. I'm not saying we'd have different solutions, but I am saying that sitting at the table trying to solve problems together, we're going to have a set of experiences that is much fuller and, therefore, is going to help us find a more reliable and effective and long-term solution.

DONNA BRAZILE

"I found that when I was coming up through the political ranks, it wasn't enough to be the only woman, or sometimes the only minority, in the room; I wanted to make sure that I was not the last. So while I sat at the table, I often told my colleagues, 'Look, if there's no room at the table, we'll just bring in folding chairs. We'll make space for women.'"

VETERAN DEMOCRATIC POLITICAL strategist Donna Brazile is an adjunct professor at Georgetown University, a syndicated newspaper columnist, a columnist for *Ms. Magazine* and *O, The Oprah Magazine,* an on-air contributor to CNN and ABC, where she regularly appears on ABC's *This Week,* and the author of the best-selling memoir *Cooking with Grease: Stirring the Pots in American Politics.* Brazile has worked on every presidential campaign from 1976 through 2000, when she became the first African American to manage a presidential campaign. She is currently on the board of the National Democratic Institute, the Congressional Black Caucus Foundation, and the Joint Center for Political and Economic Studies.

MARIANNE SCHNALL: It seems like talking about a woman president is a timely topic. Why do you think that is?

DONNA BRAZILE: This is the right time to talk about it if we're going to think about 2016 or even 2020; it always projected in my mind that it would take us till 2020. Then again, I never thought we would elect our first black president before 2020. So we've made some adjustments already, as a country. The country is ready; the electoral ground is fertile. Now it really takes a candidate, and this is a very strategic moment for women who've been thinking about this moment for the last fifty years. We thought about it in 1972 when Chisholm made her run. We thought about it when Pat Schroeder initially tossed her hat in the ring and when Elizabeth Dole tossed her hat in the ring, and of course we thought about it with the selection of Geraldine Ferraro in 1984. And then, of course, we had Hillary Clinton and Sarah Palin in 2008. So we've had moments before, but we've never had the right political ingredients to really stir up the electorate to make it happen, and we finally have them.

One of the things that will matter to this is the marketing and the strategic placement of [the next female] candidate. Back in 2008, the Clinton campaign really downplayed women's issues. They thought—I'm sure, just like Obama, downplaying race—that the first "viable female candidate" should not be a woman's candidate. We didn't really get a good, strong message out of Hillary until, honestly, I believe, until June, when she gave her concession speech. She was a tough candidate. The failure was in marketing her and making sure that she understood that you couldn't just run a primary-focus campaign; you have to do a constituent-based campaign, in which you have to focus on caucuses as well. . . . I do believe that having that early team of strategists and marketers [is important] because we live in a totally different universe than the one [that existed] when I got involved in my first presidential campaign. Back then, you still had people's names on three-by-five index cards. Nowadays, they're in your computer, with analytics driving so much of what we do in politics—knowing what people think, their preferences, what magazines they read, and what that could possibly tell us about voters . . . not just at the federal level, but also at the state and local levels, precinct levels. There's so much data out there, and the first female president will have a geek side to her. Because that's how you can tap into the richness of the new voter experience, the rising American electorate, so to speak. That's ultimately going to change American politics. This is why you saw the Republicans put out their ninety-seven-page autopsy report.

MS: Why do you think we have not, as yet, had a woman president?

DB: Because the country was not ready. The country wasn't ready in 1972 when Shirley Chisholm went out for her candidacy. The country wasn't ready in 1988 when Pat Schroeder announced her candidacy. The country wasn't ready in 2000 with Elizabeth Dole. And the country *was* ready, but Hillary Clinton fell a few votes short of securing the Democratic nomination. The country now is eager to see a woman run and compete successfully for the White House.

MS: What will it take to make it happen? Do you feel now is the time?

DB: The political environment has drastically changed. Demographic changes are under way in the country, combined with the fact that the face of leadership is no longer masculine. There are feminine traits that are now accepted, like cooperation, for example. So I do believe the country is ready, and I also believe that the political environment would support a woman seeking the highest office. Of course, it would be helpful if we had a female as a defense secretary, but even in that area—military readiness, commander in chief—women have taken steps to demonstrate that we can handle those types of issues as well.

MS: Anita Hill said something interesting to me: she wondered whether the first woman who becomes president is going to have to prove her toughness by maybe even being more likely to go to war because of the fact that there's something to prove being the first woman. Do you think there are going to be certain expectations that may not allow the first woman president to be her authentic self, that she may have to still conform to what we expect from that office?

DB: If you look around the world at other female heads of state, I don't think their voters put too much stock in their so-called military experience, but they did take a look at their role in society, their role as leaders in society, and that was a big factor. Perhaps if you look at Merkel in Germany, or even Dilma Rousseff, the current president of Brazil, when you look at models of leadership and what it took to advance women in those societies, many of them did not have the so-called military experience, but what they did have was some type of executive experience, by experiencing government that was transferrable to a new job as head of state.

MS: The fact that we do have President Obama, who now has been elected twice, do you think that makes it easier, just in terms of opening up diversity in general? Looking at this last election, do you see any hopeful shifts or paradigms emerging?

DB: When the country elected its first biracial president, we broke the mold in terms of the face of leadership. . . . I think the country is more open to looking at other types of leaders and more diversity in our leadership. We're having conversations today in 2013 that we didn't have in 2008 when we did have President Obama, as well as then–Senator Hillary Clinton. Also, if you look at media coverage in 2008, misogyny in the media was at an all-time high, but in 2012 it was a little bit tempered, perhaps because more women were out there talking as pundits and political analysts and news analysts. But the face of leadership has changed over the last four years, and it will continue to change in the coming years.

MS: With Hillary's candidacy, it was a very interesting time to see how she was covered by the media, because it was telling to watch the often-sexist coverage of her. What do you think we learned that was useful from her campaign? What emerged out of that that struck you?

DB: Well, although she hit that artificial glass ceiling, she made it possible for future candidates, including her, to put together the kind of national organization that can compete, head to head, with any man running in a race. So I think that's number one. That's never been done before. The sheer number of primaries and caucuses she won, the fact that she was able to compete, and practically, in my judgment, win all of the presidential debates (maybe with one exception). She clearly has the qualities and traits that people most admire in their national leaders—she's compelling, she's smart, she's decisive. There's a reason why for, I think, the seventeenth time [she's been given the title of] the "most admired woman" in this country, because people see her as a model of leadership, and that is a very important step in ultimately running for national office.

MS: You mentioned that women are now one-fifth of Congress, which is an important milestone and is history making, but it's nowhere near parity. Why is that?

DB: You know, right after women gained the vote in 1920, there were articles out like, "Why has it taken so long?" Well, first of all, women had to, like everybody else, figure out the political process. They had to register to vote, they had to join a political party, they had to begin to identify and build political resources. Again, we've made terrific progress since 1920, and why has it taken so long? Because, first of all, it still takes a candidate—incumbency is still a major obstacle. If you look at the years that women have won, made some significant gains in Congress, they coincided with years following redistricting or years where we saw a lot of retirement, big election years. Those years tend to be presidential years, but there have been a lot of nonpresidential years where women have made gains, so why has it taken so long? It still takes a candidate. It still takes motivating women to run for office and then following that with supporting those women candidates so that they have a good chance of winning.

MS: Speaking of which, I keep running into these studies saying that women have to really be actively coaxed and convinced to run for office. Why do you think that is?

DB: Political socialization is still a factor. Most girls don't grow up thinking that they want to be out there in the rough-and-tumble of politics. Politics is not, as they often say, for the fainthearted, but it is part of our culture to try to encourage people to seek public office in some capacity. . . . You have to go out there and encourage women. You've got to give women the tools they need in order to believe that they can be successful when they get there. Some women believe that it's important to run after they've finished their so-called child-rearing years, if that's still a matter of interest to them. Some women believe that they have to have a solid education and this, that, and the other. What they simply don't know is that most men wake up in the morning or wake up in the middle of the night, and decide, Why not? They feel very passionately. When you look at the number of women who are serving today and you go back and look at the reasons why they decided to run, often they have to do with raising their kids and wanting a better education in their community, or fighting for environmental issues. So it takes all kinds of reasons. But the good news is that I think we've turned the corner; we just can't see as far as we want to see down the road.

MS: Sometimes this is framed as almost a competition between men and women—an equality thing, as if we just want parity for parity's sake—but why is it important? Why is this not a "women's issue" but something that men should also support?

DB: Because every time that women have made progress, typically it's because some woman stepped up and stood up and said, "You know what? This has to change." Because the progress we've seen in our lifetime happened because of women who dared, women of courage—women like Olympia Snowe and Pat Schroeder and others. Because they spoke up and we got Title IX, because they spoke up and they were able to change the Family Medical Leave Act, they were able to make advancements on so many other fronts—assuring that women had access to credit cards, as my home-state congresswoman Lindy Boggs did. So it's important that women continue to see that when women run, they make a difference in our lives. They tend to be more collaborative. There was a study recently, in *The New York Times,* I believe, about the women in the United States Senate—they want to get along, they want to work across the aisle, they don't have this macho thing that they can't compromise or they can't find common ground.

MS: Regarding leadership positions, the numbers are low not just in Washington but across the board in terms of CEOs and Fortune 500 companies, as Sheryl Sandberg's book has been highlighting. How is that connected? Do you think that the more women come into other areas of power and influence in the corporate world and in these other arenas, the more it would enhance the overall acceptance of women leaders?

DB: I do believe that public service is one of the most visible forms of leadership in society, but there's no question when you look at what happened a few years ago in California, with Meg Whitman and Carly Fiorina, that was also an important step—you had two women in the corporate world stepping out into the political world. Again, when you look at most of the men who are in office—not to give them the short end of the rope—but men have had success in business and say, "I've made a great living and all. Now let's see what I can do for the country or to make the world a better place." I think for women in the corporate world, we don't have that many role models, we don't have that many mentors. And I think Sheryl Sandberg is fostering this interesting conversation on that, not just about the role of ambition, but also about mentoring and the fact that we cannot just walk in the door and shut it behind us. . . . We have to find ways to keep the door open for other women to join us in the circle of power.

MS: I interviewed Anna Deavere Smith for another series about leadership, and I remember her really stressing the fact that she thinks it's not just enough to get the women in the door—women have to reach back and also bring up other women, especially women who are in underserved communities.

DB: That's an important part. I found that when I was coming up through the political ranks, it wasn't enough to be the only woman, or sometimes the only minority, in the room; I wanted to make sure that I was not the last. So while I sat at the table, I often told my colleagues, "Look, if there's no room at the table, we'll just bring in folding chairs. We'll make space for women." The attitude is that we've got to start making space for each other. If we don't, we will never see ourselves as making real progress.

MS: What about this whole likability factor that Sheryl Sandberg talks about in her book, in terms of when you have strong, ambitious women, they're perceived as "unlikable"? Do you think that's improving? Because it seems to me that it's a hard situation for women to be in—that if you're strong and successful, you're unlikable.

DB: I used to tell people to embrace the inner bitch, because people will trample on you if you don't have any self-esteem or self-respect. People will intimidate you if you're unsure or unsteady, so embrace the inner bitch. You may want to call it the inner goddess, but whatever you call her, we've got it and we have it in abundance. My mother always said, "It's not what they call you; it's what you answer to."

MS: You have such a strong sense of self and such confidence. What gives you your drive and inner strength?

DB: First of all, I had a mother and grandparents who were simply phenomenal. They were women who just seized every opportunity. And I come from a working-class background, really poverty, and my parents were my motivation, especially my mom. I saw how she worked, and she didn't distinguish between the boys and the girls; there were nine of us, and she made us all do the same things. She made us speak up. She made us toughen up. She really gave us all what I would call the key ingredients of leadership, and because of her, I think I was so motivated, as a little girl, to go out there and do my very best.

I knew that as a black woman in the formerly segregated Deep South, I would have to pick my way and find every elevator I could, as well as a ladder, to be able to be successful . . . My grandmother, of course, made it clear to me when we were kids, "Okay, we're former slaves and that's it. No more picking cotton. It's too hard to pick cotton." And so I grew up wanting to know how women like my grandmother and so many others survived, and what I learned was, they were blessed with determination. They were blessed with courage. They were blessed with resiliency and perseverance. They're the ones who blessed me to have the seat at the table that I have today.

MS: Why is there such inequality of representation and diversity in the media, and why is this important? How do those low numbers and lack of diversity affect both the political debate and consciousness?

DB: Well, as I tell my students at Georgetown, "Visibility is viability." If you're not visible in society and you're not out there, people don't know you exist. Think about where we are today—you've got Dianne Feinstein now heading up Intelligence, Barbara Mikulski on Appropriations, Patty Murray on the Budget Committee, Mary Landrieu on the Small Business Committee, and there are probably more that I'm not remembering right now. But I'll tell you this: when you look at the fact that all these women are in all these key, remarkable positions, and yet you turn on TV and you see John McCain and Lindsey Graham, you want to scream. . . . Why are there no women? Because often we don't push ourselves to go out there. I'm serious. It's not only because we've got young men who don't know how to reach women; we also have a culture where women still don't self-promote. You know what I do once or twice a month, because I have this attitude like, who cares? I just call CNN: "What Sunday do you need me?" I do! I will pick up the phone and say, "Which Sunday do you need me? Because I'm in D.C. all week." And I don't just call one person—I call four or five. And I harass them sometimes, if I'm in the mood. I go out there every week, because it's important to go out there. I have to tell you the truth: it's not easy to do that . . . but it's worth it because I can get out there. I can talk about gay marriage. I can talk about immigration. I could talk about guns. I could talk about the budget. I could talk about 2016, and those are my topics. And if they need me for the foreign policy stuff on Syria, Cypress, and all the other topics, I would have been ready for that, too. When I push, I push. You've got to self-promote, and I know that's hard for some women and some of them simply don't like to do it, but think about John McCain and Lindsey Graham—they will self-promote in a nanosecond. Joe Biden used to self-promote. Dick Durbin self-promotes. Chuck Schumer self-promotes. It's all self-promotion. That's all it is.

MS: I have also seen studies saying that sometimes the reason why women aren't self-promoting is that they don't think they're qualified enough. This self-doubt is so subliminal—again, probably programmed into us as girls to make us doubt what we know—that it may be holding us back. I think there was some statistic that only 3 percent of women are in the top clout positions in the media. Isn't it also the responsibility on the part of the media to make sure that they're reaching out to women, too?

DB: There's no question that it's a two-way street. I think we have to do self-promotion, but we've also got to find those who are in charge of the media and stress upon them the fact that there needs to be more diversity in the newsroom. As I've said, I've been involved with CNN now for over eleven years; I've been with ABC for about seven years. I can tell you that based on my relationship with those producers, I go to [them], and I say, "Okay, I'm not available, so have you talked to Maria Cordona? Have you found out what Hillary Rosen thinks?" The other problem is we have some women who don't do that, who don't recommend other women. When I was up for a renewal, I didn't just speak up for myself. Of course I did, but I also asked, "Well, what about Maria, what about Anna, and what about Hillary?" Just because I'm sitting at the table doesn't mean I can't have additional chairs for other women. That's another problem that we have sometimes as women: we don't carry each other into the world, and also, when women are trying to impress the boss, they think about guys. Well, if I know John Kerry is available, Jesus Christ, you know who's got comparable experience to John Kerry and has been serving on the Foreign Relations Committee for all these years—you should also reach out to her. The media piece is a very difficult beat. . . . It's a tough business, even those Sunday shows. Do we watch them? Do we support them? Do we tweet about them? I mean, I try to tweet about Diane Sawyer. I try to tweet about Katie Couric. Of course I've written for Oprah's magazine. We've got to be better supporters. That goes back to this whole notion of why there are not a lot of women, when we're the majority of voters. We must ask that question of ourselves. What are *we* waiting for?

MS: I know you have done so much advocacy in promoting voters' rights and in getting young people to vote. Do you feel like that's improving in terms of citizens, common citizens, just wanting to be a part of the process and speaking up when there's something that they believe in?

DB: I do believe that we need refresher courses from time to time on what it means to be a citizen in the United States of America in the twenty-first century. I think so many people lose sight of the fact that we have a system of a Republican form of government with self-representation. And not everybody needs to run for office. Some people need to be better advocates in their neighborhood. Some people need to be better advocates when it comes to fixing up schools and keeping the community thriving. Some people need to be better advocates in terms of the environment. So there are many ways to serve and many ways that we can fulfill our role as citizens of the United States of America. But we need to understand that we have the greatest power on the planet—as citizens of the United States of America—and when we fail to utilize that, that's why we end up with the kind of government and the kind of dysfunction [we have], because we're not actively engaged as citizens. That's why, for me, voting is the lifeblood of our democracy.

MS: In terms of where women are today, I feel hopeful on one side, because it seems like there are a lot of promising signs, and then on the other side of things, you see all this pushback on things that we thought we had already settled—on contraceptives and reproductive rights, as well as some of the misinformed rhetoric about rape that was going on in the last election. How do you view the moment that we're in as it relates to the overall status of women in the United States and in the world?

DB: There are always people who are going to lag behind. When you run a race, not everyone comes in first, and when you make social change or make progress, there will be those who say, "Not now, and not ever." What you see today is a backlash—there's no question there's still a backlash. It's cultural and it's religious. Whenever there's a dry moment in the forecast, some people use that as an opportunity to try to take us back to another, bygone era. But this is another reason why we have to remain ever vigilant. Let's be honest: How many models do we have in the world to look toward? So we have to, as Gandhi often would say, "be the change that we wish to see in the world." And as women, as leaders, we have to continue to fight for those priorities and champion those issues that will ultimately make our lives better and allow us to be coequal citizens on this planet.

MS: Many people I spoke with made the point that we need to support Republican women candidates as much as we do Democrats. I want to make it clear that this is not a partisan issue.

DB: There are so many Republican women. Because, look, I don't believe that we can afford to put all our eggs in one basket. The political parties exist—and you have to have the structure, because you can't just be president without securing the nomination, so there's a role for political parties. But when it comes to promoting and pushing women in leadership positions, we should work all across the court, even women who might disagree on issues. We need to find common ground with the notion that once we get to the table, we might be able to break bread.

MS: If you could have the ear of women and girls today, what would be the one message you would most want to get out there?

DB: Believe in yourself. No one is going to give you the tools to make you the success that you want to be, so you've got to find it inside you. I often tell people that I think we already come prepackaged, but we fail to open up and become who we are because society has put so many daunting and challenging things before us. So be who you are.

MARY FALLIN

"The Republican Party has embraced women in leadership posi-tions. And I get frustrated at times when different news media outlets, and certainly the opposite party, say that Republicans don't care about women, because it's not true. We've proven that by the numbers that we have in leadership positions, not only in governor's offices, but in Congress and legislative positions."

GOVERNOR MARY FALLIN was elected November 2, 2010, during a historic election in which she became the first-ever female governor of Oklahoma. In 1994, Fallin made history by becoming the first woman and first Republican to be elected lieutenant governor of Oklahoma, an office she would hold for twelve years. Fallin used her position as president of the Oklahoma State Senate to allow the citizens of Oklahoma to vote on Right to Work, which ended the practice of compelling workers to join and pay dues to a union. In 2001, Oklahoma became the first state in the country to pass such a law in more than twenty-five years. Fallin was elected to the U.S. Congress in 2006, where she represented the Fifth District of Oklahoma. As governor, Fallin has cited job growth and retention, education reform, government modernization, and protect-ing Oklahoma from the intrusions of Washington, D.C., as top priorities. During Fallin's administration, Oklahoma has consistently ranked among the top states for job creation. She is married to Wade Christensen, an

Oklahoma City attorney who is the state's first "First Gentleman." The couple has six children between them.

MARIANNE SCHNALL: What do you think it would take to make a woman president?

MARY FALLIN: I think the biggest challenge facing our nation, as far as more women getting involved in politics, is just the fact of women stepping up and being willing to run for office—to put everything on the line, to do the hard work, to go through the process itself, to risk winning or losing, and to step up to any kind of office, whether it's president or heading up a major corporation.

MS: One of the things I'm hearing about the political pipeline, and especially leading up to the presidency, is the importance of having more female governors. Being the first female governor of Oklahoma, do you have a sense of why we don't have more female governors?

MF: Well, I think in the past, when I first started running for public office, back in 1990, there were some stereotypes of whether a woman could get the job done, whether a woman would be effective. And frankly when I ran for office back in my thirties, I was a young mother, I was a professional businesswoman, and I became frustrated with things that weren't happening at the Capitol, such as improving education and healthcare. And being a businesswoman, I thought we needed a better business environment for our state. I decided to run for office, and I was young; I was in my mid-thirties. I had a three-year-old child at the time and worked my job full time, and then I would go out nights and weekends and campaign. And several months into my own first election, I was feeling a little sick in the mornings, and there I was, working a job full time and campaigning nights and weekends and had a three-year-old, come to find out my husband and I were expecting our second child. So when I announced—even though I was already several months into my campaign—that I was pregnant, I had people come up and tell me that I wouldn't be effective, that I needed to drop out of the race, that I should have an abortion because I wouldn't be able to get the job done. And, you know, I kept focus on what I wanted to accomplish in the end, which was to go to the Capitol and make changes on these different policy issues. So I kept running my campaign, and on election night I was eight months pregnant, and then I actually had my son between the primary and the general election in September—the election was in November. And I didn't have an abortion; I, of course, continued on with my pregnancy and that was twenty-three years ago. And not only did I win the House of Representatives seat back in those early days, I was able to pass over a dozen pieces of legislation into law. And I was very much in the minority in the Oklahoma Legislature. I was one of three Republican women at that time, so I was very much in the minority as far as political party and being a female.

Then I went on to run for lieutenant governor, four years after that, and by that time my children were four and seven. And I ran for a state-wide office, which was not easy, because I had the regular things a mom does—you have to bring your children to school, picking them up and going to their after-school activities—and trying to deal with some tough issues as lieutenant governor. But I won that race and served twelve years as the first female lieutenant governor of our state. Then, in between all of that, I became single and was a single mom, and that was challenging. I also had a mother who became sick at that time and bedridden, and she was widowed so I was taking care of my mother and my children in a state-wide elected position, which was tough. But then I just kept working hard. I basically prioritized my time to where—certainly my faith is very important to me, which carried me through that time—but my children were a top priority, and then my work was my third priority and keeping that balance of what was really important in life helped me be effective. And then I ended up running for Congress and became the second woman elected to Congress. We elected our first woman in 1920, and she only made it through one term and was voted out of office. We hadn't had a woman go to Congress since 1922.

So I served four years in Congress, and it was challenging as a woman trying to live between two states. By that time, I had one child that was in college and one that was a sophomore in high school, and I was coming home every weekend, trying to take care of them and balance family and work and do my job effectively. Then after four years of doing that, I was recruited to run for governor, and that was challenging, too, trying to be in Congress and come home on the weekends to not only see my children and take care of things at home as a single woman, but also run for state-wide office again.

And to my surprise, during all that time, I reconnected with an old college friend, a wonderful man that I had known thirty years ago, and in between all of that, a life surprise came up and within a couple of months, he asked me to marry him! I was like, are you kidding? [laughs] I'm in Congress, I'm a single mom, and I'm running for governor. I've got a little bit going on in my life right now. I said, this is a serious thing, to remarry, but there are times in your life when you know that you know it's the thing to do. So we actually got married during my campaign for governor. He had four kids, I had two, so now we have six together. So I started a new family, a new phase in my life, right in the middle of running for governor and being in Congress!

You know, I've kind of gone full circle in my life and meeting life's challenges and opportunities face on, pushing through them, walking by faith that it would all work out the way it was supposed to. And here I am three years later. Later this year, I'll take over as the first Oklahoman to ever be the national chair of the Governor's Association. So I've kind of run the whole gamut of trying to balance family and work and be effective. And I've had a great time as governor. So it's been an interesting walk in life, but one that's been very rewarding—not without its challenges. It's not an easy job.

But back to your original question, I think women just have to be willing to step up, take risks, take chances, know there will be some setbacks. One of my favorite sayings is that setbacks are always an opportunity for a comeback. I think when you're willing to take those risks, no matter what they are, that it can be a very rewarding, satisfying career, no matter what business you decide to go into.

MS: Going back to the notion of having a woman president, do you think that we'll have a woman president in your lifetime? And is that a path that you have ever considered?

MF: I do think we'll have a woman president. I think a woman has to prove herself, just as a man does, that they have goals, they have ideas and solutions to problems facing people, businesses, the nation, a state. And when a woman can articulate those things and be bold and courageous, be willing to take risks, then people will follow a woman—and certainly follow a man, too—but I think if a woman demonstrates those things, she can get elected to public office. There used to be a thought, many, many years ago, that if you were a woman and you ran, people might vote for you just because you were different, because women don't always run for office that maybe you could get some votes. But I really think that people vote for women based upon their ability to get things done and their accomplishments and the respect that they have for a person. I remember back in the early 2000s, we had a major issue in front of our state, and I was the lieutenant governor at that time. And many times I would go to different meetings, or different Cabinet meetings, with the former governor, and many times I would be the only woman at the table. But we had this big issue that came up in front of the House and the Senate, and that was the issue of Right to Work, and throughout the history of Oklahoma, no one had ever been able to get Right to Work passed through the Senate and the Oklahoma Legislature, much less to the other people. And I was the president of the Senate, but it was more of a ceremonial position, because [I didn't] actually run the Senate. But anyway, they had an amendment on the floor to put the issue of Right to Work to a vote of the people, and the Senate got into a big fight and they went into recess to try to stall and hopefully kill the amendment. And I got a phone call from one of the senators saying, "You know, constitutionally you have the power to go up and sit in the Senate chair and take over the Senate. It's never been done, but you do have that power to do that. We think you should come back and take over the Senate." And it was an opposite political party that was in control, and so I said, "Sure, I'll do that. I believe in what we're trying to accomplish here." So I came back; I was out of the Capitol and I came back to town. I walked in the Senate with just a handful of my colleagues in my party and took over the chair from the opposite party of the Senate while they were out on recess and tried to get a quorum to get them to come back to just vote on allowing the issue of Right to Work to go to a vote of the people. Well, of course, the opposite party, the majority, wouldn't come in. They actually walked out for three days on us and I was sitting there with my colleagues of the Republican Party, and we sat there for three days. They had all kinds of schemes and plans that they were going to have me physically carried out of the Chamber. They were going to have me arrested. They said, "You'll never win another election again from doing some stupid stunt like this." And I can remember sitting those first couple of hours in the chair, and of course all the TV cameras and news media was there, because a lieutenant governor had never taken over the Chamber on a controversial issue like that. I remember thinking, *Boy, this could either make me or break me. I may never get elected again to any public office.* It was really a risky thing to do, but I believed in my heart it was the right thing to do for Oklahoma. And this is one of those issues that had never been able to get resolved in our state's history.

So I remember picking up my cell phone as I was sitting in the president of the Senate's chair, and I called my mother and said, "Mom, when you watch the news tonight, I've got a little something going on at the Capitol today. So I've taken over the Senate and it's going to be all over the news. It's controversial, but I'm okay, don't worry about it. I just think this is the right thing to do." And sure enough, from that point on for three days, there was a massive fight in the Senate, and senators were leaving. Finally on the third day they came back. The Senate president came in an hour ahead of time, of course. The Senate started and took over the chair of the Senate from me, and I came walking back in at the regular time it was supposed to start, and I took the chair back away from him and he told me, "We're going to play this game with you, but here's what you're going to do: you're going to recognize a certain senator, he's going to make a motion to kill this amendment on Right to Work. And when he kills it, we'll have a vote and it will go down, and then you can go back to your office and then you can be the lieutenant governor and cut ribbons around the state." This was his opening. He said, "You've got that?" I said, "I hear what you say." He said, "Well, that's what you're going to do, right?" And I said, "No, sir. Go sit down." He said, "What do you mean?" I said, "Go sit down." He said, "Well, you're going to recognize this senator." I said, "No, actually, I'm going to recognize another senator. Go sit down." So I forced him to go sit down and I called the vote and I recognized the other senator who made the motion to allow this vote to go on the floor to have the amendment go to a vote of the people. It actually fell by one vote—all pandemonium broke out on the Senate floor. But the very next year, the Senate actually ran an amendment to send Right to Work to a vote of the people, and it passed. And that's how we passed Right to Work in Oklahoma. We were the first state in twenty-five years to do that. It was really risky for me to do that, because politically I would be campaigned against by the opposition to that issue, but in actuality I think people appreciated the fact that I had the guts and the courage to try to make a change for what I thought was right. And it has been good for Oklahoma, so taking the risk, standing up for what you truly believe in, doing things that maybe people have never done before, always [believing] that you can truly earn the respect and trust of people, [will help you] to be able to make further changes later on down in your career.

MS: That's a great story.

MF: I will tell you one other little part of that story. The senators who were the opposite political party were so mad that I did that, that if you look in the histories of the journals of the Senate, which are published every day, you won't find that incident. They wouldn't publish it. They were so mad at me. It's all in the papers, you can read it in magazines and books and history books, but in the old Senate Journal, they wouldn't publish what I did.

MS: Wow, that's wild. Are there specific challenges for being a woman in the Republican Party, or do you feel like it's the same? Do you feel like there's been progress made? Do you have a sense of the situation for Republican women?

MF: Actually we have more Republican women governors in the nation than there are Democratic governors in the nation. There are four Republican women governors at this point and one Democrat. And those numbers change year to year. But the Republican Party has embraced women in leadership positions. And I get frustrated at times when different news media outlets, and certainly the opposite party, say that Republicans don't care about women, because it's not true. We've proven that by the numbers that we have in leadership positions, not only in governor's offices, but in Congress and legislative positions. My mother was mayor of a town when I was growing up, so women can get into office, once again, if they have a vision for what they want to accomplish and they're able to articulate that in the right way.

MS: When people look at the world right now, it can all feel very discouraging, especially the possibility of running for office. What makes it all worthwhile?

MF: Making a difference in people's lives. Being actually able to create change, to shift the paradigm and a challenge that's within in my state—whether it's addressing our child welfare system, whether it's being able to pass initiatives that create major changes, like the Right to Work initiative that I talked about. I've been able to have a tax cut; I'm proposing another one this year to give people back some of their hard-earned money to help improve the quality of their lives. I mean, the people of Oklahoma's per capita income has gone up in our state since I've been in office. So being able to create that change to make people's lives better. I've certainly been able to sign into law a lot of education reform to improve the education system for our children in our state, creating jobs—it's all very rewarding. And I'll just tell you, too, that from a personal standpoint, I've been elected as the vice chair of the Governors Association. I'm the only woman on the

Executive Board right now, and so I get to go meet with the president and his cabinet and sit in the West Wing with the president or have a personal phone call with the vice president or a cabinet secretary in the administration—and to have a seat at the table, as a woman, to me is a big deal. I mean, there are times I'll be sitting there with the president and his cabinet or other governors, and I'm sitting there as the only woman, thinking, This is really neat, [because I'm] a small town girl—I grew up in a town of 2,000 people. My mother and father were not wealthy people; they were just small-town, good people. But they taught me the value of hard work and public service and giving back to your community and that one person truly can make a difference if they're willing to take a risk, take a chance, and work really hard.

JOY BEHAR

"I think that humor is a powerful tool to use . . . When I first started stand-up comedy, I think part of my motivation for getting into it was that I felt powerless as a woman in this society. I was becoming invisible. I was already thirty-nine. After thirty-five you become invisible, pretty much, certainly to men. I was just becoming more and more invisible, and I was like, I have things to say. I have to do it . . . Of course, no one was going to listen to me if I was just talking, so I had to make them laugh, and then they listened to me. So I think that it has a very powerful effect on people."

JOY BEHAR IS an Emmy-winning talk-show host, comedian, best-selling author, and actress. For more than sixteen years, she cohosted ABC's *The View*, which earned her a Daytime Emmy Award as Outstanding Talk Show Host. Behar is the host of *Joy Behar: Say Anything!* on Current TV. In theater, Behar had a successful run in the off-Broadway hit *The Food Chain*, earning rave reviews in the starring role, and also in the critically acclaimed *The Vagina Monologues*. Behar received GLAAD's Excellence in Media Award, presented to media professionals who have increased the visibility and understanding of the LGBT community. She is the author of two children's books, as well as the *New York Times* Best Seller *Joy Shtick: Or What Is the Existential Vacuum and Does It Come with Attachments?*

MARIANNE SCHNALL: This book was partially inspired because right after Obama was elected, my then-eight-year-old daughter, Lotus—when I was saying how wonderful it was that we finally had our first African American president—looked at me, completely innocent, and asked, "Why haven't we ever had a woman president?" And I found that this very simple, honest, innocent question was actually more challenging to answer than you would think. So, starting there, why do you think we haven't had a woman president?

JOY BEHAR: You mean, besides the obvious answer that it's been a very sexist country for many years? I mean, women didn't even get the vote until 1920. In fact, African Americans got it before women, so they were even lower down on the respect scale. I've been around a long time now, and I remember when Gloria Steinem and the rest of them in 1970 basically started the Second Wave of the feminist movement, I think they called it. It was 1970. My daughter was born in 1970. She'll be forty-three now, and it's not that long ago. They're trying to reverse the Voting Rights Act now, in some of the states that have a history of racism, trying to prevent black people from voting, so I think that it's very hard to change these entrenched notions and ideas that people have, particularly when men are controlling everything. I'm not surprised. Are you?

MS: No, I guess it was just sort of funny, because it's become so ingrained in our psyche, we just have accepted it, that I think when you have a young girl asking you, point blank—

JB: They don't get it, exactly, because they haven't lived the lives that we have lived, and so they don't know what we had to go through. I forget where I was hearing this—in 1963 or 1964 or 1965, women couldn't get their own credit cards. This sounds like such a preposterous notion to girls today. Who would ever have thought that when I got married in 1965, the first time, a lot of girls were just in college to get their "misters"? We never even thought about what careers we would have. I had an uncle who said to me, "Why do you have to go to college? You're a girl. You're going to get married." I actually heard those words.

MS: Well, what about now? Do you think you'll see a woman president in your lifetime? Do you feel we're ready for a woman president?

JB: Yes, I do. I was hoping that it would be a liberal president, a female liberal, because England had Margaret Thatcher, but she was to the right of Ronald Reagan, and so I thought in this country, they're going to pick a woman. But it's probably going to be a conservative. Then, of course, the crop of conservative women was very disappointing. We had Michele Bachmann and Sarah Palin, and people on the right would say to me, "Well, shouldn't you support a woman just because she's a woman?" No, no. You want a woman president, but you don't want a woman president who's going to fight women and who's going to vote against women's interests. So it can't just be any woman. But I think that it's becoming clearer that Hillary Clinton is in the bull pen and she is going to be running in 2016, and I will work as hard as I can to get her in the White House if I'm able to.

I can just add that she had a very tough assignment as secretary of state. She had to show that she had as much testosterone as she had estrogen, and I think that she showed it. She was as tough as any man in the world arena, and that's why men respect her. That's why she would be a very, very good candidate.

MS: It's been a tricky balance for women—this whole question of the likability factor, of how women who are openly ambitious and confident are sometimes treated.

JB: It's a tricky road that women walk in politics. Even on television, where I work, you have to have a likability factor to survive, and that's why people like Rachel Maddow are very valuable, because she is likable and she is smart and she does have a good brain.

MS: Sometimes this gets framed as a "women's issue," but obviously, having more women in positions of power and influence isn't just about fairness or competition, but it has benefits to all of humanity, including men. What special qualities do you think women would bring to the Oval Office, or to leadership roles in general, that the world most needs today? Why is this important?

JB: You know, I'm really not sure about that, because when women get in positions of power, they can be just as bellicose as men, so I'm not sure that sort of knee-jerk [reaction of], "Oh, a woman won't be as tough," or, "A woman won't be as warlike," or what have you, is true. You know, Golda Meir was very tough and very conservative and kind of a war hawk in many ways, and so was Margaret Thatcher. Listen, Hillary voted for the Iraq War, and that pissed me off big time. So I can't say that just because you're a woman, I'm going to love everything that you do. But what special qualities does a woman bring to it? I don't know. I'm asked that same question as a comedian.

MS: Maybe the other way to frame it is also about overall diversity, in terms of our government looking more like America.

JB: That's right. That's why you need diversity. And I like the idea that someone's up there that shows other young women that they, too, can be in those positions. Sometimes I think that women are more reasonable in many ways.

MS: I feel like we're at a little bit of a confusing moment. Sometimes I feel like everybody's talking about women and the influence we had on the election—whether it's responding to sexist attacks or rape rhetoric that's misinformed—but on the other side of things, there's this whole backlash. Where do you think we are in the status of women today?

JB: I think there are always going to be people who are threatened by women's progress. And, I mean, it was so scary for a minute there, when you had these men in positions of power, talking about how the body shuts down after a rape so you can't get pregnant, and let's get a sonogram, a vaginal sonogram, before a woman wants to have an abortion. I always say, get out of my uterus! Stay in Congress, and get out of my uterus. Worry about other things. So you always have people like that, I think. But it was a beautiful thing to see how they were dismissed, summarily dismissed, by the electorate—it was great.

The second election of Obama was even more exciting to me than the first, primarily because people stepped up and they saw what these people, these others that I just mentioned, were trying to do. Not just to women, but to immigrants, poor people. And you hear stories about how long they waited in lines to vote. People heard and saw what was going on. And even Romney, he's still in shock that he didn't win, because he was tone-deaf to what was really going on in the country. And a lot of these people who tried to roll back Roe v. Wade, and roll back this and that, they also are in for a rude awakening. Now, having said that, I think that the Supreme Court is very, very precarious at the moment. They have the power to do all sorts of damage to very hard-won fights that we've made over the years. I worry about the Supreme Court. I really do.

MS: I was watching Diane Sawyer, who was interviewing all of the women senators—this was right around the time of the fiscal cliff—and they were saying that if they had all been able to sit in one room together, the whole thing would have been resolved. Do you think that's a little bit true? Again, it's so hard to make these generalizations, but if we did possibly have more women, reasonable women, in all these negotiations . . . ?

JB: I think you would. I think definitely, if you had *reasonable* women, then yes. That word would have to be very prominent. If they're reasonable women, they're going to be thinking about the pragmatic solution to what's going to happen to the country. I mean, even now, this sequester—you know, I've never even heard of this before, or the fiscal cliff. In all the years I've been voting and watching politics, this is the first time this has ever become an issue. It's almost because the extreme right wing in the Republican Party is just creating these canards to stop Obama from becoming a great president. I think it's unpatriotic, frankly, the way they have been trying to get the country to go backward and not deal with these issues. Reagan was able to work with the Democrats; Lyndon Johnson was able to work with Republicans. Come on.

MS: On *The View,* you have Elisabeth Hasselbeck representing the conservative viewpoint, and you often also have guests on the other end of the spectrum from you politically. Whether it is with Elisabeth or your guests, you seem to, at least most of the time, be able to discuss issues and diplomatically disagree. Wouldn't it be great if they could have that same type of ability in Congress? What communication advice would you offer to congresspeople to prevent the partisanship and gridlock we see today?

JB: Well, never take it personally is number one. I've had arguments on the air with Elisabeth and other Republicans, even Bill O'Reilly. But I don't take it personally. I don't feel any personal animosity to any of these people. A lot of times, what you've got is people who are very, very stuck in their positions. A lot of times, it can't be resolved. This is why the Founding Fathers made it majority rules, because sometimes that's what it's about.

MS: We were talking earlier about this whole idea of just speaking your mind. Women and girls, especially, can often feel hesitant to speak out or stand out too much, and, again, you have always seemed to have this natural ability and courage to speak your mind and just be your authentic self. You don't seem to really care so much what other people think. You have conviction in your own beliefs. Where does that come from?

JB: Sometimes girls are like that because they don't want boys not to like them. They think a mouthy girl doesn't get the date. And believe me, when you're a funny or mouthy woman, like I am, men are not attracted to that. They don't like that. You have to be willing to forfeit your Heidi Klum credentials [laughs]. Maybe she's the wrong example, but you know what I mean: a model who keeps her mouth shut and just looks gorgeous. You can't have everything. I would say to these girls, "Which is more important to you—is it more important to impress a boy, or is it more important to speak out?" I always encourage my daughter to speak out. Even when she was a kid, she used to have feminist arguments with boys in the class; I remember that. And I thought, *Good. Good for her.* The boys are not as important as her making her point. So that's one reason I think they don't. Also, I was always encouraged to talk in my family. I always say this to interviewers— they ask me this question a lot, and I always give the [same] answer: they never told me to be quiet. No one ever said, "Be quiet, Joy." And believe me,

I must have irritated them plenty. But, I don't know, they just thought I was amusing or something, and they let me just yak it up. So you don't tell girls to be quiet. Stop telling us to be quiet; we're not going to be quiet.

MS: I wanted to ask you about the role of comedy, because I think it is not just entertainment. I do think that there is something especially important about women being funny, since we often take ourselves way too seriously. I'm friends with Kathy Najimy, and she talks about how sometimes, even talking about politics, if you add a little humor, it can feel more palatable.

JB: Well, I think that [female comedians] are powerful. I think that humor is a powerful tool to use. It's a great talent to have, because you can disarm people. You can make your point. Ask anybody who has to give a speech—very often they'll say, "If I start with an anecdote and get them laughing at the beginning, I own them; then they'll listen to me." When I first started stand-up comedy, I think part of my motivation for getting into it was that I felt powerless as a woman in this society. I was becoming invisible. I was already thirty-nine. After thirty-five you become invisible, pretty much, certainly to men. I was just becoming more and more invisible, and I was like, I have things to say. I have to do it. As hard as that was, I got up on that stage with a microphone in my hand, and I went there. Of course, no one was going to listen to me if I was just talking, so I had to make them laugh, and then they listened to me. So I think that it has a very powerful effect on people.

MS: Even in the media, women hold only about 3 percent of top positions. As a media figure—through *The View* and through your talk shows—what do you think of the state of media today in terms of women's representation, both behind the scenes and as news anchors and personalities?

JB: I think there are more of us. There are a lot of women now. I was just watching MSNBC before, with S. E. Cupp and this girl Krystal Ball, and they're terrific. And then Rachel Maddow's on that station. You have Andrea Mitchell, you've got Mika Brzezinski, just on MSNBC. Then CNN has Candy Crowley, who I think is great. And, you know, Barbara Walters and Diane Sawyer and Katie Couric and those kinds of newspeople on the networks all these years have been very important. I think there's quite a few of us.

MS: I was thinking about *The View,* and it brought to mind this quote from an interview I did with Gloria Steinem. She said, "If we're by ourselves, we come to feel crazy and alone. We need to make alternate families of small groups of women who support each other, talk to each other regularly, can speak their truth and their experiences and find they're not alone in them." I think that *The View* is kind of modeling that for us. How do you see the cultural significance of what takes place on *The View* in terms of this forum for women to talk and share their opinions?

JB: I think in the beginning they were calling us a "coffee klatch" or "a bunch of hens"; somebody said one time "yentas." We've been called all sorts of things—these disparaging remarks about women sitting around a table, discussing anything they feel like talking about that day, things that are in the news. It basically is an extension of the kitchen table where we all grew up. When I grew up—I grew up in Brooklyn, in a tenement, and my grandmother lived on one floor, and my parents and I lived on another, and my aunt was on another, and we had dinners together, and we'd sit around and have dinner or coffee and just talk, play cards—we called it a neighborhood. And I think that people—because this country is so spread out—are missing that a lot. I really do believe that's one of the biggest problems, this lack of community that's going on. I hear constant complaints from people that they don't have a community, and I do my best to bring groups together all the time in my personal life. I do believe in it. And, yeah, *The View* kind of shows you what it could be like.

MS: In terms of leaders today, man or woman, what traits or qualities do you think are most important to have?

JB: Intelligence, integrity—those are the two things that come to mind. And a certain humanity, a "menschiness." That's why I like Obama. I think he has all that. You would never catch him cheating on his wife. It's not going to happen. And he's very, very smart. I think that he might be difficult at times, because they say he doesn't want to bend too easily, but you need to be flexible, too, I guess. Pragmatic—that's another thing. One of the reasons I liked him and I voted for him was that I think he's pragmatic. I think he wants to solve things.

MS: There have been all these studies saying that oftentimes it's women themselves who are sort of reluctant to aspire to leadership positions, that they have to be convinced to run for office, or even just to advocate for themselves or negotiate for a raise. What advice would you offer to girls, and young women particularly, on finding their worth, following their calling? What words of wisdom would you give?

JB: I believe that young women need to take care of their financial house. If you have a way of earning a living and you can save some money so that you can take risks, I would suggest something like that. Because, you know, women stay in bad marriages because they don't have any money. They stay in abusive relationships because they can't get out, because they don't have the ability to move or change. So I would say always make sure that you're financially stable, so that you can take a risk. You shouldn't have to stay in a job. One of the benefits of this country is that we have the freedom to move around. This is not Afghanistan. So you shouldn't stay in a situation that you hate. And the way that you get out of that is when you have some money. That's one thing I would say to them.

★ ★

WOMEN AND GIRLS IN THE MEDIA

★ ★

In 1984, NBC's Tom Brokaw described Vice Presidential Nominee Geraldine Ferraro as a "size 6" at the Democratic National Convention. On the day Condoleezza Rice became America's first African American female national security adviser in 2001, a front page New York Times *story reported that "her dress size is between a 6 and an 8." Broadcast news outlets have called Secretary of State Hillary Clinton a "bitch," "harpy," "nutcracker," "ugly," and far worse. Media outlets regularly obsess over female politicians' hair, bodies, clothing, and motherhood choices—a double standard that is virtually never applied to male politicians. When journalism treats female politicians like ladies first and leaders only a distant second, the public is led to believe that women are less qualified to lead—and less electable—than their male counterparts. The roots of this double standard go beyond the content itself, to an institutional bias within the media industry.*

— JENNIFER L. POZNER, AUTHOR, FOUNDER AND EXECUTIVE
DIRECTOR OF WOMEN IN MEDIA & NEWS

If the media shows women in a degrading, demeaning way, if violence is not taken seriously, if female candidates are covered in the context of how they look and what their hair is like and how they're dressed as opposed to how the male candidates are referred to, this has an impact on women and girls. Not always conscious, but it can't help but make us feel somehow we don't count as much. It's not a cognitive thing, it's a visceral response, I think.

— JANE FONDA

I would like to see more women in executive positions in the media. I mean, it still really is an old boy's club. It's changing, and there are increasingly more women in executive levels, but we definitely need to see more. The more women, the more minorities we have at the executive levels, the more sensitive we'll be for women and for minorities.

— LISA LING

It's hard for young women to look at the way other women are objectified in the media—how they're photoshopped to perfection—and not feel that we have to live up to this perfectionist standard. This is a phenomenon that just doesn't occur for our male counterparts. And I think once we realize that there's a perfect image we're not living up to, we begin to question ourselves in all aspects of our lives. I think it starts with reconsidering our bodies . . . but it really feeds into everything that we do.

—JULIE ZEILINGER, AUTHOR, FOUNDER AND EDITOR OF THE FBOMB BLOG

The media could do a much better job, that's for sure—especially the media that targets women. . . . Their message to women is all about consumerism, looking sexy, and pleasing men in bed. And yet they have the potential to make profound changes for the better in women's lives.

—ISABEL ALLENDE

Media are highly influential in creating and communicating societal norms about proper roles and behaviors for men and women. If more women were involved in the production of entertainment and news media, we would see more women on screen and better roles portraying women as powerful subjects instead of passive sexual objects. More images and more diverse images of women in media would lead to a revolution of identity and leadership if millions of little girls grew up thinking of themselves as fully capable, ambitious human beings instead of bodies to be worked on in order to get validation through male attention.

—CAROLINE HELDMAN, PhD, ASSOCIATE PROFESSOR OF POLITICAL SCIENCE AT OCCIDENTAL COLLEGE

ANA NAVARRO

"I think the reason that there are fewer women—that there is a gender gap in the media, there's a gender gap in elected office, there's a gender gap in high-level corporate America—it's all the same reasons. Because, until very recently, women have been the ones that bore the brunt of family and home responsibilities. And it's not been until recently that that has begun to change and we are now in an era where shared responsibilities have become the norm, not the exception."

ANA NAVARRO IS a Republican political strategist with expertise on Latin American, Florida, and Hispanic issues. She is a political contributor on CNN, CNN-Español, and CNN.com. She is a frequent speaker and commentator on political issues and current affairs. Born in Nicaragua, she and her family immigrated to the United States and resettled in Miami in 1980.

Navarro served on Governor Jeb Bush's transition team and served as his first Director of Immigration Policy in the Executive Office of the Governor. In 2001, she served as ambassador to the United Nation's Human Rights Commission where she helped pass a resolution condemning the government of Cuba for human rights abuses. She was Senator John McCain's 2008 National Hispanic Advisory Council co-chair. She has played a role in federal and state races in Florida. In 2012, she served as National Hispanic Advisory Council co-chair for Governor Jon Huntsman's campaign.

MARIANNE SCHNALL: Why do you think we've not yet had a woman president?

ANA NAVARRO: Because we haven't had the right candidate. And because it's taken years, it's taken decades, to get a deep enough stable of women elected officials to be able to have any of them turn into potential presidential candidates. I think we haven't had a woman president because we have not had enough women elected officials, until recently, that can be groomed into becoming presidential candidates, that can grow into becoming presidential candidates.

MS: Why do you think that is? Is it that not enough women are running, is it that there's a kind of glass ceiling or structural obstacles? Why do you think that it has been so challenging to have women in those positions?

AN: Well, first of all, because we got a much later start than men. We got a later start than men in having the right to vote and getting women elected. And it's been a glass ceiling that has taken effort and time to break women into public office, because of the demands—it hasn't been until recently when co-parenting and sharing of family's responsibilities has become more common, that women have been able to explore many other professions usually left to the men, including running for office.

MS: I've done a lot of interviews so far for this book, and I'm hearing a lot of people say that in addition to the structural obstacles, it also may be that psychologically men *and* women still have a hard time just because of cultural stereotypes—imagining a woman in the top office. And part of that is because of having to deal with things like war and the economy, or the perception that a woman wouldn't be tough enough to deal with a war situation. Do you think that's also part of something that has been problematic for people seeing a woman in these top leadership positions?

AN: I think we haven't had the right woman. Right now we're in the midst of reflecting over Margaret Thatcher. Margaret Thatcher was the right woman at the right time and nobody doubted her iron will and her ability to play with the boys in the toughest of situations, including facing down enemies, international enemies, and going to war. Let's not forget it was Margaret Thatcher who told then-President George Bush, "George, don't get wobbly about going into war in Iraq." I just think we have not had the right woman. The first woman to become president has to be somebody who has to have a very impressive résumé. I can't think of a woman who's in elected office right now that would get away with what Barack Obama did, getting elected after three years in the Senate. I think there's going to be higher scrutiny on a woman when it comes to issues like foreign policy, national security, and even economic issues, and it's going to have to be a woman with an impressive résumé that has shown her ability to deal with these issues.

MS: I've heard some people say that we would be more likely to elect a Republican conservative woman for our president. Do you think that is true? I interviewed [Democratic strategist] Celinda Lake and she said, "In some ways it's easier for the first woman president to be a Republican than it would be for a Democrat, because the stereotypes of a Democrat and the stereotypes of a woman are the same. The stereotypes of a Republican counteract some of the stereotypes of being a woman." It's an interesting way to put it. Do you think it is sort of the way that a conservative woman like Margaret Thatcher became the first woman prime minister, that that is something that could be a factor?

AN: You know, I really think it's going to be less about the party affilia-tion and the ideology and more about the individual woman. I don't think many people in America today doubt that Hillary Clinton can be a formi-dable presidential candidate. And I don't think anybody sees her as terribly wishy-washy on foreign policy or national security issues. So I think it's going to be less about ideology. When you said that I immediately thought about Sarah Palin, for example, who was a conservative woman, but I don't think being a conservative or being a Democrat is going to be what determines the first woman getting elected. It will be what that woman has done, shown, and proved throughout her life to get her to that point and earn the trust of the American people.

MS: You're obviously a very knowledgeable strategist and have worked with a lot of elected officials. Do you think there are unique strategies women need to consider? What would you suggest as a strategy for a woman that would be helpful?

AN: Well, I think a woman candidate is different. There might be more equality when it comes to public perception—it's changing, it has changed, and it will continue changing. But today a woman candidate has to deal with issues about her appearance, for example, and her temperament, that a male candidate would not have to deal with. Nobody thinks much about John Boehner breaking into tears in public, but if a woman did that, the reaction would be different. The reaction to a man showing emotion tends to be much different than to a woman showing the same emotion.

MS: This is such a unique conundrum for women—not just for a woman showing soft emotion—because, on the other side of the coin, women are scrutinized if they appear too ambitious or too tough . . .

AN: Yeah, women have to walk a very thin tightrope. . . . Women have to look strong, but have to do it with grace.

MS: I know the Republican Party is going through all sorts of changes, as are we all, but I was curious if you think there are any specific challenges to being a woman in the Republican Party right now?

AN: Yes. I would like to see more women in leadership. I think the Republican Party needs to make a concerted effort to bring in more women to run for office, to run the Congressional offices, and there need to be more women in leadership. There are no Republican women in leadership in the U.S. Senate today. There's one Republican woman out of the four in leadership in the House, [Cathy McMorris Rogers], and she doesn't get enough of the spotlight. There is no reason why there should only be one woman committee chair in the House right now.

MS: Why do you think that is? As hard as it is for women in the Democratic Party, if the numbers are lower in the Republican Party, what's your assessment of what the challenges are there, and what will it take to change that?

AN: I think it's demographics, the current demographics. The biggest challenge in the Republican Party right now is the demographics. For a long time there were a lot of older white men firmly in control. And why are there more women on the Democrat side? Well, because they have more younger voters. You know, this question you're asking me is almost what came first, the chicken or the egg? It's hard to elect more women when you have a smaller base of women activists and voters and local elected officials. So the Republican Party has a long-term challenge . . . because we have to turn around the perception. We have to change the perception that the Republican Party is by and for older white men, and it's not going to happen in a day.

MS: Now we have twenty women in Congress and already there was an article on the front page of *The New York Times*—it was Rob Portman, a Republican male senator, who said even that small increase in women was having a "positive impact" and that he thought that "women tend to be interested in finding common ground." Especially given the fact that things are so partisan right now, do you think that having more women on both sides can lead to a different dynamic?

AN: Listen, the men have been in charge of leadership in Congress for a long time and they don't seem to be getting it right, so we are in the midst of a sadly dysfunctional government. Our government is operating in a somewhat dysfunctional way, and I think having more women could only help. But you know . . . it really depends on the person, the individual, and not his or her gender. There are some women who are ultra-partisan. I'm not sure Nancy Pelosi would be thought of as being more of a consensus builder than Steny Hoyer. If you ask me, I think Steny Hoyer is more of a consensus builder than Nancy Pelosi. So, I think we are, ourselves, delving into stereotypes and generalizations if we think women are different than men. Women can be just as hyper-partisan as men, and men can be just as practical and consensus building as women. It just totally depends on the individual.

MS: I definitely agree with you. There was another thing Celinda Lake said that I wanted to ask you about. She said, "I firmly believe that what we need are more progressive, moderate Republican women. Now the problem is that they can't survive." You seem to me to be somewhat of a more progressive, moderate Republican woman—

AN: I don't know what the hell I am anymore. The conservative movement has changed so much. After three days at CPAC, I don't know what a conservative is anymore. I thought I knew what a conservative was. I'm telling you that when I first started in politics, conservatism had three legs. It was a three-legged stool: strong national or international defense, fiscal conservatism and small government, and strong social values. I went to CPAC and half the people are saying, "Let's be isolationists, forget aid to Egypt, forget aid to Syrian rebels." Half the people are saying, "We don't want to talk about abortion; we don't want to talk about gay marriage; we don't want to talk about social issues." . . . I'm telling you, I don't know what conservatives are anymore, so I'm not sure.

I go back to telling you, I think it's less about the ideology and more about the individual. I think one of the problems we've had, as Republicans, certainly when you look at the Republican women in the Senate in particular, Olympia Snowe, Susan Collins, Lisa Murkowski . . . they're very pragmatic women, all of them, who are less about ideology and more about policy. They do what they think is the right thing to do. In fact, if anything, moderates have been the ones getting elected, but the Republican primaries right now are equally tough for progressive, moderate men.

MS: I was curious about your perception of what the results of this last election told us about the way both our electorate and the face of our government is changing. I know you also do a lot of outreach to Hispanic communities, and obviously the larger picture isn't just about women—it's just about diversity in general. Do you see a shifting of paradigms happening toward greater diversity in Washington?

AN: It's inevitable. Anybody who doesn't acknowledge that there's a growing diversity in the American electorate lives in a cave with their head in the sand—and that means gays, it means women, it means young people, it means blacks, it means Hispanics, it means Asians.

MS: That seems hopeful. I know that you've worked on a lot of different campaigns. If you look at Washington right now, things seem really dysfunctional, and it's hard to get people motivated to want to be a part of that. But I know you're very big on trying to engage people into the process, especially minority groups. What advice or encouragement would you give in terms of trying to get people to run and to be an active part of our process?

AN: People run because they have the fire in their belly. I don't think you can persuade or advise somebody into running. Running for office requires a level of commitment, willingness to be scrutinized and lose your privacy, the sacrifice of time away from family and home . . . I think the women who run pretty much know what it entails. And I always think that running is a very personal decision. But I do think anybody who runs, regardless of gender, needs to know what's entailed, what it means.

MS: I do some writing for the Women's Media Center and they had released a report recently that was titled "Report Exposes Problem: Gender Disparity in Media is at Crisis Levels." I know that you're a regular contributor to CNN and a variety of other media outlets, but women are still very much a minority. Why there is such inequity in terms of representation and diversity in the media, and why is that important?

AN: I think the reason that there are fewer women—that there is a gender gap in the media, there's a gender gap in elected office, there's a gender gap in high-level corporate America—it's all the same reasons. Because, until very recently, women have been the ones that bore the brunt of family and home responsibilities. And it's not been until recently that that has begun to change and we are now in an era where shared responsibilities have become the norm, not the exception. That women are beginning to have just as many chances as the men to enter careers that require great commitment and time, including the media. When you take a look at the news anchors, it's got to be somebody that can hop a plane and go cover the war in Kuwait one day and hop a plane and go cover the Papal election the next. So the reason that there are fewer women in the media and corporate America and elected office is all the same reason. We've been keeping up the home front and it's not been until recently . . . that women are having the opportunity to pursue careers that are very demanding.

MS: I do think the other part of the problem is that, for example, women hold only about 3 percent of clout positions in mainstream media.

AN: I think part of it is being in the media is a twenty-four-hour-a-day [job]. Being in the media is like being a doctor on call every day. There could be a number of emergencies that just require getting covered at that moment. And I think it's not until recently when women have been able to get out, when women have been able to do more than raising children and taking care of the home duties, that they've been able to pursue that. I think that's going to change. I think we're going to see more women in every aspect of American life, because it's changed and it's going to continue to change—the notion women no longer have to feel limited or guilty about spending time on other pursuits and asking their partners to share in the responsibility of raising the children.

MS: You are somebody who is so outspoken. You've always seemed to have had the courage to speak your mind. I was very taken with the fact that you came out in support of same-sex marriage, something that many people in the Republican Party are against. Where did that inner strength and courage come from?

AN: I think it's about commitment to your principles, to what you believe in. But also I grew up in a household where I was constantly encouraged to learn, be educated, and have my own opinions. And I was educated by the Sacred Heart nuns in an all-girls school . . . and believe me when I tell you that Sacred Heart nuns are the foremost experts in encouraging the independent, strong voices.

MS: What advice would you want to give to a young girl or a young woman today? What words of wisdom would you want to instill in them?

AN: I would say, "Be open to opportunities. See the opportunities when they appear, and seize opportunities." But I also think that women need to follow their hearts. It's okay for a woman to lean in. It's also okay for a woman to lean back, if that's what she wants. I think women need to follow their hearts and their minds and not conform to social pressures. And I think we also need to be acutely aware of opportunities when they arise and seize them with both hands.

MAYA ANGELOU

"We need to be seen as well as heard. It's not sufficient to say, 'Well, we are here, and we deserve.' Because if we really think that the majority of women in the world are also always in the kitchen and in the kindergarten and in the places just to look after the young and men, then we do ourselves and everybody a disservice . . . The whole country needs to know that women are much smarter—we're more than that."

D R. MAYA ANGELOU is one of the most renowned and influential voices of our time. Hailed as a global renaissance woman, she is a celebrated poet, writer, performer, teacher, director, and civil rights activist. In addition to her groundbreaking autobiographies, beginning with I *Know Why the Caged Bird Sings*, Angelou has written two cookbooks; five poetry collections, including *I Shall Not Be Moved*; three books of essays, including *Letter to My Daughter*; and six long-form poems, including "Mother." The list of her published verse, nonfiction, and fiction now includes more than thirty best-selling titles. In her most recent work, a memoir titled *Mom & Me & Mom*, she shares the deepest personal story of her life: her relationship with her mother. A trailblazer in film and television, Angelou wrote the screenplay and composed the score for the 1972 film *Georgia, Georgia*. Her script, the first by an African American woman ever to be filmed, was nominated for a Pulitzer Prize. In 1996, she directed her first feature film, *Down in the Delta*.

Angelou has served on two presidential committees, was awarded the Presidential Medal of Arts in 2000 and the Lincoln Medal in 2008, and has received three Grammy Awards. President Clinton requested that she compose a poem to read at his inauguration in 1993. Angelou's reading of her poem "On the Pulse of the Morning" was broadcast live around the world. In 2012 she founded the Maya Angelou Center for Women's Health and Wellness in her adopted hometown of Winston-Salem, North Carolina.

MARIANNE SCHNALL: Why do you think we haven't had a woman president? And do you feel our consciousness is ready to have that happen?

MAYA ANGELOU: Well, I think we are more ready for it than we think we are. I mean, if anyone had asked you five years ago, "Do you think we're ready for a black president?" it's very likely that the wagging of the head would have been, "No, no, no—not yet." However, we're readier than we thought we were. And I think that's true about women. I supported Hillary Clinton in her bid for the White House. After a while, some of the top Democrats phoned me and asked me to ask Mrs. Clinton to step down because it seemed certain that Senator Obama was going to be the choice. So I said, "I told her twenty years ago that if she ran for anything, I had her back and would support her. When she steps down, I will step down." I think that she would make a wonderful president. But when she decided that Senator Obama was a likely candidate that she could support, she stepped down and I stepped down with her. And I went over to the Obama camp and said, "If I can be of any use, please use me."

MS: Sometimes this gets framed as just about equality—women are still such a minority, not only in Washington, but in corporate leadership. Why is it important that we have women's voices equally represented?

MA: Well, we need to be seen, all over the place. We need to be seen as well as heard. It's not sufficient to say, "Well, we are here, and we deserve." If we really think that the majority of women in the world are also always in the kitchen and in the kindergarten and in the places just to look after the young and men, then we do ourselves and everybody a disservice. Because women offer so much more than it would seem we offer. It would seem we offer kindness and the chance to be cared for and nursed in more ways than just medical. And I think that the whole country needs to know that women are much smarter—we're more than that. We're that and more than that.

MS: If you could speak to the world community, what message would you most want to deliver to humanity?

MA: I would encourage us to try our best to develop courage. It's the most important of all the virtues, because without courage, you can't practice any other virtue consistently. You can be anything erratically—kind, fair, true, generous, all that. But to be that thing time after time, you need courage. We need to develop courage, and we need to develop it in small ways first. Because we wouldn't go and say, "I'll pick up this hundred-pound weight" without knowing our capacity. So we need to say, "Oh, I'll start by picking up a five-pound weight, then a ten-pound weight, then a twenty-five-pound, and sooner or later I'll be able to pick up a one-hundred-pound weight." And I think that's true with courage. You develop a little courage, so that if you decide, "I will not stay in rooms where women are belittled; I will not stay in company where races, no matter who they are, are belittled; I will not take it; I will not sit around and accept dehumanizing other human beings"—if you decide to do that in small ways, and you continue to do it—finally you realize you've got so much courage. Imagine it—you've got so much courage that people want to be around you. They get a feeling that they will be protected in your company.

MS: What message would you most want to instill in young girls? What do you wish you had known as a child?

MA: Courage. Also, I encourage courtesy—to accept nothing less than courtesy and to give nothing less than courtesy. If we accept being talked to any kind of way, then we are telling ourselves we are not quite worth the best. And if we have the effrontery to talk to anybody with less than courtesy, we tell ourselves and the world we are not very intelligent.

MS: I saw some of your emotional appearances after Barack Obama's first win, in 2008. Did you ever imagine that you would live long enough to witness that?

MA: Never. Never. And yet somewhere, obviously, I must have known. I know that my people did, because they couldn't have survived slavery without having hope that it would get better. There are some songs from the eighteenth and nineteenth centuries that say [*sings*], "By and by, by and by, I will lay down this heavy load." I mean, so many songs that spoke of hope—amazing songs. The slaves knew that they did not have the right legally to walk within one inch away from where the slave owner dictated, and yet the same people wrote and sang with fervor, "If the Lord wants somebody, here am I, send me." It's amazing.

MS: There seems to be a growing movement around issues such as anti-war sentiment, awareness about global warming, violence against women, and world poverty—a growth in awareness and compassion and a sense of responsibility. Do you think humanity is experiencing an evolutionary shift to a new paradigm?

MA: I think so. I think we are making it very clear to people, whether they want to hear it or not, or whether they would like to think of this as some fluke of history—wrong, wrong. People are saying, "This is what I will stand for. And I will not stand for any less than this." It's amazing. We are growing up! We are growing up out of the idiocies—racism and sexism and ageism and all those ignorances.

MS: What do you think is the root cause of all the problems we have in the world today?

MA: Ignorance, of course, but mostly polarization. You see, it's a long time arranging this sort of condition. And it will not be over in one term, or even two. But we are on the right road. If you have a person enslaved, the first thing you must do is to convince yourself that the person is subhuman and won't mind the enslavement. The second thing you must do is convince your allies that the person is subhuman, so that you have some support. But the third and the unkindest cut of all is to convince that person that he or she is not quite a first-class citizen. When the complete job has been done, the initiator can go back years later and ask, "Why don't you people like yourselves more?" You see? It's been true for women, it's been true for immigrants, it's been true for Asians, it's been true for Spanish-speaking people. So now we have to undo. We can learn to see each other and see ourselves in each other and recognize that human beings are more alike than we are unalike.

MS: There are still so many ways in which we divide ourselves—by religion, race, gender, sexuality, nationality. Are you hopeful that humanity will ever come to see itself as one family?

MA: Yes, but it will be a long time. But that's all right; it's a wonderful goal to be working toward.

MS: Do you feel like women around the world are awakening to a sense of their own power and a need in the world for their influence?

MA: Yes, I think so. We can see—from California to New York, from Maine to Florida, Seattle to New Mexico—everywhere there are women's groups. Everywhere there are women who have gotten together to examine global warming and women who have gotten together to prepare each other for single parenting, women who have come together to be supportive—all sorts of gatherings of women. I mean, I look back fifty years ago and there was nothing like that, nothing.

MS: I know you have gone through some dark times in your life, but you have accomplished so much and are such a beacon of light and inspiration. Where do your own strength and courage come from?

MA: Well, I had a fabulous grandmother. And my mother. I have some sister friends. . . . They have influenced and strengthened my life. And when I want to think about what would be the right thing to do, the fair thing to do, the wise thing to do, I can just think of my grandmother. I can always hear her say, "Now, sister, you know what's right. Just do right!"

MS: Do you have a spiritual philosophy or way of looking at life that guides you?

MA: Yes. All of us know not what is expedient, not what is going to make us popular, not what the policy is—but in truth each of us knows what is the right thing to do. And that's how I am guided.

MS: What advice would you give to people who are going through something painful or are feeling frustrated or depressed? What would you say to give them hope?

MA: Well, I would say, "Look what you've already come through! Don't deny it. You've already come through some things, which are very painful. If you've been alive until you're thirty-five, you have gone through some pain. It cost you something. And you've come through it. So at least look at that. Have the sense to look at yourself and say, 'Well, wait a minute. I'm stronger than I thought I was.'" So we need to not be in denial about what we've done, what we've come through. It will help us if we all do that.

BALANCING THE MASCULINE AND FEMININE

I believe we have been living in a very masculine world; a world of singularity where we are not looking at things holistically, where we don't take in the totality of a woman. It's been a boy's club, and leadership and the way we think about it has been impacted by this. In order for things to change, we have to shift the perspective from being "either/or" to "and." It's not about women replacing men—it's about the embrace. We need masculine and feminine energies for us to move the needle forward. I have said many times that I'm fascinated by the word "woman," and that's because when you really look at the word, you see how there is a man in every woman. I think this is incredibly symbolic, as the feminine and the masculine need to be in harmony. I feel that there is a dynamic shift that is happening and that a balance needs to be restored.

— DONNA KARAN

Let's face it: we could have a woman president and it might not be any different if the woman, in order to get up the ladder, has armored her heart and become like a man. . . . So while it would be great to have a woman president, what may be more important is her consciousness. Whether it's a man or a woman, do they have a feminist consciousness? And, of course, what we would have to contend with if there was a man running who had the consciousness, well, we know the names that would be hurled at him, and given our culture, it would be really hard. He'd be called a pansy, effete, and on and on and on. It takes a lot of courage for a man in this culture to claim his emotional literacy and his heart. And we have to rally around both genders. It's less about gender sometimes and more about consciousness.

— JANE FONDA

Sometimes I feel like it's a bit of fallacy to say men are violent and women are non-violent, because I don't think that's necessarily true. But I do think there is a sort of natural balance in nature between men and women, and that it's being thrown off balance by the social and economic inequities between men and women. And one of the reasons FINCA [the organization I'm an ambassador for] is primarily women is because in many places when they would have mixed groups of men and women together, the women just wouldn't run for office; they wouldn't try to be president or vice president. You see that so often, and that's something that's totally socialized. I read some study when I was in college about how in the United States, if you see class president elections, it's like all girls, and then in eighth grade, no girls run. It's like, what happens in there that tells girls to be quiet, be submissive, be meek? It's ridiculous—we're missing out on 50 percent of our potential great people.

—NATALIE PORTMAN

I think calling it masculine or feminine is being trapped in the old patriarchal model. I think I see a desire coming forward of human qualities in both men and women, and it's up against this division of human qualities into masculine and feminine. The problem is that with that division, I would say, neither men nor women can be leaders, because you can't be a leader if you can't join thought and emotion, and you can't be a leader if you don't understand how to live in relationships with people.

—CAROL GILLIGAN, PhD, AUTHOR AND PSYCHOLOGIST

The feminine has to rise in order for there to be any hope of continuation of the species. And I think that most people actually feel that on some level. . . . Anything that encourages women to accept themselves as who they are and what they are and to honor the feminine in them, would be very, very helpful for the world's healing.

—ALICE WALKER

MICHAEL KIMMEL

"I have found that since I've begun to support gender equality—since I've tried to do it at home, as well as in my professional work—my life is much better. My relationship with my family, with my children, with my parents, with my friends, with my colleagues, is so much richer. So the argument that I make consistently to men is that gender equality is not a zero-sum game—it is a win-win. And, in fact, gender equality is the only way you're going to be able to have the kinds of relationships you say you want to have, so it's in our interest to support it."

MICHAEL S. KIMMEL is University Distinguished Professor of Sociology at SUNY at Stony Brook. He is the author of *Guyland: The Perilous World Where Boys Become Men*, which was featured on *The Today Show* and *Good Morning America* and in more than one hundred radio, newspaper, and blog reviews. Some of his other books include *Changing Men, Men's Lives, The Politics of Manhood, The Gendered Society, Misframing Men,* and, most recently, *The Guy's Guide to Feminism*. He is the founder and editor of *Men and Masculinities,* the field's premier scholarly journal, a book series on gender and sexuality at New York University Press. He was also one of the founders of the National Organization for Men Against Sexism.

MARIANNE SCHNALL: Just to start with, why do you think we haven't had a woman president so far?

MICHAEL KIMMEL: I think there are two reasons. Obviously, the easiest answer to this is the overconscious prejudice that people believe that women aren't as competent around leadership, that leadership requires being a man—being willing to push the button, being willing to let our sons go into harm's way, to stand up to our rivals and our enemies. So there's always been the feeling that in some ways women weren't qualified, that there was an essential difference between women and men, and that categorically, women should be excluded. I mean, it's not that long ago that women just barely got the right to vote. So there's still a tremendous amount of prejudice, it seems to me, and this results from the kind of essential-difference argument.

Now, it is also true that if I make an essential-difference argument with my students, if I say to them, "Women and men are so fundamentally different that women should never, ever be elected to higher office," my students immediately would respond, "But what about Golda Meir? What about Margaret Thatcher? What about Indira Gandhi?" I mean, there are a lot of women who are really qualified and certainly as capable leaders as any man. So my students are willing to suspend it if they're challenged, I think, but what I've come to believe is that a lot of this "discrimination" is soft discrimination, by which I mean that if you could find a counterexample, they'll believe you. What happened to Hillary Clinton in 2008 seems a really good example. She was defeminized because she seemed so competent: "Okay, right, she could definitely be president, but she's not a real lady" [laughs].

So that's the first thing. It's the obvious answer, it's the right answer, but I think there's another answer as well. There was a breakthrough essay written by an art historian named Linda Nochlin in the early 1970s. The article basically posed a question as women were beginning to criticize the art canon, the canon of great artists, and she wrote an essay with the title "Why Have There Been No Great Women Artists?" And the answer, of course, that everyone had been given is this overt discrimination that women weren't good enough, capable enough, couldn't hold the brush right, whatever. And she said, you know, it is really facile and probably wrong for us to go back through the old pages of the history of art or music or literature, searching for the female Shakespeare or Rembrandt or Mozart. The truth is, there haven't been any great women artists. The question is not to sort of dredge up some second-rate artist or musician and try to proclaim them to be as great as Mozart or Shakespeare. The question is, Why? And there, she says, the answer is that women were excluded from the schools that created the great artists to begin with. She looked at French painting in the eighteenth century, and she said what happened in France was that there were three levels of painting: there was genre painting, there was landscape painting, and then there was portrait painting. And portrait painting was, of course, the most elevated. But, of course, in order to paint a portrait, you have to actually see a model, and women were way too delicate—they were excluded from the live-model studios—therefore, they never could paint portraits; therefore, they never became the great artists. So she said it's not enough to just throw it on bad men or bad ideas and prejudice; it's also the fact that women are excluded from the very places that train you to be that kind of person. So if women are not in the great military schools, if they don't get into the great law schools, or whatever, that prepare people for careers in politics, then of course they're not going to be those kinds of leaders. Now, that answer means that we haven't had a woman president yet. But clearly now there are women at West Point. There are women at all the major colleges and universities and all of the premier law schools. In fact, over half of the students are women, so it does seem to me now that after having these centuries of exclusion, what we're dealing with are the remnants of this prejudice. I personally believe we will have, in 2016, our first female president. I'm actually a big believer that now that these structural obstacles have been removed, there is enough of an erosion of this old prejudice that, in fact, we're about to see something quite remarkable: the first black president, followed by the first female president. And America is really the outlier on this, Marianne, as you know. Countries that we keep denigrating because they treat women so badly, like Pakistan, have had two! They're right to say, "Who are you to talk?" [*laughs*] Because we've had zero. We've barely had a woman come close. So my answer [pertains to both structure] and the remnants of prejudice, and I believe that now that those structural barriers have begun to fall, the prejudices are also beginning to erode. I think the percentage of people, male and female, who believe that by definition a woman is unqualified for public office has shrunk to single digits. It's never been lower. I would imagine, although I don't have the numbers in front of me, that the numbers were probably close to 30 or 40 percent only forty years ago. That's a pretty big change.

MS: You devote much of your work to and write a lot about gender roles, and we were talking a little bit about what happened with Hillary—the conundrum women face of having to be confident, powerful, and ambitious to get to a place where they can be considered good leaders, while dealing with all the negative backlash against women who do act in that way. What are your thoughts on that conundrum for women?

MK: One of the things about Hillary's candidacy that I think was made most evident in her campaign was that sexism is still more permissible in our culture than racism. I don't want us to get too self-congratulatory here. I don't think that we're there yet, although I think that we're closer than we ever have been. You remember that "iron my shirt" moment. What's interesting, I have to say, is that my students just didn't know about that. When I talk about that in lectures, when I say, "And you will remember the time when those guys held up that sign that said GO IRON MY SHIRT," most people look at me like, *What? No, we never heard of that.* I thought that was interesting, because that was a pretty obvious moment in the disability of sexism—and those ideas were still alive and well. And I thought to myself, *What would have happened if, instead of some men holding up a sign that said Go IRON MY SHIRT, some white guy at an Obama rally had held up a sign that said GO SHINE MY SHOES?* The entire campaign would have come to a screeching halt. Every single media outlet would have covered it, big-time. It would have been the major news story, and every candidate, including the Republicans, would have said, "Okay, stop everything. That's wrong." The fact that it passed without notice is an indication that that kind of sexism, those kinds of prejudices, are still more visible than racism, still more permissible.

MS: What qualities do you think women would bring to leadership that are most needed in the United States and around the world now? Why would you like to see this? Why is it important?

MK: There are two answers to this question—one of them depends upon a kind of gender-similarity hypothesis, and one of them depends on a gender-difference hypothesis. The gender-similarity hypothesis would say I don't really care what gender the person is—what I'm looking for is somebody who is really qualified to lead the country, to help us restore the economy, to rein in rapacious corporations, to be more equitable in our tax policies, to make sure that there is an adequate social safety net, and to lead us as the leader of the world. Now I want to know who that person is. And most voters, I believe, don't really care about the gender package that comes in. So that's the gender-similarity argument.

The gender-difference argument is, now, what I've just said are gender traits, so we want to say to everybody that we should share the burden, we should seek peace, we should be safe, we should make sure that everybody has enough, that the hungry should be fed—those are traditionally feminine attributes. In the old way that we coded traits, attitudes, and behaviors, those were coded as feminine. It's moms who say to children who are fighting, "Now, wait a minute—let's share that toy and use your words." And then there are the dads who say, "Draw a line in the sand and stand up for yourself." So which one is more likely to go to war?

Either way you go, a woman would be a reasonable candidate. If you believe women and men are basically, fundamentally different, you should vote for a woman, because you would be much safer and you'd be much less likely to go to war with a female president—if you believe in the gender-difference hypothesis. If you believe in the gender-similarity hypothesis, which I do, you'd simply look for the person who would be more likely to enact those kinds of things.

MS: When we were talking about the milestone of Obama becoming president, I think in some ways, in addition to the fact that he's paved the way for having a minority become president, he also does embody a slightly more "feminine" way of being—in the way he tries sometimes to negotiate, reach across the aisles, and he also is very vocal about taking time for his family. Is this also just a push to have the more "feminine values"—not necessarily that women always embody that—enter into the paradigm of leadership?

MK: I think that's right. First, there's Obama's personal style. Secondly, there's the demand. What we demand from a black candidate is, of course, that he remain utterly and completely even-tempered and never get angry, because the last thing that people would vote for in this country is an *angry* black man. So his temperament, plus the demands of unconscious racism in the electorate, led Obama, I think, to be far more conciliatory. And, of course, everybody criticized him because the right wing, the Republicans, dug in and they were intransigent, and he tried to compromise. That didn't work, and so he became equally bellicose. Why? Because he had to.

MS: It seems to me, even with men—and you being a perfect example of this—men are starting to become supportive of women's equality, not for the sake of fairness but because they do think that women have something to contribute. Is it your sense that men are starting to also realize how important it is that women's voices and perspectives are equally represented in all sectors, including politics?

MK: You know what? I don't think so. At our best, I think currently we're becoming more gender blind. I don't think men would sit there and say women embody these characteristics, therefore we should vote for them. I don't think that that's true. I think the liberal position is to be more gender blind.

MS: That's really interesting. I actually like what you're saying. I think it is maybe true that hopefully it isn't about all these divisions and classifications, but just about looking at the person inside us. I would love to be moving to a place like that. How did you come to be who you are and being able to raise a son in the way you're raising your son? Did you have a certain influence on you that allowed you to be this way, or is this something that you had to learn, in terms of your awareness and activism around these issues?

MK: My experience is a combination of all of the different ways in which men come to believe in gender equality. I think we come to believe in gender equality in three fundamental ways. First—because the first one is what you might call the ethical imperative—I'm an American. This is what my son, Zachary, said yesterday about why he thinks men should support feminism. He said, "I'm an American. We believe in equality and fairness and justice for all. That's the foundation of our country." Of course I believe in that. To me, the weird thing is people who don't believe in that. So gender equality is right and fair and just, and—being an American and studying America's society—I believe that. I believe that firmly, and it's made me an antiracist activist and a profeminist activist, because I believe that's what America stands for. That's the first thing.

The second thing is, it's been part of my experience to meet and listen to the experiences of people who have been harmed by gender inequality—just as I've talked to people who have been harmed by racial inequality or sexual inequality—and listening to those stories sometimes breaks your heart. Sometimes it makes you feel angry. Sometimes it makes you disgusted. How is this possible in this country that people have to endure these kinds of things? I think that's one of the other reasons that men get involved in this, because they have some personal experience with the women in their lives being discriminated against or subject to violence or whatever.

And the third thing, and this is the part that I take on the road most often, is that I have found that since I've begun to support gender equality—since I've tried to do it at home, as well as in my professional work—my life is much better. My relationship with my family, with my children, with my parents, with my friends, with my colleagues, is so much richer. So the argument that I make consistently to men is that gender equality is not a zero-sum game—it is a win-win. And, in fact, gender equality is the only way you're going to be able to have the kinds of relationships you say you want to have, so it's in our interest to support it.

MS: I don't know if you saw the film *Miss Representation,* about the media's impact on our perception and what that results in. It makes me think—especially for you, as the father of a boy—of how boys are just inundated with images of women and girls as sex objects. You have a son whom you are raising who can obviously see past this, but how do we raise our boys to see women as leaders and not as pretty things?

MK: I want to say first, this is exactly what Zachary has written about in his SPARK Summit blog post: the effect of the media's sexualization of girls on boys. And he says, "When I'm hanging around with my guy friends, they all talk about girls in exactly those ways," and he realizes it's really destructive. He told a story yesterday—he said he went to see a movie with some friends, another boy and two other girls, and they were all sitting there, and they had a trailer for the *Twilight* movie. And when Taylor Lautner ripped off his shirt, all the girls went, "Oh!" and he said, "I felt really terrible about my body, and I immediately went home and did a hundred sit-ups" [*laughs*]. So boys are being constructed to have the same kind of view of their bodies as girls do. So he understands completely the effect of these media images on boys, as well as girls.

So how do we combat this? First, media are not monolithic. There are many, many alternatives, and especially in this era of Internet proliferation and critical engagement with media and social media, for every awful image that we encounter, there are also positive ones, or positive ones to be abstracted from the things that we're watching. I think that the key to parenting is not to use media as free babysitting—that is to say, park your kid in front of it and go off and do what you want to do. The thing to do is, of course, to engage with your kids, to help your kids develop a kind of critical engagement, a critical capacity to engage with the media that they're looking at. So I've watched *Toy Story,* for example, probably fifty times. I've memorized it. Why? Because when Zachary was three and four, we watched it several times a day [*laughs*], and, yes, like many parents, I was bored to death after a while. But he was mastering how narrative works, how a story develops, how you move from one idea to another, and so it was important to watch it over and over and over and over again. And so once he had the idea of how a story goes, we were able to have conversations about what else might have happened, or what do you think of this character. And to develop that, I think, requires what children actually really need, which is a lot of time, a lot of attention, and a lot of love. The form that that comes in—a heterosexual couple, a gay couple, a lesbian couple, a single mom, a single dad, whatever—is a lot less important than the context. That's what kids need, and that kind of media engagement is very critical.

MS: You said you thought we would have a woman president in 2016. What do you think are the most important areas to focus on or to change in these next few years to allow that milestone to happen, to pave the way?

MK: I am congenitally optimistic. I don't think you can be an educator without being an optimist, because I have to believe that if my students engage critically with their world, their lives will be better for it, so my job is to help them engage more critically. And I can't be a political activist without believing that change is possible. And, frankly, just look around— the evidence of this is pretty incontestable. Five years ago, I stood in front of my students and I said to them that there will be marriage equality in the United States by the end of this century. "You will live to see it," I said to them, "but I won't." I was so wrong. We will have marriage equality in this country by the end of this decade, maybe even by the end of this year. The old barriers are falling faster than many of us ever expected, and, yes, of course, there's tremendous backlash, lots of obstacles—I'm not Pollyanna about this, but I am optimistic. I do believe, as Martin Luther

King, Jr., said and as Obama keeps quoting, that the arc of history points toward greater equality and greater justice.

What will be the markers to me of whether or not there will be a viable female candidate in 2016? My guess is the public reaction when people start announcing their candidacy, and the biggest, most hopeful moment I can point to that would tell you this—you'll find this ironic—is, nobody really raised an eyebrow when Michele Bachmann declared. Nobody said, "Oh, but she's a woman." Nobody seemed to pay any attention to that. "She's a lunatic"—that's what people said. That's what they paid attention to. I'm serious! Nobody really said, "Well, she's a woman, she's not qualified." So, as the new slates are going to be forming in 2014, probably earlier, even, we'll begin to have the exploratory committees—let's see where the conversation goes. I have a feeling that if Hillary Clinton and Michele Bachmann or Sarah Palin begin to form exploratory committees—or some of these other women who I think are really potentially at this point perhaps vice-presidential material—it's very possible that in the next round, we'll have some women who are potential presidential candidates or potential vice-presidential candidates. So maybe we're not talking 2016—maybe we're talking about 2024—but still, as this develops, what I think we will see is less and less of, "Well, no, she couldn't possibly be president, because she's a woman." We won't hear that. It won't even register, and that's how we'll know it's time.

I think it's really important for feminists to understand that patriarchy takes aim at girls' voices, but it takes aim at boys' hearts. And it happens really early with boys, like five. Just really wrapping ourselves around that will open our hearts with empathy to boys and men. . . . Feminism is for men as well as women. I cannot emphasize that enough. And the only way we are going to make it is if we understand it and speak about it. You know, I do a lot of public speaking, and I look out at the audience, and there's always men as well as women, and when I talk about this, I can just see the tension go out of the men's shoulders. It's like, "I'm included. I'm included in this." What we can do for men is help them see that this is not attacking men. On the contrary. And it's like the opposite of patriarchy is not matriarchy—it's democracy.

—JANE FONDA

More and more men are calling themselves feminists, openly calling themselves feminists. The president of the United States does. . . . It's definitely increasing, increasing, increasing. We use the word feminist more because we do think that men themselves must change, it's not just the women.

—ELEANOR SMEAL, COFOUNDER AND PRESIDENT OF
FEMINIST MAJORITY FOUNDATION

We have to do a lot more educating of men, and I know that many feminists feel like they're tired of that and they can't do that, and da, da, da, da, da. And nobody's more tired than some of us, but it seems to be really important— especially if we're thinking of our sisters' and daughters' health. And not only that, so many of us by now have these wonderful feminist sons and grandsons who really are allies, and we should give them the respect as allies in changing a lot of the things that are wrong and done against women in the world.

—ALICE WALKER

Men can be feminists, too! Many men are feminists. We need feminism. It's not against men. It's about the empowerment of women. It's the respect of women. Giving women equal rights, the same opportunities.

—ANNIE LENNOX

What I've noticed, just in my own personal life, is that young men sort of have the same reaction toward feminists that young women do. But then when you push them, when you ask them if they support equality and about pointed issues, they will also say that they align themselves with a feminist agenda. I think we've definitely reached a point in our society where men are very open to those ideas and are supportive of those ideas, especially in conversations about family life. Men today see themselves as being involved fathers and really want to have a balance in their homes. These are all very important issues.

—JULIE ZEILINGER, AUTHOR, FOUNDER AND EDITOR OF THE FBOMB BLOG

I don't want us to, in our eagerness for men to finally put an oar in and row their share, become openly grateful, which is a woman's tendency. There's no reason to be grateful to people who are doing what they should have already been doing all along. As a white person who's privileged in a white, racist society, I don't expect African American friends or acquaintances or strangers to be grateful that I'm trying to fight racism. That's what I should have been doing all along. . . . I think, in other words, measured celebration is in order, and continued vigilance. This is a case where—and I rarely do quote Ronald Reagan, you can imagine—this is "trust, but verify."

—ROBIN MORGAN, AUTHOR, COFOUNDER OF WOMEN'S MEDIA CENTER

BARBARA LEE

"I think it takes a while for women to realize what their power is, because we haven't been part of this for very long. But I think what I have seen is that when women know their power, they really do know how to use it, not for their personal gain, but for the good of the country."

R EPRESENTATIVE BARBARA LEE is a forceful and progressive voice in Congress, dedicated to social and economic justice, international peace, and civil and human rights. She proudly represents California's 13th Congressional District. She serves on the Appropriations and Budget Committees, is a member of the Democratic Steering and Policy Committee, is a senior Democratic whip, chair of the Democratic Whip's Task Force on Poverty and Opportunity, and a co-chair of the Congressional HIV/AIDS Caucus. Lee has been a strong proponent of safe communities, affordable housing, the homeless, low-income energy assistance, job training, making health care affordable and universal, just immigration policies, the establishment of a living wage, and protection of the right of women to make decisions about their reproductive health.

First elected in 1998 to represent California's 9th Congressional District, the Democratic lawmaker has established a reputation for principled and independent stands, unafraid to take on the tough issues and speak her mind for her constituents, for a more just America, and for a safer world. As a social worker by profession, being an advocate for people in dealing with the federal bureaucracy has been a priority. She has aggressively represented the needs of the underserved and vulnerable people in her district and throughout the U.S., vigorously advocating for a wide range of social and economic concerns and bread-and-butter issues that affect their daily lives. Her accomplishments are many, including authoring or co-authoring every major piece of legislation dealing with global HIV/AIDS issues since she was elected to Congress.

MARIANNE SCHNALL: Why do you think we have not yet had a woman president?

BARBARA LEE: Well, I tell you, there are real barriers. Women have had to really fight to reduce systemic and institutional barriers on all fronts. When you look at even the pay equity at this point and the gap in terms of how much a woman makes versus a man—we're still fighting that battle. And so, we've come a long way since women gained the right to vote, but we have a long way to go. Our struggle for equal rights is not over and I think that's reflected in all levels of government and in the private sector.

MS: Do you feel hopeful that you'll see a woman president in your life-time? What will it take, do you think, to make that milestone happen?

BL: I think the country is ready for a woman to be president. Let me just say, I think we were ready, we just didn't vote en masse when Shirley Chisholm ran, and that's how I got involved in politics. She was the first woman to seriously run for president, the first African American to run, and I am telling you, the country was excited. I remember working with NOW and all of the feminist organizations and women and communities of color throughout the country, and we were close then. It's just . . . Shirley didn't have the money, and the media was against her, so she had all of the uphill battles to climb, but I think that she really paved the way. She charted the course for a woman to be president, and I think because of her and because of the movement, the country is about ready.

MS: What do the results of the last election tell us about the way our electorate and the face of our government are changing? Do you see a shifting in paradigms happening, not just in terms of having more women now in Congress, but just diversity in general? What trends interest you?

BL: Sure. Young people are really making a difference, and I'm doing everything I can do to help keep them involved. And we're seeing coalitions being put together that beforehand didn't really work together—when you look at coalitions of communities of color—the black, Latino, Asian-Pacific American coalitions, when you look at the progressive coalitions, when you look at the peace and justice coalitions. First, I think the country is very progressive, when you look at what it took to elect President Barack Obama, and so it's the natural next step to keep this coalition together to elect a woman, because I think it's these voters who have said that no longer will we have these barriers that would prevent a woman from becoming president.

MS: I know that there are sometimes psychological factors—for both men and women—in terms of seeing a woman in that highest office, being able to handle issues like national security or a situation like war. Do you think that in terms of our culture we are ready to see a woman that way?

BL: Absolutely. Even though I didn't agree with Secretary of State Condoleezza Rice, I mean, she was an African American woman as secretary of state, and I firmly disagreed with her 95 percent of the time on policy. When you look at Secretary of State Hillary Clinton, when you look at Madeleine Albright, when you look at Susan Rice, our ambassador—when you look at women and the key roles that they have played, it's almost now the norm. I think we must be vigilant, though, and the subtleties will begin to creep in, like what happened with Ambassador Rice and how they denied her even the opportunity to be considered for secretary of state, because the guys over there in the Senate found every which way to try to stop her—and I really am convinced they would not have done that to a man. So I think that there are a lot of impediments still, subconsciously, that we have to be very vigilant with.

MS: We did have a history-making election in terms of women's representation in Congress, yet it's still far from parity. We've made advancements in so many other areas—what specific obstacles are there, in terms of women in politics, and what can we do to make that easier for more women?

BL: Well, I'll tell you, I've got to start with money. This money and politics is obscene. And we have to get the public financing of campaigns to level the playing field. Right now, of course, it's been a man's world and so they have the access to the resources, in many ways, much more than women. So we've got to have a campaign finance system that really allows for equality. And I think, at this point, that system is not fair and that's a real factor in federal elections.

MS: Aside from just equality for equality's sake, why is it important that we have more women, more diversity in general, in terms of representation in Washington?

BL: Well, of course, a woman's perspective is very, very important, in terms of fixing the problems that we have in the world. When women really see a problem, they'll analyze it much quicker, they'll try to figure out a fix and then move on to fix it. And I think it's important to have people who are doers, who are intellectually very smart—you know, women are smart. And so you have that combination of a woman's head and her heart and her ability to figure out how to get from A to Z. Women are good strategists, they're good tacticians, and a lot of it may have to do with a lot of the work that we have done in our past—just personally myself, raising two young boys as a single mother on public assistance. That gave me a really good handle on what to look for when we talk about the safety net and welfare reform and healthcare and social security and childcare and all of the issues that allow for women, children, and families to move from living in poverty into the middle class. You know, a lot of women have been through this, and to be able, again, for me personally, to use experiences that I have had to try to say, you know, I'm going to make this better so that the next generation won't have to go through what I went through.

MS: A lot of times I think women have felt a little bit detached from what happens in Washington, and then all of a sudden in this last election, there was so much conversation—whether it was over contraception or reproductive rights or even some of the misinformed remarks about rape. Do you think that this last election was a little bit of a wake-up call, that there's legislation that is directly impacting women's rights? Women have to be a part of this process now.

BL: Absolutely, and I believe there is a war on women. And when you look at what has happened here in the House, in terms of the effort to erode women's rights, women's healthcare, women's right to privacy, to an abortion, to pay equity—when you look at everything, there are assaults on women each and every day. Women are fed up with these assaults. And the war on women . . . which I actually coined! At a press conference I was just so frustrated and I was trying to think of what to say about these attacks, and I said, "You know, this seems like a war on women." And I think that this caught on, and I think women, whether they agree with it being a war or not, they know that every day they are systematically being attacked here in Congress.

MS: Do you notice a change with having more women in Congress? I've seen a couple of articles recently that actually say it's already changing the tone. Even having a slight increase in women, do you think it has a tangible impact in terms of the dynamics there?

BL: Yeah, definitely I do. I think what happens, though, is naturally women get dug into their party position, but I think that the tone in terms of having more women keeps it a little more civil than what it has been in the past. And with Republican women, you know, we have a bipartisan women's caucus, and we try to find common ground on some issues, but there are some that we just can't work together on. We acknowledge that and try to find common ground on other issues. And so it has changed some, but it hasn't changed to the point where we could figure out how to solve the big problems together, because of our values as Democrats versus Republicans.

MS: What advice would you have for a woman new to Congress on how best to operate and navigate in an old boys' club, in the sense of being a minority? I remember when I interviewed Nancy Pelosi and she was talking about the "marble ceiling." As women are moving up in leadership positions, not just in politics but everywhere, that can be a little daunting. Do you have insight on that?

BL: It really can be, but what I would say is—and this is what Shirley Chisholm told me in '72—don't let this daunting task fool you and take you away from the real mission and that is you've got to not only play by *their* rules, but change their rules, because the rules of the game may not have been created for women, or by women. And so when you get here, if you see something that's old school, that's part of the good old boys' network, don't go along to get along—get in here and try to change it. We've got to shatter these rules here in Congress. We've got to make the structural and systemic changes here, just as we have to do on the outside. And so, yes, it is daunting, but we can't let that overtake us.

MS: That's such an important point. And actually in terms of paradigms that are changing, the other one that I think is changing from that last election is the whole notion of how we think about and use power. Because I think, in addition to the debates over women's reproductive rights, there was also an awareness, in terms of the responsibility that we have to not just serve the privileged communities, but to make sure that we are helping all people. I know a big part of your work is making sure that we're helping underserved communities. Do you think that the whole notion of how we view and use power has to change, as well?

BL: I think it does, because so many don't even know their power, and the title of Nancy Pelosi's book was great: *Know Your Power*. I think it takes a while for women to realize what their power is, because we haven't been part of this for very long. But I think what I have seen is that when women know their power, they really do know how to use it, not for their personal gain, but for the good of the country and the good of their constituents. There's a big difference there between how women operate versus how men operate. Women know how to wield their power, but from what I see, it's almost always for the greater good. I think that's a very important lesson that men can learn. So you could be a wheeler and a dealer and make whatever compromises are necessary, but you have to remember why you're doing this and who it's for and what good is going to come out of it, instead of seeing it as a personal gain.

MS: What inspires you? Obviously this is not the easiest job to have. A lot of people look at Washington and it looks dysfunctional—it's not the most attractive career sometimes for people to pursue. But what are the rewards, and what personally inspires you and your service?

BL: Marianne, that question comes up a lot, because this is a very tough place—and with the Tea Party in control, it's even tougher. But I think as an African American woman, you have to kind of look at women like me who are here. We have some phenomenal black women in caucus. And as an African American . . . we've been through so much in this country. You know, when I started school, I couldn't go to public schools. You know why? They were segregated. My dad was in the military. He was a military officer, fought in two wars, came back here, we couldn't even go to eat in a restaurant or go to a public theater. You know what I mean? We had to drink out of the water fountain that said COLOREDS ONLY. I mean, this is not in the distant past. I went through that. And look how far I've come, look how far we've come. And so there's no way I can get tired or frustrated or depressed or angry about what's going on, because I have to remember the past. I have to remember so many people fought and died for the right to vote. So many people did so much just to get me where I am. So it's my duty and my responsibility to take on this fight and to be part of the resistance movement and to really try to make this a better world. And so that keeps me going. I think as a black woman, my perspective—and I talk to a lot of women who are non-black and who are white and other guys, white guys—and I try to share with them, when they get down, it's like, "Come on! You've got to walk in my shoes a little bit. Don't get weary."

MS: You talk about looking at things historically. It is sort of astounding to think that women only relatively recently got even the right to vote. Where do you see the status of women, where we are now in the United States and around the world? And what is the current call to action for women?

BL: Oh boy, we haven't passed the ERA yet, have we? [*laughs*] I mean, it's like come on. Oh, my God. So, I think we have a long way to go in this country to catch up with the movement of women around the world, on some fronts. And yet we're leading on other fronts, so pay equity, gender equity, campaign finance reform, ensuring the quality of life for women who are single moms who want to raise their kids, who want to move ahead in their lives but don't have the resources—I think there are a lot of structural issues that need to be addressed, so that women can really gain equality. And we've got the LGBT community . . . we've got a lot of issues that we have to look at in terms of equality and fairness and justice. And so we haven't gotten there yet, but we're getting there, and it's almost like we're at that moment where we're taking some quantum leaps. But I think we've got to move quicker. I have three granddaughters; I don't want them to go through this [*laughs*]. I don't want them to even *think* about reproductive rights or contraception or losing those rights. I don't even want them to even have a notion that that's even possible. I don't even want them to think that they may not be able to do what they want to do because the deck is stacked against them because of money and because of these structural barriers. So . . . it's a defining moment, I would say.

MS: You're talking about your granddaughters. I have two daughters. The way that our society and culture raises girls and young women is not always to necessarily see themselves as leaders. What would you want to say to girls and young women today in terms of valuing their voices and believing that they have what it takes to follow their calling, or what it takes to be a leader?

BL: That's a really good question, because when I was a child—and my mother is eighty-eight years old and we were raised with my grandfather and my dad who was in the military. And my grandfather, I mean, he would get furious if I ever acted like I couldn't do something because I was a girl. It was like, "You're just as good as those boys. What's wrong with you?" And my mother would say, "So what if there's a boy trying to beat you in this or that? You better study hard so you can beat this guy and make a better grade than that boy next door." You know what I mean? That was early on. It was like I had no options [laughs]. So thank goodness my family were feminists, even the men in my family, at an early age. Not every girl has that kind of encouragement early on. And so I think what is important is that at an early age, young girls have an educational environment and the family support systems in place where everything is equal to boys and that they're told early on that there is no difference in terms of their abilities and their intellectual capabilities and their opportunities. This has to be taught early. And then we have to make sure that the opportunities are there and that we *don't* discriminate against those girls and we *do* have what it takes for girls to succeed in school. I fortunately went to an all-women's college, which was great. By the time I got to Mills College, I was so far ahead of most of my counterparts and my friends in school because I had had this upbringing. But the support that was there for me as a young girl and as a teenager and a young mom and all, it was just always, "You're no different from this guy in terms of your ability or capacity. Just work hard and know that you're going to hit some ceilings that you've got to shatter. But you better do it, or else" [laughs].

CLAIRE MCCASKILL

"The more voices, the more different voices, that are involved in public policy, the more sound the public policy is going to be. And frankly, our system of government depends on the acceptance of Americans, that they are being represented in an effective way. So the more Washington reflects how our country actually looks, the more confidence the American people are going to have in it, and therefore our democracy will continue to be the strongest in the world."

A DAUGHTER OF RURAL Missouri, Democrat Claire McCaskill has earned a reputation in the U.S. Senate as an independent, plain-spoken fighter for accountability in government, fiscal responsibility, and better opportunities for America's middle class families. McCaskill started out as a young assistant prosecutor in Kansas City, where she specialized in prosecuting arson and sex crimes. Later, as the first woman to serve as Jackson County Prosecutor, she established a first-of-its kind domestic violence unit for the Kansas City region. McCaskill continued raising the level of accountability in Missouri as the state's auditor, and later took on her own party establishment, becoming the first person to ever defeat a sitting Missouri governor in a primary election.

In 2006, when McCaskill became the first woman elected to the U.S. Senate from Missouri, she brought that same fight for accountability to the halls of Congress. As a senior member of the Senate Armed Services

Committee, McCaskill has led the effort to confront sexual assault in the military, and better protect survivors. And McCaskill has recently helped lead the effort to renew the Violence Against Women Act.

McCaskill was resoundingly reelected to the Senate in 2012, winning her race by more than 15 percentage points—the biggest margin for a Missouri Senate candidate in nearly two decades. Claire has pledged to use the next six years to continue her fight for stronger accountability in government, and for better opportunities for America's families.

MARIANNE SCHNALL: Why do you think it is that we have not yet had a woman president?

CLAIRE MCCASKILL: Well, I think that some of the typical socialization that women go through in this country has not always encouraged some of the traits that are incredibly important in our political system. Now, I've had a front-row seat and I feel blessed to have had the front-row seat to see a lot of changes in this regard, but when I began in politics over thirty years ago, there really weren't a huge number of mentors that were women in elective office. There were a few, but they were an anomaly. They were not really part of the fabric of elective office holders in this country. And that has changed over these thirty years.

But I was taught as a young girl that it was impolite to talk about money. I was taught that it's not something you inquired about and that it would be a sign of failure if you needed to ask someone for money. Well, clearly you cannot be successful in modern politics if you do not get very comfortable with talking about money and the notion of asking complete strangers for checks with commas in them. This is as essential to success as breathing, especially in a race like president of the United States. And to get to be a candidate for president of the United States, you have to demonstrate your ability at other offices, and that obviously entails fundraising also. So that skill was, and still is, [a factor]—whether it is the reluctance of women to be donors or the reluctance of women to "close" on fundraising.

MS: What can we do? What do you think are some concrete steps or changes that would help in terms of encouraging women, both into the political pipeline and certainly advancing through it?

CM: Well, I think one, which is related to socialization, [is that] women have to be taught that ambition is ladylike, that women need to learn that having ambition is important for their families. As I like to say to potential women donors . . . the same women that won't hesitate to buy a blouse on sale, whether it's on sale for $99 or whether it's on sale for $19. A woman will buy a blouse on sale, thinking it is such a good bargain, and it will sit in her closet because it gaps in front or it isn't exactly the right color. It might sit in her closet for a year with the tag still on it. Those same women are reluctant to write a check for that same amount to a political candidate. And part of that is that we are naturally wired to be nurturers, protectors, and we see our security as really important. So spending money on a politician's race, how does that get you security? That's not tangible. That's not like a savings account. It's not an insurance policy. And so what women have to realize is that power is the *ultimate* security. Power brings about a much broader type of security for their children and for their grandchildren. So getting comfortable around the notion of participating fully in the process *and* that ambition is something that should be admired in a woman. And there shouldn't be a tsk tsk. You know, I've had tsk tsks through my life. I remember when I was very young and a state representative, and they wrote a feature about me for the Kansas City paper and they titled it "Blonde Ambition," and I remember cringing when I saw the headline. And then I caught myself and thought, *Well now, why are you so worried that they're saying you are ambitious?* [*laughs*] I was naturally uncomfortable that somebody had called me out on being ambitious. So I think our young ladies, our young women, my daughters, their daughters, all need to understand that ambition is an important form of getting security for you and your family and for the values that you are committed to.

MS: What is the larger picture here? You were just talking about the importance of women supporting other women candidates, and certainly this is also something that we hope men will get behind. Why is it important that we have more women's voices represented in Washington?

CM: Well, I think it's very important because the more voices, the more different voices, that are involved in public policy, the more sound the public policy is going to be. And frankly, our system of government depends on the acceptance of Americans, that they are being represented in an effective way. So the more Washington reflects how our country actually looks, the more confidence the American people are going to have in it, and therefore our democracy will continue to be the strongest in the world. So it's for the health of our democracy; it's for the ability of Washington to work collaboratively. You know, I joke with some of my male colleagues . . . I think we all want to make sure that everyone understands that some of the perceived differences between men and women are just wrong, actually wrong and stereotyping and inappropriate. On the other hand, I never in my life have had the urge to punch anyone. Now a lot of my male colleagues and my husband scratch their head at that, because they've had the urge to punch someone. And so, that difference, you know, we sometimes call it the testosterone-driven leadership, holds us back sometimes, particularly when you have a real challenge with coming together because of the polarization that is occurring in our political system. You've got the far right and the far left, camping out and really not wanting to give much deference to the middle. And I think women are really comfortable with compromise. We want everyone to get along. You know, I want my kids not to fight with one another. I can hear my husband's words, "Let them go." I'm going, "No! I don't want them to fight" [*laughs*]. And I think there is this collaborative desire that we have as women that we want to find that common ground and the consensus and make progress and really try to solve a problem, rather than just posturing.

MS: Do you actually see that playing out? I saw a great roundtable that Diane Sawyer had on ABC News where she brought all the female senators together. In that interview, you called Washington a "combative place" and said that it's almost like a team sport. I saw an article in *The New York Times* recently, in which Republican Senator Rob Portman said that just with having a slight increase in women there is having a positive impact because "women tend to be interested in finding the common ground." Do you actually see that it does lead to more consensus? And what is the approach to working with, let's say, even the Republican women in Congress?

CM: Well, if you noticed in that dialogue, I think it was Kay Bailey Hutchison that was the one who spoke out and said, "I think we would do a better job in terms of leading the Senate." And that wasn't a progressive, feminist, Democratic, liberal woman senator from a blue state—that was Kay Bailey Hutchison from Texas [*laughs*]. So I do think you saw in that interview, and we see in our work on a daily basis, that whether it's Lisa Murkowski, or whether it's Susan Collins, or whether it's Kelly Ayotte. . . . I've certainly worked with Olympia Snowe—we worked on a number of things together. I think we do; we get together, we talk. I think we are most comfortable trying to gravitate toward what we have in common, rather than underlining what separates us. And that's the beginning of how you get there, that you're comfortable gravitating toward the common ground, rather than toward the confrontational, political differences.

MS: I have heard that the Senate women all get together regularly for bipartisan dinners. Is that still going on?

CM: Oh, yeah.

MS: What is the purpose of those dinners? I just love that concept.

CM: Well, it was going on before I got here, and we try to do it at least once a quarter. We sometimes do it more frequently than that if we have a special reason to get together. For example, we all got together for dinner at Secretary Clinton's home, celebrating Susan Collins's wedding, a shower/dinner honoring her nuptials. And we have a special dinner for the women on the Supreme Court on an annual basis, where the women senators and the women justices get together—just us, no staff—and dish [*laughs*], eat and dish. And it's great! We do it, and we talk about a lot of things. I mean, we're known to get off topic and visit about our children, or visit about challenges that we're having personally, but we also get to some policy stuff and kind of pick each other's brains about where we are on issues and what we can do to move things forward. The last dinner we had, there was a discussion about us working together on some human trafficking issues, on a bipartisan basis. And so, yeah, they're great. So we all try to go out of our way to get to those to the extent that we can, and they're terrific.

MS: I know that it's important to have more women in Congress, but it's also important to get the women who are there to head up committees and have more positions of power there. I had done an interview with Nancy Pelosi, and I remember her calling it a "marble ceiling." Do you feel that way? Do you feel the weight of the obstacles? And do you have a sense that it is improving? Do you see signs of progress, especially since this last election?

CM: Yeah, oh yeah. I mean, if you've been doing this for as long as I have, it would be *really* irresponsible to say we haven't made major progress. My campaign manager—and it was one of the most difficult and high-profile races in the country—the person who ran the whole show was a woman. That didn't happen thirty years ago in U.S. Senate campaigns. You look at our leadership team and you've got Patty Murray heading up the Gang of Six to try to get a solution to the fiscal problem, and then you have her as chairman of the Budget Committee handling the budget on the floor of the Senate. Obviously, there has never been a woman Budget chair before. We now have women chairing a number of committees that are not what I used to call, when I was a young legislator in my state capitol, "the soft stuff." We have a man on Health and Labor and Welfare, but we have a woman chairing the Intelligence Committee. And we have a woman chairing the Appropriations Committee for the first time in the history of the Senate. We have a woman chairing the Budget Committee for the first time in the history of the Senate. So there are clearly opportunities that are opening up and women are stepping up to handle these jobs. I just think it's a matter of time. I'm very hopeful we get a woman president in 2016. I'm very hopeful that Secretary Clinton decides to run. I think all of us are very excited about that.

MS: I'm hopeful we will reach those milestones, too. Now, part of this book is to help encourage women to pursue leadership positions and certainly to enter politics. It can seem very daunting and also a little dispiriting. Some people look at Washington right now and say it's so dysfunctional and such a hard process to run for office. What words of advice or encouragement would you have for a young woman who is considering pursuing this?

CM: As I tell kids when I give high school graduation speeches, success is not what you have, it is loving what you do. For thirty-plus years I've looked forward to getting out of bed because of what the day would bring. It is an intellectual challenge, it is incredibly interesting, very different, it's *impossible* to become bored, nothing is ever routine—just when you think you've seen it all, something else happens that's extraordinary and different. You have a real chance to see and touch things you've been able to change that have made a positive impact on people's lives. I just don't know that it gets any better than that. Now, does it suck? Yeah. There are parts of it that are terrible. The guilt that I had was not unlike what any working mom feels. I did everything in public office—I married, I had children, I divorced, I remarried. My children are now . . . the youngest is twenty-one. Did I feel bad that I couldn't be at everything that they were doing? Yeah, I did; I felt terrible. On the other hand, I in some ways had more flexibility than many of my peers that were working in big law firms, because if you are going to take off in the middle of the day at a law firm, you're accountable to someone. You've got to go say to your partner that you're working with, "I need to go to my daughter's Valentine's Day homeroom party because I'm bringing the cupcakes." You know, I could do that and there wasn't really a "boss" I had to check in with. Now, I also had to get up on Saturday morning and load all the kids in the car and take them to give a speech with me. And one of my favorite stories is when my son, my oldest, was about six and his younger sister was four. You know, when kids are that age, they think they're whispering and they're not really whispering very well, and he was trying to whisper in the next room, and he said, "Now listen, Maddy, if she says we're going to a party, ask her if somebody's going to make a speech, because if they make a speech, it's not a party" [laughs]. They were used to me loading them in the car and saying, "Come on, we've got to go to a party," and of course, we'd get there and the three of them would be going, "Uh, Mom, not so much." So, you know, yes, I had to work at night, and I was a single mom for nine years of that period, when my kids were young, so it was challenging. But it's no more challenging for somebody in elected office than it is for any woman who decides to have a career working outside the home. You've got to be very organized. You've got to not sweat the small stuff. And you have to learn to live with some guilt. That lifts like a magic cloud when they all are off at college [laughs]. And you get the wonderful moment that I've had with all three of my children, who have said to me, "Thank you for giving us the confidence to be independent," and they all are out doing their own thing in far-flung places and have been incredibly self-sufficient and confident. And they're nice enough to say—it may not be true—but they're nice enough to say to me that they think in part that was because they were expected to do things on their own from a fairly young age. And part of that was because they had to [laughs].

But I really think women should be much more excited about a career in elective office. It's a tough business, yes, but most are, and there is just an incredible upside. And it is achievable. Really, a lower office, which is where you start . . . my race for state representative, I didn't have any money. I had no particular family pedigree that put me on a path to winning. Nobody ever tapped me on the shoulder and said it was my turn. I learned that knocking on doors was essential, and I knocked on 11,432 doors. And I won! And at the lower levels, offices like city council and school board and state representative and mayor in smaller size communities—you can do a lot of it with shoe leather, and especially now with social media, which was not available to me in the late seventies and early eighties. I just really hope that women—as they see more and more women in the United States Senate, and hopefully as president—I hope they aspire to holding elective office. Our country really needs it.

MS: As you're saying, a career in elected office does require a lot of work and you have to have fuel for that. Where do your own passion and commitment come from? What drives you? What's the source of your energy?

CM: That's a really good question, and I really do think that God blessed me with a high level of energy. I've always been kind of pushing from a fairly young age—I was trying to figure out a way to organize things, or to do more. And I'm intellectually curious, and I did figure out very early on that knowledge was power. So this thirst for knowing more about a lot of things is a real natural way to feed my work on public policy, so they kind of feed off each other. When you have the opportunity to impact public policy, the fact that you're very interested in it is an engine—whether it's fixing the sexual assault problem in our military, or whether it's solving the contracting problem that our Federal Government has . . . and then I guess you kind of get addicted to when it works and you actually can [make a change]. I was part of the initial drug court movement and I watched drug courts go from a good idea to literally a worldwide phenom that changed drug treatment in this country forever. You know, that's *extraordinarily* special that you have a chance to be part of something like that. And it gets you all jazzed for the next great big moment of finding the good idea that can help people.

OLYMPIA SNOWE

"Young people, mostly young females, want to immerse them-selves in public service or to engage in some kind of either public or civic aspect of life, but they're not so sure where they can measure their contributions in political office, and whether or not they can contribute to the extent that they desire to contribute in public service. They see there are other forms of public service that might be more rewarding and enriching and fulfilling than serving in political office where you are accomplishing little. But I tell them we can't change without them."

FORMER U.S. SENATOR Olympia J. Snowe served in the U.S. Senate from 1995–2013 and as a member of the U.S. House of Representatives, representing Maine's Second Congressional District, from 1979–1995. She was the first woman in American history to serve in both houses of a state legislature and both houses of Congress. When first elected to Congress in 1978, at the age of thirty-one, Olympia Snowe was the youngest Republican woman, and the first Greek American woman, ever elected to Congress. While in the House, she co-chaired the Congressional Caucus on Women's Issues for ten years.

During Snowe's distinguished career, she served as chair and then ranking member of the Senate Committee on Small Business and Entrepreneurship, became the first Republican woman ever to secure a full-term seat on the Senate Finance Committee, and was also the first woman senator to chair the Subcommittee on Seapower of the Senate Armed Services Committee, which oversees the Navy and Marine Corps. In 2005 she was named the 54th most powerful woman in the world by *Forbes* magazine. In 2006 *Time* magazine named her one of the top ten U.S. senators. She is currently chairman and CEO of Olympia Snowe, LLC, through which she provides communications and policy advice, and a senior fellow at the Bipartisan Policy Center in Washington, D.C. She is the author of *Fighting for Common Ground: How We Can Fix the Stalemate in Congress.*

MARIANNE SCHNALL: Why do you think we've not yet had a woman president, and what do you think it will take to make that happen? Do you think we're ready for that?

OLYMPIA SNOWE: Well, I do think we're ready and prepared. I think in the past, if we look back over the campaigns, there hasn't been a sufficient number to have run or frankly, in a place to run. I think in looking back at history, you have to have more women running to even get to a place where the country is focused on a female candidate for president. And there have been too few women in public office—that would be one of the areas in which a candidate obviously could begin that process. Certainly that's been true for men over the years; not necessarily the prerequisite to running for the presidency, but certainly from one of the positions of public office—whether it was a United States senator, or it was governor, or from a higher position on the outside—but for the most part, they were catapulted from positions of high public office that put them in a position to run for the presidency. So I think in the past, we just haven't had a sufficient number of women in a position to run, frankly. You just didn't have a bench, in some ways, and secondly, there just weren't enough women serving in public office that might have been a natural pivot point for the presidency. I think that obviously has changed, and I think that one person who has illustrated that change was Hillary Clinton.

MS: I think about the fact that you were on the Senate Armed Services Committee—I think that women also being seen on those kinds of committees is really important and is maybe why we can envision Hillary there, so we can envision a woman as commander in chief or think she is tough enough to be in that role.

OS: I think it's going to depend on the person; I really do. And ultimately the breadth of experience that they bring to that position. I think that's important. Having served on Foreign Intelligence and Armed Services, Foreign Affairs for the better part of my career, probably twenty-four years worth, I have the experience in those categories—people aren't exposed to women with those views, as much as they are men. I think it's interesting—could women today have as little experience going in to run for the presidency? That will be the test. In fact, even President Obama or other candidates, President Bush, if you think about it, had to have the same or equivalent experience to run for public office and be viewed as a credible candidate for office. I think a lot will depend on how [women] perform and what their positions are. Much more so because the exposure today is so much different than it was in the past.

MS: Do you think it's more challenging for women? Do you think there are specific challenges for Republican women?

OS: I would say, yes. We're not doing well with women, but the same is true within the party. We've got a lot of work to do. I think that's true for where they have women in positions in the party, you know, whether it's chairs of committees. Frankly, in the House of Representatives, I think that in terms of current positions of leadership, they have a ways to go.

MS: Looking at this last election, everyone talked about how history-making it was to have twenty women in the Senate, and yet it is still obviously so far from parity. There's definitely been progress, but what are some of the reasons that the numbers are so low? What is your assessment?

OS: You know, it could be for a number of reasons. I'm not so sure there's any one reason—whether or not it's a matter of interest or choice. It could be that women, in the way in which they are pursuing their careers, raising families, it may be more difficult to have it dovetail with their own lives. When I was first running, I think oftentimes we used to say that women didn't have then the Rolodex, didn't have that built-in network within either the communities or within a political party organization that would have been critical and indispensable to being a candidate for high public office. So often men were in a position to have that network of support, both organizationally and financially. That made a huge difference; they could launch their candidacies and get the support of the power brokers in communities, or throughout the state, that became more of a natural alliance for men. But women did not have similar networks of support. They didn't have that kind of organization or entries that would have provided the access and the opportunities to run for public office.

MS: When you were there, did you feel that you were a minority? Were there certain challenges or experiences specific to being a woman there? I was really touched by the relationship of all the female senators from both parties, the fact that they regularly get together for bipartisan dinners, for example.

OS: Yes, they have these dinners; I'm sure they talked to you about that, about having the monthly dinners which has been a long-standing tradition among the women, because it builds camaraderie and collegiality and collaboration, a better understanding of one another's perspectives of what brought them to this point, of their life experiences that obviously can characterize someone's approach to how they address the issues in the United States Senate. So I think it's an ideal example of how you can build bridges within the institution that can result in greater benefits in the future, because that collegiality and familiarity with one another on a personal level can result in substantive results in the legislative arena. So that's what I think is so essential and lacking, unfortunately, in the current political environment is we don't have that ability to interact and to get to know our colleagues on a personal level that can help break down those barriers that will allow you to work on issues across the political aisle. So there's a bond there among women, irrespective of whether or not you have differences on issues—it's just a general connection and bonding and mutual understanding. Because with all the different life experiences, there's a specific disposition to how we approach life in general: much more practical in our thinking; less about the fight and more about the solution.

MS: I feel like you vote your beliefs. You've never been hesitant to vote across party lines or to do things that don't always go with your party. Do you think that type of courage is required—to not always be so black and white in terms of going along with your party?

OS: Yes, that's right. You see that everything isn't just in black-and-white terms, but there are gray areas. So I think women—obviously it's very difficult to stereotype—but I think there is a collaborative facet to women in the way in which they approach legislative solutions, similar to life. When you're having to juggle family demands and the professional life, you sort of [figure out] how are you going to solve these problems on a day-to-day basis. And I think it's sort of that same inclination in the legislative process. In my case, I look at the practicality of what we're trying to achieve, and how can we solve this problem. When I hear about a problem, whether it's for the country or my constituents or for an individual, my immediate reaction is, well, how can we solve this? What are the facts? So much of the nonsense that goes on today in the political arena does nothing to solve the problem. It might make good theater, but it does nothing to reach a practical end result. And I think women are much more practical. I think that's sort of a connection among us: we're looking at the practicality of how we can get something done, how can we accomplish it and move forward, because we're juggling so many different things in our daily lives. From that standpoint, I think, yes, women bring those indispensable ingredients to the legislative process, and that's why it's healthier for governing institutions to be more reflective of the broader society and certainly to include more women in the political process. And having those voices heard in all facets of the Senate or in the House of Representatives on the various committees is also critically important to have that dimension and that view represented on respective committees.

In the House of Representatives, if we had a woman serving on that committee, for example, we had that voice weighing in on that particular issue. So it does matter to have more women serving in public office, because that means that you have that particular voice lending itself to having a more balanced view when it comes to considering or advancing various pieces of legislation. I mean, look at the sexual assault in the military. Somehow the military hasn't gotten it straight—about where the accountability lies and a process in place to hold them accountable and have zero tolerance for this kind of behavior. I was working on these issues in the Armed Services in the 1990s, but there are many issues that the women carried that mantle of leadership on various questions, because they were in a position to do so. That's the point. It's adding the voice to those issues and that perspective that otherwise would be absent.

MS: One of the things we keep hearing about is the challenge of juggling work and family for women everywhere—in the corporate world and certainly in Washington—especially women with young children. But if we did have more women in Washington, would there be better policies to support women and families?

OS: You're right. This whole juggling work and family, sure, it's reality, it's a difficult endeavor day-to-day. We live in a busy world that everybody lives in, and trying to meet that demand and making sure your children are taken care of is difficult. And is there adequate childcare? I worked a lot on that issue over the years: affordable, accessible, quality childcare. That makes a profound difference in the working lives of women and, yes, men. Ultimately the way to allay the fears of someone who's going to work, in any event, let alone running for public office, is to know that they have the ability to provide that kind of support to their children and to their families. But you're absolutely right, you get more focus on those issues. We actually made historic achievement in the time when we focused on these issues in the Congressional Caucus in the 1980s. We made historic progress because we just really ensured that we were driving that train on key questions, so that they didn't languish on the back burner, but they were on the front burner for action. But it took time. I mean, I think family and medical leave, for example, to become federal law required the better part of seven years' endeavor to be successful on that front. But it's driving those efforts and making sure that they stay in the forefront of public attention and legislative action. It takes, I think, a great deal of persistence and dedication and drive. So that is why it makes a difference whether or not you have women in positions of high public office and, yes, makes a difference about running for president. I think the country is prepared. I don't doubt that for a moment, and honestly I think it clearly is just a matter of time. You just have to have more women running for that position where ultimately it will work.

MS: You've always seemed to have the courage and confidence to speak your truth. There are so many influences that try to get girls to want to please and be liked and focus on how they look, so it takes a lot for women to believe in themselves and put themselves out there. How did you get to be the bold person you are today?

OS: You know, it's interesting—when I review my own life, probably I wouldn't have been a likely candidate in many ways, but I'm passionate about what I believe in. And perhaps it's that drive from my upbringing and circumstances that compelled me to stand on my own two feet early and think for myself and depend on myself, for better or for worse, in many ways. I ended up running for a public office and state legislature right after my first husband died, and I stayed in the legislative branch for forty years, and that wasn't exactly what I anticipated. I just feel that the strength of my convictions and believing strongly in what you're doing becomes the ultimate force and the overriding interest in being strong about various positions. So it's just my natural independence to begin with. And then, secondly, as I tell young people, be passionate about what you believe in and do not be afraid to stand alone, because you may find yourself in a position one day where you have to stand alone. When you know it's that important, don't be afraid. That doesn't mean it's easy; it isn't. But if you know that if you feel strongly about a certain position and certain values or a certain view, and if you believe you're right, then you should be able to stand alone. And I just think my own experiences and my personal circumstances in life helped to contribute to how I weighed in in the legislative arena. I always attached it to personal experiences of my constituency, or the facts of an issue, and tried to appreciate and understand the dimensions of a problem and how could we solve it, and whether or not it was in our purview *to* solve it. So that's what I think gave me the strength to just build independence and to be passionate about what I view to be important. That's all part of leadership, frankly, and I think it's having a strong belief in yourself and having the confidence to do that. But whether I would have known that early on in my life, I do not know. It's just that I ended up oftentimes having to make decisions for myself—having lost my parents early and so on—but I think it all contributed to one, surviving; two, persevering; three, being independent; four, I'm passionate about what I believe in; five, I don't hesitate to drive that train; and six, to anticipate the future and anticipate problems and try to preempt them and to address them. It doesn't mean it's easy. I understand that there are so many complicating factors for young women and growing up and what the influences are and the world in which they are living today and many competing pressures to excel in so many ways. I think it's difficult. There's no doubt about it. I'm so impressed by all the young women I have met on these campuses. Wow, they're so talented.

MS: That's wonderful to hear. Sometimes there's this impression that young people, particularly young women, are maybe not as engaged, but I always think that's a misconception.

OS: I have just met some very impressive young women on these campuses who are so committed to the future and what they want to accomplish—goal-oriented and centered, not just on themselves, but the world around them. And they want to know how best they can contribute in that fashion and in the careers they intend to pursue. Most of them are going into the sciences or to pursue a medical career. I mean, it's amazing. I've been on four different campuses in the last two weeks, so I have had a chance to meet a lot of students, male and female, but I'm so impressed with these highly accomplished women. And honestly, I encouraged them—I asked them if they had an interest in public office. I'm not hearing any resonating yeses. This is what's happening: they want to, but they don't think that's the best way they can contribute. They want to contribute in other ways because of what they see happening in Washington . . . there are some who are fascinated by it and they're going to work in Washington, and hopefully it leads to public office. I always tell them, "You know what? When I was your age I had a strong interest in public service, but I certainly wasn't expecting that one day I would become a United States senator! So you never know." It is important to encourage young women just to think about public service as an option.

But I think we're seeing more women now; for example, having twenty women in the United States Senate. That makes a difference because you have more women in high-profile positions whom young women can emulate and who can serve as role models and examples of what can be accomplished when you aspire to those heights. At some point it could dovetail or integrate with their lives. That doesn't mean they have to necessarily start at a young age, like I did. I also underscore that because I want them to at least understand that it doesn't necessarily mean they have to start at the beginning and devote their whole lives to it, but rather at some point when it works, to consider it as a potential option, a possibility, and not to ever remove it entirely from their list of options throughout life. Because it may not work now, but it may work at some point in the future, and oftentimes women do raise their children and then decide to run for public office, and so many have. And there are others who are raising their young children and making it work alongside their public service. So it's whatever works and it's the flexibility, if you adapt and adopt in order to hopefully keep that option open for the future. So I encourage them to think about it and not think it's out of their realm, because it's very much within their realm. And the fact is there's a cause and effect between what happens and doesn't happen in their own lives—and that's true for women and true for society, as a whole. It's a cause and effect, and if you get involved, you can make a difference and make your voice heard.

MS: I've been hearing different kinds of assessments of where women are, some very optimistic and encouraged, some feeling very discouraged that we're stagnating. Where do you think we are in terms of the status of women in the world today?

OS: You know, I think it's interesting—I think we've made progress in some respects, and then in other cases, I'm not so sure. If you think about the debates that have taken place, for example, on contraception—maybe it's because I've been in Congress for three decades and have put some of these issues to rest, and then they're resurrected and revived, as if we're back in the seventies, or the fifties for that matter. So it often leaves me in a quandary, thinking, *Okay, have we made progress or where are we?* Or when you hear the debates about CEOs like Marissa Mayer talking about the focus and the attention that was paid to her when she was pregnant and the Family Medical Leave and the policies and what she was doing and so on. I think about all those questions, and the same type of attention isn't devoted to male CEOs. So I think, yes, there's been progress, and then on the other hand, I am not so sure what is a safe standard to use in which to measure women. The fact is that there still aren't enough women yet, either in the political arena or in the corporate arena or in the board room, in America. I mean, you know people talk about having more women on boards, but if it's maybe 17 percent; I think, give or take, 4 percent of CEOs of big corporations are women. And the same is true in the political arena, as well as in the legislatures. And in the U.S. Senate, we've made progress, but that's only been recent. So I guess on one hand, yes, we've changed many of the laws to address and remedy some of the discriminatory practices that existed in law, but on the other hand, we still have a ways to go. We still don't earn dollar for dollar for what a man earns. We've made strides, but there are obviously more that have to be made. So I think there are more opportunities for women. In the 1980s, when we were talking about the discriminatory policies at the National Institutes of Health, when they excluded women from clinical study trials, there were very few women that were in medical school, and that much has changed. So I think you see the opportunities that open up for professions who no longer think of that . . . or the military in the sense that we couldn't have an all-volunteer force without women serving in the military. I was fighting for gender integrated training in the military back in the late nineties and I was on the Armed Services Committee. . . . They have to fight the way they're trained. They have to train alongside each other. But that was a major battle. Today women are integral to an all-volunteer force; in fact you couldn't have a military without them.

So, yes, I think we have made significant advancements and they have opened doors for women in so many spheres of society. And that will continue, because the contributions are immeasurable, and I think that our country has benefited enormously and the value has been abundantly evident in so many realms. Title IX is a good example—and I've been a long-ranging and strong champion of Title IX—but think about the doors that that has opened that allows equalities when it comes to sports and education. It's no longer a question of women in sports, and I just love it when I hear young girls and young women talking about the sports that they're participating in and the championships that they've won or the teams that they're on; it's just second nature. In my generation, it wasn't second nature; you had to fight for that change and that equality and that right and that access. The expenditure of dollars for women's sports, as well as for men, it just didn't happen until Title IX. So many young women today now have the benefit of that competition. It's not as much a matter of winning or losing, but the fact that you're in the arena, you know what it takes, the ups and downs, and that you get up and you do it again and you learn from that experience, the give and take and the team playing—it all contributes to addressing all dimensions of your experiences and life's experiences. There's no substitute for that. So I just love hearing them talk about whatever they do, playing soccer or basketball, whatever the case is. It's just wonderful! Those doors weren't open, to much extent, even in my generation, but it just puts them on a level playing field with their male peers and counterparts, because those are assets and qualities that transcend in your life, for the remainder of your life. You know what it's like—you're down one day, and you have to get up the next. So you lose one game, but you know if you come back you can win the next time. That's important to experience, the winning and losing. It's the give and take in life—those things happen, and you can rebound from them and succeed. Those are irreplaceable experiences and qualities that we want for young women. [So that's a perfect example of] how the types of policies and laws that are in place matter. There are advantages for everybody in society and advantages ultimately for the entire country. It's that full participation in our society, and that's why our institutions have to reflect a broader sector of our country.

★ ★

HOW CAN WE ENCOURAGE GIRLS AND YOUNG WOMEN TO HAVE EXPANSIVE GOALS AND KNOW THEIR WORTH?

★ ★

It's really important for girls to be reminded that the sky is the limit, and anything they want to do is possible.

— AMY POEHLER

As we think to help our girls . . . what we want them to do is not be restricted or restrained by "you have to do this," or "you have to do that," or pushed too much one way or another. I think there is a confidence that comes with being comfortable with who you are and what you're about. You do not doubt yourself. And as girls grow into young women and are looking for career advancement, when they do not doubt themselves—when they know at their core they're firm and what they're really good at, and then also have an understanding of what they're challenged by—then they are going to do a better job of pushing forward and expanding the boundaries for other women who are going to be coming behind them.

— REPRESENTATIVE MARSHA BLACKBURN (R)

I think it's twofold. I think we have to make sure that they do realize there are still systematic barriers for women. Even though it doesn't apply to them personally, because they might be a more privileged child, they have to understand the different outcomes in life for women around the world and in the United States and realize that there are both important fights going on and important barriers to grapple with. And then, beyond that, they have to realize that they are the generation that can fix a lot of it, and that they can have a big impact on these concerns. So it's not a defeating proposition to realize this, but [they need] to understand that when we say, "You can be anything you want to be when you grow up" or, "You can do anything you want to do," that's true, but you have to realize what kind of challenges you face in doing that. So it's both politicization and empowerment that have to happen.

— SANDRA FLUKE, ATTORNEY, SOCIAL-JUSTICE ADVOCATE

The thing that I always say is, we spend an enormous amount of time practicing things that we think, or that we've been told, are going to help us be successful—maybe that's science or maybe that's soccer or maybe that's a useful instrument that you play. But if we spent a tenth of the time that we put into those kinds of practice, focusing instead on our relationships and our communication and the way we handle failure, I think we would be a lot better off. I just feel like we really need girls to take some of that inner résumé work into their own hands. Because I think a lot of young women are just thinking like, "I can't ask for a raise; I don't know how to do that. I'm afraid," or "I can't raise my hand and say something in class if I don't know the right answer." And I just think that these are things that you can learn, as long as you practice and set small goals and try. But I don't think that's communicated to girls; I don't think we prioritize that.

—RACHEL SIMMONS, AUTHOR, COFOUNDER OF THE GIRLS LEADERSHIP INSTITUTE

I would say "go for it," which is really cliché, but the thing that I notice most often about my generation is that we have all the tools. I think we have the intelligence, the drive, we have everything going for us. But—this idea goes with the whole Lean In *conversation—I see so many young girls just feeling like they're defeated already, that they're not special enough, they could never possibly accomplish the things that they want to. . . . I really think that one of the biggest things my generation needs to work on is putting ourselves out there and believing in ourselves.*

—JULIE ZEILINGER, AUTHOR, FOUNDER AND EDITOR OF THE FBOMB BLOG

We talk about America being this land of opportunity, but a lot of times we don't even know what those opportunities are. I would encourage young women to just go explore. Take advantage of the internships and the fellowships, and go travel and explore what's out there before you make your decision. See where you really find your passion and where you find fulfillment.

—REPRESENTATIVE CATHY MCMORRIS RODGERS (R)

GAVIN NEWSOM

"Why is it that men can't be recognized for being outstanding advocates for women? You don't need to be gay to be a great advocate for the LGBT community. In every aspect of life, you can maintain your empathy and your advocacy. . . . I think people are realizing that we're not two separate tribes, we're all in this together, and that men have a responsibility to be advocates for women, women advocates for men and boys."

A S A MEMBER of the San Francisco Board of Supervisors, then as mayor of San Francisco, and now as lieutenant governor of California, Gavin Newsom has been a visionary on issues of equality, the environment, homelessness, and healthcare. Policies he has initiated and implemented have been duplicated in cities across the nation.

During his seven-year tenure as mayor, he led San Francisco to an economic recovery, balancing seven consecutive budgets without laying off a single teacher, police officer, or firefighter. Thirty-six days into his first mayoral term in 2004, Newsom threw himself into one of the most divisive issues in U.S. politics by allowing same-sex couples to marry in violation of state law. Newsom is the author of the recently released *Citizenville*, which explores the intersection of democracy and technology in this ever-connected world. The book has been widely accepted by both Democrats and Republicans as a blueprint to government innovation and reform. He is married to filmmaker Jennifer Siebel Newsom, writer and director of *Miss Representation,* a documentary that examines the portrayal of women in the media.

MARIANNE SCHNALL: I always like to start by saying that this book was partially inspired by my eight-year-old daughter, Lotus. After Barack Obama was elected, we were talking about how remarkable it was that we had our first African American president, and she looked at me and asked, "Why haven't we had a woman president?" It was this very simple, innocent question, yet it was somewhat challenging to answer. Why do you think we've not yet had a woman president? What do you think it will take to make that happen?

GAVIN NEWSOM: At the peril of repeating some of the things that perhaps my wife already said, we had a similar interaction with our daughter, Montana, who's three and a half, and this was a few weeks ago. My wife casually mentioned something about a woman being president and my daughter—after all the indoctrination from birth on down around gender equality issues—says, "A woman can never be president." And that's in a household where we're trying to teach her and reinforce those opportunities. And our mouths dropped. It was to the old adage, as we heard from Pat Mitchell in *Miss Representation,* making the case that you can't be what you can't see. And the point being, my daughter, every time Obama comes on TV, goes "Obama, Obama, Obama!" So her image is so reinforced that it's a man, not just an African American man—she doesn't even get that—but it's a boy, it's a man. So from the earliest moments of her childhood, you can imagine how that manifests in families all across the country and it creates a limiting belief and it creates a barrier of consciousness. We all know that Roger Bannister theory of life, the guy who broke the four-minute mile—what was fascinating about that is that no one in human history had ever broken the four-minute mile, and he didn't listen to all the experts. He didn't know what he didn't know. And he broke it, and within two years, dozens and dozens of people around the world broke the four-minute mile. It turned out it was a psychological barrier, by definition; it wasn't a physical barrier. And I think about that: the psychological barrier that exists in a lot of positions of power—police chiefs, fire chiefs, heads of Homeland Security in the past—all these dominant male figures come to mind and how so many have struggled to break those stereotypes and those limitations, in terms of consciousness, and how profoundly important those things are.

I appointed our city's first female fire chief, and immediately—I'll never forget—when it came out everyone said, "Oh, you're just doing that because she's a woman." I said, "No, she's the most qualified." They said, "Okay, we'll take you at your word." A few weeks later, I appointed the first female police chief, and that's when I got a call from a well-known elected official. *She* called me, saying, "I got the fire chief. Your point was made. This is getting ridiculous." I said, "What do you mean, ridiculous?" She said, "Look, you made your point, good for you, reaching out and getting a woman in the office." I said, "You're missing the point. I didn't do it because she was a woman, either one of them." And this was from a well known, never to be named elected official who was a woman, who thought I was doing it for purely political spectacle, not for substantive reasons. It was a big eye-opener for me. But it became profound, I mean, how many events I attended with my fire chief and police chief, and all these young girls running up to them that had never seen a woman police chief or a woman fire chief, and now, all of a sudden, in their subconscious is the capacity for them to see themselves in that position. It raises their bar of expectations. Public safety now, which has sort of been that eternal daddy figure in the past, now is a maternal mother figure in the present and future in their mind. I imagine it changes their mindset at home about all kinds of things. I think these things are incredibly important on the substance, but also the symbolism. And so when we do have a woman president, I think it will be profound, more profound than having a person of a different race in many ways.

MS: This is often framed as being about equality for equality's sake, but why is this important to everybody—to men and women—to have more women's voices represented and in positions of influence?

GN: In the broadest sense, I'm sitting here in an incubator, at my lieutenant governor's office in San Francisco, surrounded by forty start-ups, all these young folks with their laptops. And I look around the room and see remarkable diversity, and with that diversity comes people that are forming new connections, making new distinctions—thus the innovation you see, particularly out here and other parts of our country. And it comes from people from different walks of life, sharing their unique experiences and perspectives. Women bring, frankly, likely so much more to the table. I grew up with a single mother who raised two kids, worked her tail off at two-and-a-half jobs. . . . She never complained. She never explained her lot in life as some negative. She had the ability to multitask, to be able to navigate the responsibilities at work and the responsibilities at home. And I contrast that to, frankly, a lot of the male members of my family. It's not an indictment of my father—I'm still very close to him—but he divorced and moved away. [Men] have a remarkable incapacity at times to multitask [and] are remarkably good at complaining. . . . I don't mean to be trivializing the point of gender diversity, but just my own experience—with my sister and certainly with my wife, Jen, and so many women in my life—it's this remarkable capacity that women provide empathy and connection and the ability to, as that wonderful book *Built to Last* said, to recognize the genius of "and" versus the tyranny of "or"; the ability to do this "and" that. But back to my original point—not just forming distinctions, but fixing connections in people and in opportunity.

MS: I see a positive shift happening in the sense that now these issues are not being framed as much as "women's issues," that there has been lately a trend toward seeing the empowering and educating of women and girls as being something that would uplift all of humanity. Do you feel that more men are recognizing that and feeling comfortable being advocates for women?

GN: Your question is a good one. Why is it that men can't be recognized for being outstanding advocates for women? You don't need to be gay to be a great advocate for the LGBT community. In every aspect of life, you can maintain your empathy and your advocacy. So I think you're seeing that, and I think it's a great thing. I think people are realizing that we're not two separate tribes, we're all in this together, and that men have a responsibility to be advocates for women, women advocates for men and boys. So in this case, we have a lot more to do to support women in leadership positions and women have a lot more to achieve in that respect, so it's right to prioritize that. Men cannot be let off the hook in terms of that advocacy. Nor can young boys. So I think you're going to see a lot more of that advocacy, because you make the point fundamentally in terms of the interdependence. These issues are not isolated issues. Women's issues are fundamental issues to *all* of our lives and they're not wholly unique and distinctive. Women's issues just basically become family issues, and family issues, especially with pay equity, become issues that affect all of us in society.

MS: What type of leaders do you think we need today, either male or female? What do you think are the ingredients to successful leadership that the world needs right now?

GN: We need courage, we need conviction, we need people that are willing to risk their comfort, risk their status, risk potential reward to stand firmly on the foundation of whatever principle they believe in. At the same time, always remembering that none of us have exclusivity to the truth or exclusivity to what's right; we have to maintain a willingness to reach out and engage those that disagree with us and maintain an openness to argument. The most difficult thing is the rigidity of those that are ideological on both sides of the aisle and are unwilling to break with their dogma. So I think real leadership requires people to be willing to listen to different points of view and to form whatever opinion the facts can persuade them to form.

MS: What advice or words of wisdom would you have for someone, a woman or a man, who is considering pursuing a career in public service or running for office?

GN: Two points: One, in every respect I want to encourage and support people in leadership positions. Two, I think it's important to remind everyone there are two paths. And you can argue that one is not necessarily superior to the other—that is, in your book the premise is formal authority, being president, being elected into a position of influence and power. But one can make a legitimate argument that that may not necessarily be the most influential place to be. There are two points of authority, and that's moral versus formal authority. When you think about guys like Václav Havel or Dr. Martin Luther King, Jr., or Gandhi, people like Mandela, you can argue that at the peak of their influence when they had the most impact in the world and in their countries, they shared two things in common:

one was jail time, and two was that none of them had formal authority at the peak of their influence. You can make a very good case that when Mandela became president for his one term and Václav Havel—Havel made this case when he was president, as well—that they lost a little bit of their authority, even though they became presidents of their respective countries, because their voices were so much more powerful when they were exercised autonomously from the formal connections within governing organizations, with all of those rules and regulations and all of the limitations and formal laws of governing. So for me, leadership is not about being something in order to do something. And I think it's incredibly important for women to recognize that you don't need to be president, you don't need to be governor, you don't need to be mayor, you don't even need to be in elected office to be a leader and aspire to influence. I mean, what's the purpose of leadership? It's to move people to a cause greater than themselves and to have an impact that transcends. You can manifest that in so many different ways; you don't have to limit yourself to formal authority. So as important as it is to be a mayor, a governor, a president, whatever it may be, one could argue that it may not be the apex of leadership, that there are other ways to truly change the world that perhaps have even more meaning and impact. And so I just hope we encourage our young girls to aspire to that consideration and not just to the limited consideration of a formal role in society.

MS: This relates to your new book, *Citizenville*. I think sometimes people feel very disconnected about what's happening in our government. Many times people don't realize or even utilize the power that we all have, even as citizens. What advice and encouragement would you offer on just becoming an active, informed citizen?

GN: Well, you've got it. I mean, in so many ways, to pull from what I was just arguing, something profound is happening. I'm just noticing book after book coming out week after week, and there's a new narrative being formed about what technology is fundamentally doing, and that's decentralizing power. It's devolving the power and it allows more involvement and allows democratization of information and voices. And that is profound. It's the old pyramid that is now being flipped upside down, where the people are on top and those that traditionally have been in those formal roles of authority are on the bottom. So that's the leveling impact of technology and this notion that I talk about in the book that small is getting big and big is getting small. Now we have such a powerful tool in our pocket, in our hands, that we never could have imagined five, ten, fifteen years ago, that allows us to participate and to connect and to influence in ways we never could have imagined. So my whole book is about active citizen engagement. It's about stepping up and stepping in. It's about leaning in and participating and making the case that every one of our voices matter and that every one of our expressions is unique. So all of these things fit nicely into the larger schematic of gender equality and provide new points of access and tools, certainly for women and girls to connect. In many ways—and this is the long-winded point—I see these technologies fitting nicely, and perhaps more seamlessly, into the hands of women and girls that naturally are forming more connections, that are building more relationships. And the tools of technology amplify that. I just think women have the profound advantage in this hyper-connected world to [utilize] these new platforms that are forming to truly empower and to organize. Again, this is not my crystal ball, but the trend lines are extraordinarily pivotal for women and girls in every respect.

MS: I remember in *Miss Representation,* you said this line and it was shocking to hear: "If more people knew that Cuba, China, Iraq, and Afghanistan have more women in government than the United States of America, that would get some people upset." Why do you think the United States is lagging behind other countries on this?

GN: There's obviously historical context and the issues of the equal rights movement and the challenges that remain, like pay equity and the limitations in terms of national public policy, state and local policy as it relates to celebrating families and engendering a rational policy to support families and to support women as the dominant caregivers within those families—all of those things have created limitations by definition and need to be reconciled. I think the greatest inhibitor—it's a little simplistic, and I acknowledge the simplicity—but the greatest inhibitor for women and girls are men, by definition. There is selfishness, and I've experienced it with my wife, in terms of my expectations from her, particularly with our newborns, to spend the amount of time that I think she needs to spend with them versus the amount of time that I feel I need to spend with them. It's not a source of friction because we've sort of figured it out, but I'm starting to recognize the unfairness of my wife sitting there breastfeeding and having to be up every few hours. And the luxury that I have of not having to breastfeed and not being up every few hours, that connection she has in those early months, those early few years that is formed as a consequence. My connection is there, but with more independence, more latitude, more ability to navigate my professional life and career versus my wife's. I just think, in particular for young mothers, it remains a vexing and challenging issue. And public policy needs to catch up. When I was mayor, we were the only city in America with paid sick leave. We had universal healthcare well before the Affordable Care Act. We tried to do those things from a policy perspective, but at the end of the day, they're still not good enough. They remain huge issues and, of course, issues of pay equity, that's just disgraceful.

My final point is the point you were making. We're an enlightened country and at the same time remarkably naïve for the world we're living in. I literally have to send back-up information—I get in these, hardly fights, but in these arguments with people that don't believe me when I make the case, as I made in Jen's film *Miss Representation,* as it relates to representation in legislative bodies and executive bodies for women in countries that so many of us feel are oppressive, where women have a much stronger voice in the orbit of affairs of state. It's incredibly important to remind people how far we've come and how far we need to go. Just because Nancy Pelosi was Speaker and just because I'm out in a state with two women that are senators, doesn't mean that this state has achieved the pinnacle of gender equality. Particularly in the legislature, not dissimilar to Congress, they actually lost more seats than they gained for women. We continue to struggle—and I think you've noted this in some of your work— even more dismally at the local level with encouraging women. And when women run, they win. It's not just a question of convincing more women of a career in politics. And many are smart just to say, "Why would I ever want to?" And so I don't think it's to be critiqued when a woman says, "It's not for me." Again, there are so many other ways to contribute and to lead and to change the world. You don't have to be in elected office, though it remains powerfully important and we need to encourage more.

MS: I feel like there are a lot of changing paradigms—look what's happening around gay marriage, and we have elected an African American president for the second time, and there's a historic number of women serving in Congress. What shifts do you see happening that encourage you? Do you feel like there are some new paradigms that are being born?

GN: I think the most profound is this 'Net generation, this millennial generation. It's the first global generation, the most empathetic and connected generation in history, people thirty and younger. And again, I think it's a generation that forms less distinction and more connection. It's a generation that is more civically minded. It's the most educated generation. . . . And there's a recognition that we don't just tolerate diversity, that we celebrate it. I see that generational shift and generational attitudes, less defined by Democrat/Republican, there's a different diversity that's being formed, and I just think that it's going to bode extraordinarily well and very favorably toward the shift to gender equality and advancing the rights of women and girls. So I'm with you on the optimism. And again, there's a demographic shift in this country taking shape, and when you twin the demographic shift with these tools of technology—you merge IT and the demographic changes and the globalization—that is something that we've never experienced in human history and the rate of change is exponential and so, on this one, fasten your seat belts. I mean, I don't think we're looking at the traditional trajectory of change, as it relates to empathy and understanding and capacity building that we've seen in the past. I think that change is going to be much more acute and much more intense. So I don't want to be Pollyannaish about this, or naïve, but I really feel there is a tsunami here and in the future . . . I remain extraordinarily optimistic about it.

★ ★

WHAT OBSTACLES, STRUCTURAL OR PSYCHOLOGICAL, ARE
PREVENTING WOMEN FROM ENTERING INTO LEADERSHIP ROLES?

★ ★

*I think one of the major obstacles we face is that we keep thinking there's going
to be a perfect moment where someone is going to come to us and say, "Wow,
you would be perfect to run for the United States Senate," or "I really think
we should put you forward for state House or to become governor." We think
there's a perfect moment in which our children will be the right age, we'll have
all the correct degrees, know the right people, we'll have had all the correct
experiences—and that simply isn't how life works. And as women we're so
caught up in doing everything right that I think we are sort of pre-conditioned
to wait for the perfect time, and it just doesn't happen. And I still see that.
Actually, I just spoke to a bunch of young women in Washington, hundreds
of young women who are politically active and in their twenties, and I said,
"Look, the most important thing to learn is to just say 'yes.' Whenever the
next opportunity comes to you, don't think about whether you have the right
clothes or you have the right degree; just say 'yes.'" And it was like dropping a
match on kindling. I feel like for all of them, too, they just need permission, to
just go out and do the next thing. And it is hard for women to do.*

—CECILE RICHARDS, PRESIDENT OF PLANNED PARENTHOOD

*Stereotypes. If a man says something clearly and with conviction, he's just a
clear thinker. If a woman says something clearly and with conviction, she's
emotional or aggressive or a bitch—all the labels we already know. I think that
the issue is changing, but not enough and not fast enough.*

—JODY WILLIAMS, NOBEL PEACE LAUREATE

*The media, and society in general, are so much harder on women who try to
enter politics than men and that makes running for office seem unappealing. It
would take a really determined and self-confident young woman to view that
treatment and want to subject herself to it. I think that just on a personal level,
no one wants to be bullied, no one wants to put themselves in that position,
and that's the position we have put female politicians in. Also, just in terms*

of leadership more generally, I think there are still gender stereotypes that encourage women to remain silent. I see this in the classroom all the time, even on the collegiate level, where boys are constantly the ones raising their hands to say just about anything, and young women either don't really speak at all, or only speak when they feel like have some perfectly formulated answer and something really valuable to say. And they don't participate in the same way and they don't put themselves out there in the same way, and I think that's a huge factor in determining if they want to become a leader or not.

—JULIE ZEILINGER, AUTHOR, FOUNDER AND EDITOR OF THE FBOMB BLOG

The truth of the matter is, a lot of it has to do with incumbency. We're in a political environment in the United States where incumbency is the most powerful of things. I tell our women candidates that the best way to get elected is to get elected once before [laughs]. You're in a much better place once you get in, and it's hard to get in there, unless we're looking at open seats or swing districts where you've got a shot. And the problem right now is we're very divided as a nation, and so we don't have a lot of opportunities to get into open seats. There is a structural challenge, not just for women but for people of color, because the current make-up of how this is set up is in fact geared toward incumbents and, of course, who are the incumbents for the last 250 years? That is part of the problem.

—STEPHANIE SCHRIOCK, PRESIDENT OF EMILY'S LIST

NANCY PELOSI

"It's about equality, but it's not just about equality. And the reason it's necessary to have more voices is because that strengthens the debate and it strengthens the decisions. It isn't that women coming in are better than men; they're different from men. And I always say the beauty is in the mix. To have diversity of opinion in the debate strengthens the outcome and you get a better result."

NANCY PELOSI, THE Democratic leader of the U.S. House of Representatives for the 113th Congress, is focused on strengthening America's middle class and creating jobs, reforming the political system to create clean campaigns and fair elections, enacting comprehensive immigration reform, and ensuring safety in America's communities, neighborhoods, and schools. From 2007 to 2011, Pelosi served as Speaker of the House, the first woman to do so in American history.

For twenty-five years, Pelosi has represented San Francisco, California's 12th District, in Congress. She first made history when House Democrats elected her the first woman to lead a major political party. She has led House Democrats for a decade and previously served as House Democratic Whip.

Under the leadership of Pelosi, the 111th Congress was heralded as "one of the most productive Congresses in history" by congressional scholar Norman Ornstein. President Barack Obama called Speaker Pelosi "an extraordinary leader for the American people," and the *Christian Science Monitor* wrote: "Make no mistake: Nancy Pelosi is the most powerful woman in American politics and the most powerful House Speaker since Sam Rayburn a half century ago."

Pelosi brings to her leadership position a distinguished record of legislative accomplishment. She led Congress in passing historic health insurance reform, key investments in college aid, clean energy and innovation, and initiatives to help small businesses and veterans. She has been a powerful voice for civil rights and human rights around the world for decades. Pelosi comes from strong family tradition of public service in Baltimore. Married to Paul Pelosi, she is a mother of five and grandmother of nine.

MARIANNE SCHNALL: Why do you think we've not yet had a woman president? What do you think it will take to make that happen?

NANCY PELOSI: Well, [there are] two reasons why we will, and one is there are plenty of talented women—one in particular, Hillary Clinton, who I think would go into the White House as one of the most well-prepared leaders in modern history. She has the full package of having served in the White House and as a senator and secretary of state. She knows the issues in depth and she has great values, a good political sense, and is highly respected by the American people. So . . . how long will it take? Just as soon as she makes her decision! [*laughs*] That would be the shortcut—it isn't a shortcut, it's over two hundred years due. Why I think it will also happen is the American people are very, very ready for a woman president. They're far ahead of the politicians, and that may be why we haven't had a woman president. I always thought it would be much easier to elect a woman president of the United States than Speaker of the House, because the people are far ahead, as I say, of the electeds, on the subject of a woman being president. And in Congress, you know, as I said on the day I was sworn in, you have to break the *marble* ceiling—forget glass, the marble ceiling that is there of just a very male-oriented society where they had a pecking order and they thought that would be the way it always was and they would always be in charge, and, "Let me know how I can help you, but don't expect to take the reins of power." So it was interesting to me that we were able to elect a woman Speaker, and it wasn't because I was a woman. That's the last thing I could ask my members: to vote for me because I was a woman. But I just had to get there in the way that a woman would get to be president; not because she's a woman—says she immodestly—but because she has the talent and the know-how and inspires confidence that she can do the job, whatever that job happens to be. In this case we're talking about president of the United States.

MS: Looking at the bigger picture, because sometimes this gets framed as equality for equality's sake, but why is this important to have more women represented and women's voices—not just ultimately in the presidency, but in Congress and in Washington?

NP: Well, I think you're right—it's about equality, but it's not just about equality. And the reason it's necessary to have more voices is because that strengthens the debate and it strengthens the decisions. It isn't that women coming in are better than men; they're different from men. And I always say the beauty is in the mix. To have diversity of opinion in the debate strengthens the outcome and you get a better result. I do think that women bring a tendency, an inclination, toward consensus building that is stronger among women than men, as I have seen it so far.

MS: Women have made progress, and certainly it was history-making in terms of the number of women in Congress from this last election, but it's still very far from parity. As women have seemed to make strides in so many other areas, why do you think progress for women in Washington has been so slow?

NP: Well, we've had a woman Speaker of the House. I don't think enough appreciation was given to that, because I think a lot of people didn't know what the Speaker of the House was. Now they do because they see an obstructionist one. Not to toot my own horn, but that's a very big deal. President, vice president, Speaker of the House—you're not there because the president chose you, you are there with your power derived from the membership of the Congress of the United States, so you go to the table as a full partner in the balance of power. And our checks and balances . . . the legislative branch is the first branch, the executive branch is second, and then the others. But more fundamental, what we have in our House—and it was a decision we made to make it so, and we want to do more—is our caucus is a majority of women, minorities, and LGBT. That is, 54 percent of the House Democratic caucus is not white male. In the history of civilization, you have never seen a representative body for a leading party that was so diverse. And the majority not being the so-called majority, as previously conceived.

Also, our committees will lead—should we win—but even in the minority, our top Democrats on these committees are a majority of women and minorities. Now, getting just to women and why aren't there more . . . I'm drawing some conclusions the last few years when we've pushed and pushed and we've gained more, but in order for us to really kick open the door, we have to change the environment we're in. The environment I would like to see is one where the role of money is reduced and the level of civility is heightened. If you have less money and more civility, you will have more women. And that's one of the reasons—not the only reason, but to protect our democracy—that we are pushing for campaign finance reform to reduce the role of money in politics. If you bring more women, more young people, more minorities, more diversity, more of a face of America to public office and to public service, just speaking in terms of women, I can guarantee you: if you lower money and increase civility, you will have many more women. And that's what we have to do: create our own environment. We've been operating in an environment that has not been friendly to the advancement of women, especially now that it's become so harsh and so money driven.

MS: Looking at the landscape right now, it does look very daunting to run, and even when you get to Washington, very challenging. What advice or encouragement would you want to offer to a woman who is considering pursuing elected office but feels discouraged?

NP: Well, one of the things that was very disappointing when they went after me in such a major way, is women would come say to me, "I'm not subjecting my family to that." And I say, you have to know what you believe and how important it is to you, how urgent it is for the country, and then that doesn't matter. You've stepped into the arena, you're in the fight, you throw a punch, you're going to get one thrown at you, and vice versa. They throw one at you, you've got to be ready to throw one at them [*laughs*], because it's a rough terrain. It shouldn't be that way, but that's what it is now.

So what I tell women is, "This is not for the faint of heart, but you have to have a commitment as to why you want to engage in public service." We want people who have plenty of options in life to engage in public service—not anybody where this is the only job they could get. So we're competing for their time, and their time, their priority decision will be made as to how important it is for them to make their mark, whether it's on issues that relate to the economy, national security, family issues, education, healthcare, and those kinds of things. But I consider every issue a women's issue. So you have to believe in who you are and what difference you can make. You have to care about the urgency and the difference it will make to your community, and you have to, again, have confidence in the contribution that you can make. You believe, you care, you have confidence in the difference that you can make. And that's not to be egotistical, it's just to be confident.

I tell women . . . "If you have a vision about what you believe about America, about our country and our families, you have to have knowledge about the situation. You don't want to be a notion monger, you want to be an idea creator. So you have a vision, you know your subject—you don't have to know every subject—you can focus, whether it's foreign policy or whatever. Vision, knowledge, judgment springing from that knowledge, confidence, a plan, thinking strategically about how you would get this accomplished. When you tell the story of your vision with your knowledge and how you plan to get it done, you will be so eloquent, you will attract support. You will be lifted up and you will lift others up."

MS: You have written a whole book about knowing your power. Do you think part of the problem is that women and girls today don't know their power? And what can we do to change that, for even women to know that they have a vision worth pursuing?

NP: Well, here's the thing: I wrote that book—it's like just a little puff—because people were saying I always wanted to be Speaker since I was five years old; I had no interest in running for office when I was five years old, nor when I was a teenager, nor when I was forty years old. I had an interest in politics, but not in running for office. So I thought I sort of had to keep the record straight. But for that reason, I was able to say to people, "Be ready. Just be ready. Take inventory of what your skills are. And if that means being a mom and all the diplomacy, interpersonal skills, management of time—all the rest that is involved in that—value that." How many times do you ask somebody, "What do you do?" "I'm just a housewife." Just a housewife? No, proudly a housewife, or a homemaker, or whatever the term is these days. But that's what women used to say when I was young, and I'd say, "Don't say that! I'm a stay-at-home mom, too, but I don't think I'm just a housewife!" So in any event, take inventory of what your possibilities are and have confidence in that. . . . And what you have—as I say with the vision, knowledge, et cetera—you have your own authenticity that is very sincere and very convincing. So be proud of the unique contribution that only you can make. That really is what I want people to think—to enjoy why they're attracted to a certain issue, to savor learning more about it, that they can have opinions that are respected, they have standing on the issue, a plan for how they can implement something to make progress for our country and our families . . . and that argument will always win the day.

MS: You were the first female Speaker of the House, which is a huge milestone. What advice or perspective can you offer on breaking through glass ceilings, or as you say, "marble ceilings" and being the first or one of very few women in the room and the pressure that comes with that?

NP: The only time I'm the only woman in the room is when I go to the leadership meeting. But by and large I have made sure that women were chairing our committees when I was Speaker, or the senior Democrat on each of the committees, where I had the jurisdiction, because I think it's really important for people to know: it's not just about one woman, it's about women. And it's about the issues that we care about and the reinforcement of a message, not just one person saying it. The Speaker has awesome power, there's no question about it. That role, number three—president, vice president, Speaker of the House—they are the highest positions in the country. But the fact is that, again, it's not about one woman, it's about what this means in the lives of women. So the interaction of women on these issues was [more] important for the members than the reinforcement on how we see our role. We're there for our country, we're there for our districts, but women in America see us partially as their own, even if we don't represent them officially.

MS: Did you feel the magnitude of being in that position? Because being the first is something that's significant, even thinking about what the pressure's going to be on the first woman president. Did you feel that you could be there and be your authentic self, or did you feel the weight of people's expectations?

NP: Marianne, I want to tell you something, and as I think back on it, I was so busy. I was so busy. We had an agenda to get done for the American people. And while I never set out to be Speaker and I never even envisioned it, one thing led to another and there I was, but I just knew I had a responsibility. As I look back on it, maybe I should have taken time to just sit there and say, "Wow," but I didn't even have a second to do that. I'm looking at President Bush's library, and he used to say, "You're number three." He'd point to himself, one, point to Cheney, two, [point to me], three. Yes, it would be driven home to me that I was in this very exalted position, but it was only important to the extent that I could involve other women at the proper level, so that it wasn't just about one person. It's pretty thrilling to be Speaker, no question about that. But, again, right away we had sent the president the Lilly Ledbetter [Fair Pay Act], and one week and one day after his inaugural address we sent him the American

Reinvestment and Recovery Act. I mean, that's when we had President Obama, but when we won, President Bush was president and we had a 100-hour agenda—the first 100 hours we raised the minimum wage; it hadn't been raised in eleven years. We had our "Six for '06" [agenda], most of which became the law of the land. So we were on a schedule. There wasn't really too much time to think of how important I was. It was really more important for our members and our women to take ownership of the issues that build consensus around where we would go from here.

MS: Well, you did a wonderful job. And actually, I have heard your name come up many times, not only just being such an admired woman leader, but also as somebody who could potentially run for president or would make a great president. Is that something that you would ever consider?

NP: No. Here's the thing: I didn't even focus on becoming Speaker, but I knew—as whip, and as leader, and then as Speaker and then leader again—that the cooperation you get from members, which is everything— how you build consensus—has to have no doubt associated with it that it's anything but for the good of the country. That there isn't even a slight tinge that there might be some other political agenda at work. This is not for the faint of heart, any of it. You take a vote, you make friends and foes, and everybody has to know that this is a consensus that we build together. I think that's really important. And nothing could be more of a thrill to me than to represent the people of San Francisco in Congress. To be speaker and have that recognition from my colleagues, and to be the first woman—I'm honored by that. I thought it would be not in further-ance of reaching all of our goals if there was any doubt that I wanted to run for any other office. And I didn't, so that was easy [laughs]. There was no contrivance there; it was like, "Make no mistake: I've reached my height" [laughs].

MS: When you were talking about the importance of a consensus—and certainly in this current climate, that seems really important—what advice do you have on working with people across the aisle whose opinions you may disagree with but who you have to interact with?

NP: We come to Congress representing our own district. And so does everybody else, so even if you disagree with the manner in which some people present their views and how negative they may be, the fact is, you respect the people who sent them there. They are there, a House of Representatives, and so it's unimportant what you think of somebody; what is important is that you respect their constituents and the right of that person to represent them. Now, having said that, you know you're in the marketplace of ideas; that's how our founders had intended. You depend on the strength of the power of your ideas, the strength of your argument, to compete in this marketplace of ideas to prevail. You know that if you're going to do something that's going to have sustainability that you're going to have to try to build consensus across the aisle, if possible. Go to find common ground; where you can't, you stand your ground, as I always say. But you always try.

MS: Looking at Washington right now, it can seem very daunting and it looks like a lot of work to people. What would you say are the positives? What drives you and fuels your work and motivates you every day? What are the joys of doing the work that you're doing?

NP: Well, again, there are 435 members in the House, only one from my district, from each of our districts, so that's a great honor—that is a tremendous honor to be able to speak for the people of your district. So that's always a joy, and when it isn't, it's time to go home. To represent your district in the people's House—how thrilling, how thrilling. I think that people have some thought that this gridlock has been there for a long time. It really hasn't. It's largely something that has obstructed progress from when President Obama came in and the Republicans declared that they would stop his success, and they did that in a way that I think was harmful to the American people. So it's not about the niceties of debate; it's about what are we here to do? If they're standing in the way of jobs for the American people, then we have to make that fight. And we have differences of opinion on the role of government in whatever it is—the education of our children, the safety and good health of our neighborhoods and of our people, you know, all of that. We believe what we believe, and we respect that other people have different beliefs, but we don't just roll over and say, "Okay, we all sign up for obstruction." We just can't. We can't govern . . . we're called the legislative branch; we came to legislate and that's what we should do. So when people say this and that, I say, "You know what, understand this: the House has always been a competitive arena for the battle of ideas. Anybody who's here to obstruct progress for our country really should be held accountable for that." And that's what we're dealing with right now.

MS: Women and young girls can feel very hesitant to speak out or stand out too much. It seems like you've always had the courage to speak out for what you believe in. You don't hold anything back. Where does that come from? How did you develop your inner leader?

NP: Well, I think a couple of things. I went to all-girls' schools my whole life, so every model of leadership that I saw was a young girl or a woman, and so there was never any hesitation that women could lead. I know what I believe. And I really think—says she immodestly—one quality that I bring to my role is that I've been in Congress awhile, I know the issues, so I think I have good judgment as to what works or what doesn't and an institutional memory of what has worked and what hasn't. It's also that I have a clear view of what I think our purpose is and that is to make the future better for all of our children, in every way, and that involves national security, our economy, every subject you can name, including those that are directly related, like health and education and environment.

MS: Are there concrete changes that you would like to see that you think would help foster more women leaders, not just in Washington, but in general? Are there things that you think we can do to increase the numbers?

NP: Well, I think that really lies inside of every woman. They have to really have confidence in themselves. If women have confidence in themselves, they will have confidence in other women. Sometimes we wonder, what is the support of women, for women? It's by and large, very large, I think, but sometimes it's not always there. And sometimes I think it's because, "Well, I can do that. Why is *she* doing it?" You know, it's not a zero-sum game—there's plenty of opportunity for everyone, so there's no reason to worry about somebody else's success, either saying you couldn't do this so she's better than you, or she's doing it so you can't. No, she's doing it so you *can*. Every piece of advice I give to people is, "Be yourself, know your power, have confidence in what you have to contribute." If you have all of that, you will respect that in other women and we can just advance this. Now I've said to you before: reduce the role of money, increase the level of civility, and women will take these responsibilities. And many more women will say, "Okay, I'll run. I'm not afraid of needing the money or being . . ." shall we say, "smeared." A little girl interviewed me this morning, she said, "How did your family deal with all the negative things that the Republicans said about you?" I said, "Well, they didn't really care that much, because I didn't really care that much." What I do care about is that it's an obstacle to other women entering politics, because they'll say, "Why would I do that? I have plenty of options." And women with plenty of options are just the women that we want to be in politics and government.

MS: It's been brought up how remarkable it is that it was not that long ago that women didn't even have the right to vote. It's almost surreal to think about that. Where do you see the current status of women in the United States and around the world right now? What do you see is the current call to action for women today?

NP: I think that women have to know how important they are. Not that women are better than men, but the mix is a beautiful thing and you get a better result. I think that we will have a woman president soon. I hope that Hillary Clinton will decide to run, because I think that will bring that day closer to us. . . . I do think that we will be required to be taken into a direction where the American people are so far ahead of the Congress. And as I said to you before, I always thought we would have a woman president before we would have a woman speaker of the House, because of the way this system has been so male-dominated and the American people are far ahead on that score. So I see us on a path. I think it will be very important to our country, to women and little girls in our country, and to everyone in our country and the world, to see our country join the ranks of those who have women leaders.

★ ★

HOW DO YOU VIEW THE STATUS OF WOMEN TODAY?
ARE YOU OPTIMISTIC?

★ ★

I have the strongest belief—not just hope, belief—that we are now undergoing, in this area of women's rights and violence toward women, we are on the threshold of a transformation. . . . I'm tremendously hopeful.

—PATRICK STEWART

I believe that it is only a matter of time before the structural barriers to women or minorities are effectively dismantled. I look forward to the day when I am thought of as the 102nd Supreme Court Justice rather than the first female Supreme Court Justice.

—SANDRA DAY O'CONNOR

It fascinates me. What appears to be the most obvious is not. Living in New York City, I see women in power everywhere, but this is not the rule—this remains the exception. When you look at things from a global perspective it becomes so clear that we need to shift the paradigm so that opportunities and access are available to all women. We know women are a key part of the answer, and we need both men and women to fully embrace this. Change is scary but it is also necessary.

—DONNA KARAN

I think the world is realizing that [empowering and educating girls and women] is incredibly important and that we need to do more and more to support women, because in many parts of the developing world their power is often very limited . . . And yet in so many cases, the power they have to make decisions is the key to their families' future . . . I think people need to remember that empowering women to determine their future should not be controversial, no matter where you are.

—MELINDA GATES

It's unbelievable that we're applauding winning what is really a miserly amount of number of women who are in the House, and we think, Oh, wow, look at this high number. *I mean, you've got to look at where we started from and where we are now. Granted, if you just had a fresh pair of eyes looking at the numbers, you would say this is pathetic. This is nowhere near a reflection of the demographics of the United States of America, but that's true for every population, whether it's Hispanic or African American or women. I mean, we've come far, but we certainly have a long way to go. But considering where we were just a few years ago, it's really changing. It's moving in the right direction.*

—REPRESENTATIVE ILEANA ROS-LEHTINEN (R)

Well, [we're] far better off than we were, but a long way still to go. It's very easy to get discouraged. It's very easy for people to pull out bad statistics, but overall it's in our direction and it's coming. But you can't take it for granted. You've got to work very hard to make the change. The women's movement now is global; it is worldwide in every aspect. . . . You name the country, and there's a vibrant women's movement and they're gaining in strength. And certainly here we are so much bigger and so much more diversified than we ever have been. It's very exciting. . . . Now [the Feminist Majority Foundation leadership program] is on campuses all over the world—I'm not talking just the United States. We're on about 900 college campuses. At Ms. Magazine, we do a whole women's studies edition and get everybody there . . . it's thousands upon thousands upon thousands of students, males and females, learning about the status of women and equality and gender roles and history and language and so many things. . . . They bring with them the passion and the energy to make sure there will be equality and justice. And that, to me, is just so exciting I can't even tell you. And I see them all the time. The energy for this is just boundless, and we'll see far more than we ever have.

—ELEANOR SMEAL, COFOUNDER AND PRESIDENT OF FEMINIST MAJORITY FOUNDATION

DON MCPHERSON

"Sometimes when I talk to people and they want to debate the severity of sexism in our culture, I remind them that I, as a black man, at one point in this country, was livestock. And I got the right to vote before [women] did. That should tell you the severity of sexism in our democracy."

F OR MORE THAN twenty-five years, Don McPherson has used the power and appeal of sport to address complex social justice issues. He has created innovative programs, supported community service providers, and has provided educational seminars and lectures throughout North America. Don has twice testified before the United States Congress and has worked closely with the U.S. Departments of Education and Defense on issues of sexual violence in education and the military, respectively. He has provided commentary on numerous news programs and was featured in O, *The Oprah Magazine* and appeared on *The Oprah Winfrey Show*. McPherson has served as a board member, consultant, and advisor for several national organizations including the Ms. Foundation for Women and the National Football Foundation. Recently, McPherson joined the board of directors of the U.S. National Committee for UN Women. As an athlete, McPherson was a unanimous All-America quarterback at Syracuse University. As captain of the undefeated 1987 Syracuse football team, McPherson set twenty-two school records, led the nation in passing, and won more than eighteen national "player of the year" awards. His professional football career included playing for the NFL's Philadelphia Eagles and Houston Oilers, then going up north to join the Canadian Football League's Hamilton Tiger-Cats and Ottawa Rough-Riders. He was runner-up for the Heisman Trophy. In 2009, McPherson was enshrined into the College Football Hall of Fame. McPherson has worked as a college football analyst for ESPN, BET, and NBC and is currently the studio analyst for Sportsnet New York's coverage of Big East Football.

MARIANNE SCHNALL: Why do you think we have not yet had a woman president?

DON MCPHERSON: Wow. It's funny . . . you're asking this question, and there are about five or six different ways in my head that I can already think of answering it. We live in this incredibly sexist and misogynistic society—that's an easy statement to make—but it's more. I think when you really start to drill down into American culture, we're the greatest hypocrites going. We say things like "equality," and yet we laugh in the face of that at times. We still have unequal pay for equal work. We still have these glaring things in our culture that we have yet to address. We have not ratified certain agreements, even the rights of a child. We are so hypocritical: we live these very Judeo-Christian values on the one hand, but on the second hand, the capitalism that drives our culture is so loaded with gender inequities and use of sexual behavior and sexual innuendo in this supposed Christian culture. It's subtly powerful. Even if you look at our current political structure, there are so many whys. Why haven't we had a Jewish president? The hypocrisy of our culture sometimes . . . we talk about being fair and just, but we are sexist and homophobic. So that's sort of my first gut reaction.

MS: In connection to that, that's why I always think it's not just about electing a woman president, but the fact that we've elected Barack Obama twice, just in terms of changing the paradigms by having greater diversity up at the top is still a very positive sign.

DM: It is, but sometimes when I talk to people and they want to debate the severity of sexism in our culture, I remind them that I, as a black man, at one point in this country, was livestock. And I got the right to vote before [women] did. That should tell you the severity of sexism in our democracy. And so Barack Obama is part of the boy's club. Even though he's a black man, even though he's a black man named Barack Hussein Obama. He's not a black man named George Jefferson, as was famously George Jefferson [*laughs*]. But this guy—Barack Hussein Obama—and he made it to the presidency before [a woman did].

MS: Do you think that we're ready yet, to elect a woman president? Do you think men especially are ready?

DM: I think that person has to be so special and so unique. I think that Hillary is probably the only woman right now that we know of. And I say that only because of the way the political process works, that there's all the internal vetting of the party that she would have to go through in our dysfunctional two-party system, and no one's going to challenge her. So I do think the country is ready for Hillary, but there's a reason why I think that men are ready for her: She's put up with more crap than any woman has ever had to in public office. And everything that she put up with, publicly and privately, I think she has had to go through that to earn the respect of especially men. She couldn't just come up and be a brilliant woman who has great political instinct and is well studied on foreign relationships. She had to go through everything she went through. She had to go through the moment when . . . she cried, in New Hampshire, it was all these charges of her gender that somehow mattered. So even that—Obama never had to deal with anything like that. He didn't have to deal with anything that was specific to his race. In fact, everyone walked on eggshells around his race, whereas any moment where Hillary showed her gender, she was attacked. And what I love about her is that I think she honored both the men and women who love her and respect her and support her, because she did it with such grace and power. She never gave into the hate and the sexism.

MS: When I had interviewed Gloria Steinem, she said in the 2008 election she didn't think we were ready for a woman president, but she thinks we are now. She said that part of the issue was that men, especially, are not used to seeing women as authority figures and leaders. She gave me this quote, and I was just interested in your reaction: "We were raised by women and so we associate women with childhood. Men, especially, may feel regressed when they see a powerful woman. The last time they saw one they were eight. So one of the most helpful things we can do in the long term, is to make sure that kids have loving, nurturing, male figures, as well as female figures, and authoritative and expert female figures, as well as male figures." I'm just curious if you think, in terms of talking about some of these gender roles, if that is part of the issue? That men have issues with seeing powerful women?

DM: Yes. To your point about what happens with our boys . . . I always say that boys who are raised by women, as you mentioned, there comes a point when they are told, explicitly, that what your mother does is beneath you. And what she does is less than what your father does, or has less value, and you're not to do those things. And we laugh about it. We joke about this. Boys don't do laundry, they don't cook. You hear a guy say he cooks, you're like, "What? You cook?" "Yes, I prepare food for the family to eat." And yet that's beneath boys, and it's all the behaviors and all the things they see their mothers doing. My daughters put on my shoes and clog around the house, but if I had a son, would he put on his mother's shoes and clog around the house? Our homophobia tells that boy, "No, that's wrong." And we learn this as boys. We learn this at a very, very early age. For a lot of boys, it's troubling. It's like, What do you mean? This is the woman who bathed me, who fed me, who does all these things—still does all these things—and I'm being told that who she is, is less than. And that is a very real expression; I hear it almost daily. I have two children who are seven and nine years old, so I hear it in their peers of families on a regular basis. And so boys are learning that women are less than. And as they grow, that just gets reinforced in so many ways. It's the mom is a cook, but Dad is a chef. Your elementary school teacher is a woman. Your middle school teacher is a woman. Your high school teacher is a man. Your college professor is a man. So it's all these different things—as we get older, the more serious roles are men.

MS: So how can we fix this or change this?

DM: I actually think that as dramatic as that just sounded, I think it is one of the areas where we are far in advance of what we think. What I mean by that is, as I said, I have two daughters. And my two daughters know they can be just about anything. And they've asked that question about a woman president. And because of the media the way that it is now, I do think that this is a very interesting time where a lot of challenges to convention are happening at a very, very rapid pace because of technology and media. I was just having this conversation yesterday with the Breakthrough office about why this time is so interesting. It's that the conversation right now at the Supreme Court level with Prop 8 and DOMA is one where we're seeing how twenty years ago the Supreme

Court moved at a snail's pace, Congress moves at a car's pace, and society moves at a jet's—and that was twenty years ago. Today, it's Congress and the Supreme Court are still the same, but society is at light speed. It used to be that people left small towns and little places to come to New York or San Francisco to be gay or to look at the world in a more loving social justice lens that was more accepting of all, and now you don't need that. People are connecting without having to move to those locations, so we're seeing this collective consciousness that is being supported by media. . . . And generationally, because of that being more connected, more aware, more conscious, I think that those things are moving us toward a woman president, toward a lot of things. I think there are a lot of things that are happening rapidly, that are challenging the convention of all white men.

MS: One of the things that I've heard you say, which I think is always so important to keep in mind, is that we sometimes mistakenly think of gender stereotypes as fixed attributes, like men have an innate propensity toward violence and women more toward peace, when the truth is a lot of that has been cultural conditioning. Isn't it really that men and boys have been directed dysfunctionally that way, not that they're naturally that way? I have heard you talk about, as a man, trying to embrace your wholeness. I like that you call those qualities of being loving and nurturing and peaceful part of your humanness, rather than feminine. Those are qualities that exist in men and boys, as well, but they've been conditioned to turn those off by society. The fact that women aren't represented in positions of power and authority may also have to do with these "feminine" and "human" traits associated with women that have been suppressed in the world.

DM: That's patriarchy. Because what it's doing is taking those qualities that we see as weak or that we associate with weakness. I'm just thinking of myself in some ways, but I think of men in general, when we *feel*, we feel weak and we feel vulnerable. And it is a horrible feeling, but what's amazing about that horrible feeling is that's where we grow. And men are typically violent toward that growth and toward that feeling.

MS: In my interview with Patrick Stewart recently, I thought one of the most powerful things he talked about was how he came to understand why his father was violent toward his mother. He learned after his father's death that his father had actually been suffering from post-traumatic stress after returning from the military following World War II, which was never properly diagnosed or treated. While that doesn't excuse his father's actions, it may help explain his coping problems and propensity toward violence. It's the idea that men, too, need help, that men have been taught to suppress their emotions, not to reach out for help and may only know how to deal with conflict through violence. So men need this help dealing with constrictive gender roles and stereotypes, too.

DM: You're exactly right. The other day I was in Dallas for a rally, and a guy named Dale Hansen—he's been on the air doing sports in Dallas for so long, I know who he is and I don't even live in Dallas. He's a big man and he spoke at a rally the other day, and he talked about his father who was the biggest, strongest man he's ever known. He talked about his father winning the Strong Man Competition in the carnival that used to come through his town when he was a boy, and his father was this big, burly man. And he watched his father punch his mother in the face and break her nose. At this rally, he told that story, and he cried telling the story. After the rally, I was talking to a woman who runs a domestic violence shelter in Dallas, so we started talking about young boys and at what age boys begin to learn to suppress their feelings, and it's so much a part of them—it's half of who they are. And she says, "What happens to those boys? What happens to guys?" I said, "Well, we become Dale Hansen." We become this sixty-year-old man, this seventy-year-old man, who still recalls with vivid recollection that moment when the biggest man he knew, in his words, became so small in a child's eyes. But you suppress that and you keep pushing it back. It doesn't go away and you are that man, as Dale Hansen is—this big man who is this high-profile sports announcer in Dallas, who's living with this and has lived with this. And so, yes, for Dale Hansen that moment was cathartic for him to be able to stand up in front of other men and tell that story.

So, yes, I used to always say, "I am a man in recovery," because you are constantly trying to unlearn behaviors and attitudes and feelings that were nurtured into you your entire life. Not only were they nurtured into you, but you were told that they mattered and that they made you important, they made you strong. And I said that even as a black person, nothing was more damaging to my life than masculinity. . . . And I go back to Obama: his race didn't hold him back. He's president of the United States! And yet it is my gender as a man that has made me less functional in relationships. It has made me less functional in my own health. It has given me a very narrow lens on the world. Again, because I'm a man in a patriarchal society, I never had to address that.

I don't know if you saw the news today, but there was a case of a basketball coach at Rutgers University who was recently fired for being extremely abusive—standing two feet away from one of his players and hitting him very hard with a basketball and using homophobic slurs, and it was a horrible, horrible display of humanity. My friend at CNN.com asked me if I would write something on this, and I started to write about how there's this creed in sports—and this is very much again a part of that masculinity zero-sum game, living in a meritocracy—"I win, you lose." And that's very much this narrow masculinity; we're not going to have a broad conversation around feelings and respect of others and all that. It's

"I win, you lose." So I'm writing this article and I started to put the quote that's most often attributed to Vince Lombardi that says, "Winning isn't everything. It's the only thing." As a player, that's the "I win, you lose," but as a human being, stepping off of that field—as a father, as a brother, as a husband, as a son, as an employer, as an employee—if I live my life by that same mentality, then I'm a bully. I'm an abuser. But that's the other part of that creed of masculinity: you're supposed to be in charge. So boys learn this at a very early age.

MS: I think that's so interesting. It does seem like there needs to be more of a forum for men to talk about these things. I think one of the few positive things that have been coming out of, for example, the Steubenville rape case, is that it does seem like men speaking out about violence against women has been a specific way for men to begin to have these conversations. Because, as you've often said, violence against women isn't a "women's issue." Do you think getting involved in the effort to stop violence against women has provided a way for men to begin to have this conversation?

DM: I've said this for a long time, and I believe it's from my first introduction to this work, that what is necessary for a lot of reasons—and primarily just from the perspective of working to end men's violence against women, but for a whole host of other reasons—is that men need to have this conversation *without* women, and not driven by women. What needs to happen is that needs to be a conversation led by men about men, and we have to move away from even the discussion about this is about preventing violence against women. In other words, we agree that, okay, rape is wrong. Okay all these other things are bad—pornography is bad, strip clubs are bad—but when do we get to the stuff about who we are, as men? When do we get to the conversation not about masculinity, but about masculinities, that we accept our gay brothers as our brothers; that we accept all forms of masculinity; that we allow all men their masculinity as they define it? And we're not even close to that. It's like I always say, when do men have these conversations? When do men have the conversation around violence against women? It's after there's been violence against women. So there are a couple of problems with that. One is that all men in that subsequent conversation represent the perpetrator, so men are defensive. And then our conversation is around addressing that issue, so even in the room, knowing that we're here because of Steubenville, and so we have to work on preventing Steubenvilles. We have to address narrow masculinity and violent masculinity, but we don't necessarily address vulnerable masculinity. We don't necessarily address loving masculinity. We don't address the wholeness of masculinity. I think that is ultimately the problem that we have right now in the conversation.

MS: Are you optimistic? What is the consciousness of the world that we're aiming for, in having this conversation, in terms of having men and women reach their human potential? What is the grand vision that you think we are looking to achieve?

DM: The grand vision . . . without being too over the top, right? Because you have to get there; you don't stop short. It's utopia. It's a loving society. And I say that, not as a religious person, but isn't that the question? Why are we here, so to speak? What's it all about? I think that's the great question. And that's why in all the issues—I started doing work on drunk driving when I first started as an activist and speaker on different social issues with kids, back when I was in college—and that's why that whole conversation on gender to me was like the final frontier, because it answered so many of the other ills that we inflict on one another. Because if I choose to take a drug, it's me, it's my hand that lifts the glass up to my lips or puts the needle in my arm or brings that joint to my mouth, or whatever it is—it's my hand that does that. So if I am violent toward someone, it's my hand on someone else. Violence works because violence controls what we cannot control. We can't control nature, so we have to be violent to it. But nature's more powerful than that; nature comes through. And so violence is typically used to suppress those things that we cannot control. So I do believe that when you start looking at a different form of masculinity, that no longer defines control by oppression, or suppression, then you are looking at a world that is going to be less violent. And a world that is less violent is more of a world that is peaceful and loving . . . and isn't that utopia?

As leaders, we must also encourage other women to step up to positions of leadership and fight to elect more women to public office. Women who understand the glass ceiling that still exists for us in the workplace and in every aspect of our lives and who are committed to helping us shatter that ceiling once and for all. Consider an eye-opening statistic: In the entire history of the United States, only 296 women have ever served in Congress. Compare that with the number of men who've been elected—more than 12,000. Ladies, we have some serious catching up to do!

But I know that taking that first step can be tough. As women, we face more obstacles than most. We face skepticism and doubt from others and from ourselves. It's no secret that throughout life, people will always try to sell you on shortcuts and the easy way out, and as women, they will tell you what you cannot do. It was true for me, and it was true for all the women who came before me: There will always be naysayers. There will always be people telling you that the timing just isn't quite right, that the work just isn't important, and that the world just isn't ready. You know what we have to do? Prove them wrong! Because what we really need are more women opening doors in every aspect of our society—more women practicing law, more women researching cures for cancer, more women in information technology, and more women in public office!

—Representative Debbie Wasserman Schultz (D)

I think it's really what Sheryl Sandberg says to women, you know, "Don't leave before you leave." Stay engaged. If you are going to take time off to have children, that's great, but don't leave until that happens. And stay engaged at whatever level—it doesn't have to be elected office. There are many ways to be a leader.

—Arianna Huffington, president and editor-in-chief of the Huffington Post Media Group

If you don't strive for a seat at the table, you can't complain about what is decided there.

—TINA BROWN, EDITOR-IN-CHIEF OF *THE DAILY BEAST*
AND FOUNDER OF WOMEN IN THE WORLD

There are multiple levels of leadership. Your leadership in your own family, your community, how you lead your life, how you present yourself in the world as one who is willing to use what you have to give to others. That to me [is] the defining meaning of what it takes to be a leader.

—OPRAH WINFREY

Lord knows it's scary to step out in this culture, isn't it? It's scary to take the road less travelled. It's scary to upend your life, and flip up your life, or walk into a room and say, "I'd like to be the leader of this." This is a scary, scary, thing. Who you are, and how you think and how you feel and how you remember and how you process does come from the brain. And women's and men's brains are different. Who you decide you are and want to be comes from your experiences and how you process them and how you believe your life should go. I think that's all really important. It's really hard to go and lead if you don't know who you are.

—MARIA SHRIVER

We need women to speak up. Women are the creators and, in my opinion, the leadership qualities that are needed to really propel things forward are feminine, and both men and women need to draw on these attributes because the times are calling for it. You know, I've always had a thing for "C" words. Create. Connect. Collaborate. Communicate. Change. Compassion. Community. These are the words I've leaned on in my own experience as a leader, and when I really look at these words I see how how they are all about feminine leadership.

—DONNA KARAN

SOLEDAD O'BRIEN

"I look at my daughter, who, as little as she is, has a sense that women can do anything. In her lifetime—since she's been old enough to pay attention—she's only known a black president and a woman who was very close to being president. I think that has changed her perspective on what is possible. . . . I think that her sense of expectation is an incredible, powerful thing, because she walks into a room with, 'Of course I can do this!' So I think you have a generation that thinks that way, as opposed to one person who feels that way. I think that's very powerful."

S OLEDAD O'BRIEN IS an award winning journalist, documentarian, news anchor, and producer. She was previously a special correspondent for CNN and the anchor of CNN's *Starting Point*. O'Brien was the originator of the highly successful documentary series *Black in America* and *Latino in America*. In June 2013 she launched Starfish Media Group, a multi-platform media production and distribution company dedicated to uncovering and producing empowering stories that take a challenging look at the often divisive issues of race, class, wealth, and poverty. Also through Starfish Media Group, O'Brien will contribute short-form segments for the upcoming Al Jazeera America news program *America Tonight*. She is also a regular contributor to *Real Sports with Bryant Gumbel*.

O'Brien has reported on breaking news from around the globe. She won an Emmy for her coverage of the earthquake in Haiti and a George

Foster Peabody award for her coverage of Hurricane Katrina. O'Brien was named journalist of the year by the National Association of Black Journalists and one of *Newsweek*'s "10 People who Make America Great." O'Brien and her husband run the Soledad O'Brien & Brad Raymond Foundation, which sends young women to and through college.

MARIANNE SCHNALL: This book is about a woman president as a symbol, but much more generally just about the need to encourage women and girls into leadership positions and the changing paradigms in politics and in our culture at large. It actually came to be through a question from my then eight-year-old daughter. It was right after Obama was elected president and we were talking, as a family, about how amazing it was that we had an African American president and my daughter, Lotus, looked at me and said, "Why haven't we ever had a woman president?" And it seemed like this very simple, obvious question, and yet I found it somewhat difficult to answer. So I always like to start by saying, how would you explain it? Why do you think we've never had a woman president?

SOLEDAD O'BRIEN: I had a very similar conversation with my daughter, Cecilia, in 2008. She was six years old at the time. She almost couldn't believe me. She kept saying, "So he's the *first* black president?" And I said, "Yeah!" She said, "But the *first?*" "Yeah, it's the first!" As if I had been lying to her all these years. And then she said, "Well, how many girls have we had?" And I'm like, "No girls. There have been no girls." She never went on to ask the why, but of course, the question of the why not is inherent. And you know, I think that some of it is opportunities for women. And . . . I guess it's sort of both sides of the coin, right? Some of it is external—people have to be ready for that, the electorate has to be ready for that. And then, women have to be ready to assume the mantle to lead. I think we've made a good amount of progress on that; we see women in leadership positions across the board. And I think we also made a lot of progress on people being ready for women to be in leadership positions in a very visible place. So I think we're very close to that.

MS: What factors or conditions do you think need to be in place to make a woman president? And do you think, in terms of our consciousness, we're ready for that?

SO: Yeah, again, I think that the very fact that a six-year-old girl, who's now a ten-year-old, is saying, "Well, how many girls?" because she's used to girls doing everything. And some of that is just the accepted norms of her life. I think it's a generational issue, more than anything else.

MS: Yes, that reminds me of sometimes this notion that girls, or younger women, can be complacent just because they haven't known as much about the struggles women have faced. Do you think that can have a negative impact in terms of being complacent or not being as activist, because they're not as aware that these kinds of barriers exist?

SO: I actually think there's a certain amount of activism in this sense of expectation. I think there's a tremendous amount of power when there's a sense of expectation that you are in line to run a company. It is possible for you to be president. So I think there is a real power in that. I don't know that it's all about marching, shouting activism. I think some of it is that, but there's a certain amount of making people ready to lead. I look at my daughter, who, as little as she is, has a sense that women can do anything. In her lifetime—since she's been old enough to pay attention—she's only known a black president and a woman who was very close to being president.

MS: That's very true.

SO: I think that has changed her perspective on what is possible. She's only known high-level executives who are women. My husband is an investment banker. She knows lots of women who run things in investment banking and who are her teachers and who are people who are at high levels in every field, mostly because I run around and interview them. So I think that her sense of expectation is an incredible, powerful thing, because she walks into a room with, "Of course I can do this!" So I think you have a generation that thinks that way, as opposed to one person who feels that way. I think that's very powerful.

MS: I know that part of this whole conversation about encouraging women into leadership positions is also about getting men on board for this and reframing it not as a "women's issue," but about the benefits to everyone of having equality and balance in leadership positions. I know sometimes it's hard to answer these questions without making generalizations, but what special qualities do you think a woman president, or women in positions of influence in general, would bring to the table that the world most needs now?

SO: You know, I think there's been a lot of research into how men and women lead differently, and you certainly can pull all that. But what I have found in the documentaries I've done, which focus on people who are sort of outsiders to the process—whether it was the documentary that we did about the women at Ground Zero, women who worked as rescue workers during 9/11—they were outsiders who brought a different perspective.

[In the documentaries] *Black in America, Latino in America*—it's often we talk about the outsiders trying to figure out how to navigate sort of the bigger inside. So I think that the bulk of your answer is in the research that tells you women do this and they're more collaborative, and I've read a bunch of that. But what I think is more powerful is you come from this outsider perspective, so when you take your seat at the table you don't necessarily ask all the same questions that other people would. You don't necessarily bring with you all the same people that other people would. You bring a different perspective, you bring a different background.

I remember having a male colleague who would look at pregnant women and sort of roll his eyes, like "Ugh, it's going to be such a drag." He was a super nice guy; it wasn't that he was a bad person. I think he treated everybody very fairly, but I think our take on what that symbolized was very different. I know that pregnant women, once they have the baby, they get much more done. I remember being like that when I had a young child. I would have been happy to surround myself with women. In fact, most of my friends are women with small children. We're all in the same boat. We are very efficient. I think you just bring a different mindset to the table than other people, and certainly in my business, that expands the storytelling that you are able to do.

MS: The lack of women in leadership roles extends beyond Washington, where women are only 18 percent of Congress. Women hold just 14 percent of executive officer positions, 16 percent of corporate board seats and are only in 3 percent of clout positions in the media. How do you think the lack of women in leadership positions in other arenas is connected to the lack of women in Washington?

SO: I think it's connected in very tangible ways when it comes to money and support. The problem of the pipeline issue is a genuine and important one: in order to be able to run stuff, you have to have run stuff, right? You need to be on boards in order to have credibility. And you need to be on corporate boards, because those are people who are powerful and make a lot of money. Those are important, high level, networking kinds of people who are important to your support, whatever you're going to do in your career, whether it's going to be in the corporate environment or you're going to be in Washington, D.C. So it's not just that it would be nice but irrelevant. It's not irrelevant. I think there is absolute correlation—it's a certain amassing of power in a corporate level that we all know then translates very handily to Washington, D.C.

MS: Do you think that, in terms of being a milestone for women and the world, having a woman in the Oval Office would have the same impact that electing Barack Obama had for African American people? How symbolic do you think it would be to have a woman as president?

SO: I think it would be huge. I just think it's huge in the sense of, back to my six-year-old, where ultimately it's the optics of this is what's possible. This is the kind of thing that's possible. We know it's always tough being the first, but once you've gotten to the first, then you're really in a position to move the needle.

MS: In this last election there was obviously increased diversity, not just for women but in general. What did the results of this last election tell us about the way our electorate and the face of our government is changing? Were there particular trends that interest you that you thought were hopeful?

SO: Yeah, I think that there are two big takeaways and they almost are a mirror reflection of each other. Number one, the nation is very divided. We're really very, very partisan. And number two, the nation is becoming more diverse, and I think the GOP has clearly recognized that if it can't figure out how to appeal to that more diverse nation, they're going to have some big problems. If you look at the turnout, it was higher than what anybody expected. Where the models were off was that the models predicted that fewer people would turn out—fewer black people, fewer Latinos. The economy is down, fewer would turn out. And that was just not the case. So if you can't figure out how to break through that model, you're not going to win.

MS: So what do you credit that to? Do you feel like people are awakening to a sense of their own responsibility and the importance of being an active part of our democracy and realizing our power as citizens?

SO: I think certain things resonated with people, and I think people felt like they were fighting social issues that had already been decided. Contraception was one, the idea that all these comments about rape . . . I think they were very hurtful to the GOP, that even if you had these outliers who were not necessarily espousing a position that was held by the particular party, they wouldn't come out against them either. Ultimately it was very damaging to them, that we were sort of re-discussing what was really rape, and should women really have access to contraception? Those were kind of these crazy conversations we were having on our morning show. So I think whenever you get knee-deep in social issues, you really do motivate people. I think immigration was a big, big emotional debate for people that spurred them to the polls.

MS: I know you have your own foundation that provides scholarships to women. The mission statement at your site is, "We provide young women with a bridge between obstacles and opportunity by giving them the resources to overcome barriers and reach their highest potential." What inspired you to found that organization, and what is the role of education in terms of this conversation, about grooming future women leaders?

SO: Well, you absolutely cannot move anywhere without education. Education is that bridge. We really focus on education because I can't think of a better way to help women. Most of our girls are in poverty situations or situations where they just cannot afford their college education. The best possible way to help them move from one category into the next, out of struggling and into solid opportunity, is through education. So that's why that was the focus for our foundation. And then with that, of course, along came the tuition payments and things like that, but also wraparound services—they need mentoring, they need ways to see women being successful. Our biggest challenge was that these girls aim very low and they just don't see what's possible because they really haven't had that opportunity to know what's possible.

MS: That was one thing that I wanted to ask you, because you've done some amazing work to bring up issues surrounding race through *Black In America* and other work that you do. As hard as it is for women generally to reach leadership positions, obviously minority groups face additional challenges. What is the situation, in particular for African American women and women of other minority groups? What specific challenges do they face and what support do they need?

SO: I think it's the same—I think women just need to have somebody to guide them. A group called the XX Project asked me to speak yesterday. It's a new group of women who are basically having speakers talk about the challenges for women in business. And so we had this exact conversation yesterday. We talked a little bit about my foundation and then we were talking about women in business. Everybody needs some kind of mentor to figure out how to navigate what they're trying to get to. People like to hire who they look like—whether you're talking gender or race—and breaking through that can be very, very challenging. Figuring out how you juggle all that and juggle a personal life, as well, and a healthy family—I think that's really very hard and it requires a lot of mentoring. Being great at your job is not enough.

MS: I'm close with Pat Mitchell and I loved watching you on her PBS series, *She's Making News*. One of the interesting things that you were talking about was being the daughter of a black, Cuban mother and your father who's white and Australian. That you're a product not only of mixed races, but also a woman, how did that affect your understanding of your identity and sense of self? Because in our culture and society, one of the problems is we like to label everybody, and it's so divisive. What did you learn from having that perspective?

SO: I guess what I thought my parents were really great at was, on one hand, absolutely embracing the label: that's what I am. Especially growing up in an all-white neighborhood, where you really stuck out, there was no alternative to that. But at the same time, that label was not meant to be limiting, that label didn't have to be the only definition of who you were. My parents were very much self-created—they came to this country, they built a life, they built a family, they did what they wanted to do. So I think the message I took from my parents was, "This is who you are and be proud of that, but don't let other people decide who you are and what that means. You would be insane to do so."

MS: I think back to when I interviewed Anna Deavere Smith recently and she was talking about the need for women, as they go up higher on the ladder, to make sure they bring other women up as well. When I think about you, you've done so much wonderful humanitarian work and you're now using your influence and resources to empower others through your foundation and the other work that you do. Do you think women who do reach positions of power and influence have a responsibility to use it to uplift other women and underserved communities? Do you think that's an important part of this?

SO: Absolutely. I don't know that you can make people do it, but the bulk of the women that I have dealt with, whether it's just on panels, or just having opportunities at Time Warner and CNN and NBC, women were always incredibly gracious and helpful. My best friends in this business, mostly, are women. So it's funny, last night at this event, people were talking about how women are just so negative and that their worst experiences have been with women, picking them apart and beating them down. I was so surprised—it's just not been my experience. It's weird. In TV news, I've felt very supported. . . . My dearest, best, most supportive cheerleaders in this business are women who really back each other up, all the time. I look at myself and I look at other women—we're on panels, we're running around, hosting people, mentoring people, sitting down and having lunches with young people. That's what we do. Most of my girlfriends do the same thing that I do, and we do it a lot. We do it right before we run home to pick up our kids from school, or run out to some parent/teacher conference. I see tons of examples of women doing that.

MS: I definitely see that, too. You do such wonderful work on the many outlets you work with and everything that you do. The media is obviously such a big force in shaping our culture, our consciousness, and political debate. Do you think diversity in the media is improving?

SO: Diversity in the media is . . . I don't know that it's improving. I think that the media is expanding and people have this opportunity, with better access to technology and the price point coming way down, to be able to express themselves. Right now, one of the most amazing things is when a celebrity hops on Twitter to defend themselves, they don't go through their publicist anymore. So I think you're able to hear directly from people and a lot of having your own voice is that, right? You get to say what your perspective is. I have arguments with people on Twitter all the time. I can defend myself or say whatever I want to say. So I think if you look at the traditional media, no, I don't see dramatic changes at all. I do think there are so many women who have struck out to do on their own what they want to do, and I think that they're in media. I think Pat Mitchell's a really great example of that. She just creates this center where she's like, "Here are the voices that I want to hear, and I'm going to help these women all get to know each other, so that when they're later looking for funding or looking for support or looking for networking, here it is. It's right here." She makes herself so incredibly available to everybody. I don't know how she does it. And I'm someone who does it a lot. It's something she feels very passionately about, that you have this connection of women. Everybody I know knows Pat Mitchell. Pat Mitchell has had lunch with every single woman in the city it sometimes feels like. That's a very intentional strategy to truly building power—it's not let's amass X number of people at X number of women at X company. It's really about creating these organizations that can help women network and support each other.

MS: When I interviewed Gloria Steinem, we were talking about how gender roles, in general, need to be reshaped, not just for us to be able to see women and girls as being in positions of authority, but also for men and boys to learn to be caretakers and nurturers. I know you have twin sons. How do you groom them not only to respect and encourage women, but also to embrace their own wholeness, all of their attributes? How can we help boys break out of their own gender programming, which is rarely talked about?

SO: I think the only way to do it is to do it. I don't know how to help my boys, other than to have a dad who does all that he's supposed to do. And letting them see options that are good options, right? How do you explain to a girl that she can be a scientist, except say, "Look, there's a female scientist and there's one and, in fact, I'm going to bring to meet you this one and I'm going to help you to get an internship with that one." It's very possible. It's very doable. It is not magic. It's the same thing with boys. What do you want to do and be? There's a world of possibility out there, not just in terms of jobs, but in terms of the kind of life you want to lead and your gender roles. You can do anything. I think people need to actually live that. I don't think you can sit there and espouse it and not really believe it. If there's one thing that children are, they are finely honed bullshit detectors.

MS: I find that very much true. Do you think we will have a woman president in your lifetime?

SO: Oh, sure, absolutely. Without having a doubt.

MS: And what do you think are the ingredients to successful leadership, for a man or woman? How do you define leadership?

SO: You know, that's a really good question. My husband and I talk about this a lot, whenever there's a "Corner Office" article in *The New York Times,* we sit down and discuss it. I think that really great leaders figure out how to let the people hierarchically beneath them shine. You bring the best out of people. If you can do that, then you are a really great leader. And so what makes a great leader is understanding where you're trying to get to, but also having great faith in your people and wanting to see the best out of them. I think being a really good leader, is really, really hard for most people.

MS: There are so many destructive messages that are hurled at girls all the time. What message would you most want to convey to girls and young women today in terms of advice on succeeding?

SO: My mother used to give great advice, and her advice was this: "Lovey," she calls me Lovey, "most people are idiots." And I think part of that advice was whenever I would complain to her about something that had been hurled at me, she would be like, "And? What? You're going to take advice from people who are idiots? Ergo, you're a bigger idiot. Most people are idiots, so ignore the advice and figure out how to get from point A to point B, if that's what you're trying to do. But don't come back here and complain to me, 'Boohoo, someone said something mean to me.' I don't want to hear it. Most people are idiots. Move on. Don't sit there and listen to them, then you're a bigger idiot!" I've got to tell you, that was great advice, because every time I would pause to listen to somebody, what became very clear was . . . they haven't done it, they haven't researched it, they have no idea what they're talking about.

It really was great. Whenever my daughters to this day complain about something, I say, "Well, they don't know what they're talking about. Most people are idiots." You have to really remember that. Most people have no idea what they're talking about yet they're happy to give you advice about it. My mother used to smile at people so nicely like, "Oh, mmm hmm, yeah, mmm hmm," and I could tell, Oh, God, they think they're getting through to my mom and she is completely not listening to them—she totally tuned them out. And the minute they turned their head, she'd just take whatever they handed to her, throw it in the garbage, and keep going.

WHAT CHARACTERISTICS DO WOMEN BRING TO LEADERSHIP?

The world is looking at women now and saying, "This is your moment," in everything from studies by Ernst & Young and McKinsey and many others that tell us businesses that have more women in top leadership positions make more money, to a constant flow of leadership-oriented books, articles, and speeches that say the characteristics that women bring to the workplace are exactly the kind of leadership we need today, in politics, in business, in any sphere of life. The attention to relationships. The tendency to want to collabo-rate. The notion that power doesn't have to be about power over someone, but rather it's the power to. It's the power of possibility. It's the power of making good things happen. Making the world better for my family, my kids, my com-munity, my world. That's how women can really make a difference.

— GLORIA FELDT, AUTHOR AND FORMER PRESIDENT OF
  PLANNED PARENTHOOD

There are a lot of biological processes that make women more equipped to handle change. Women experience life as cyclical right in their own bodies, and I think this makes them more adept at going with the flow, adapting, and being able to move from one thing to the next. There is a nurturing aspect to women that is probably hardwired hormonally and is definitely enhanced by our cul-ture. This generally leads us to have a greater sense of compassion. Society also forces women to grow in a way that men aren't required to. Many women have had to and continue to have to work hard to survive, whether juggling life-or-death situations or juggling families and jobs. Women are responsible for managing things and doing them all as well as they possibly can.

— SALLY FIELD

As women, our DNA is just different. Of course, we are all necessary and as human beings we are equal, but this does not mean we are the same. Women bring so much more than just our brains into the decision making process. I think this is incredibly powerful.

— DONNA KARAN

Repeated polls suggest women inspire more trust in public office and are considered more honest, especially on fiscal issues. Women tend to be consensus builders and multitaskers in their management styles and more in tune with kitchen-table issues, since women do over 80 percent of the family budgeting, health care, education, et cetera.

— MARY MATALIN, REPUBLICAN POLITICAL CONSULTANT
AND TV/RADIO HOST

I think one of the big challenges we have in how we talk about electing women to office, generally—and the ramifications of it are one of the reasons why it's harder to elect a female president—is that we talk about how if we elect women, they'll govern differently. I know there's research about this as well, but I think it's problematic messaging to be using. Because, for one thing, when we say that women will compromise more or women will be more collaborative, they'll get more done in legislatures and they'll focus on issues that women care about, they'll focus on early childhood education and violence against women—and all these types of things—it lets all of our male legislators off the hook. And it has that impact on how we see women, because we're categorizing them as different by our language, and [saying] that we should elect them to focus on those "women's" issues, which, it seems to me, automatically implies that they're not necessarily the right people to focus on military issues or economics or national security, things like that. And those are the types of issues that we tend to sometimes associate more with the presidency . . . so I think that's problematic.

— SANDRA FLUKE, ATTORNEY, SOCIAL-JUSTICE ADVOCATE

We bring all the qualities that men bring, and then some! We are the descendants of Ginger Rogers dancing in high heels and backwards. Fred Astaire was great, but can he dance in high heels and backwards and in a floor-length gown? In addition to grace, beauty, intellect, leadership, we bring a connection to each other and Mother Earth. We bring our intuition, compassion, instincts. . . . Whatever it is, however it works, we are in tune and we are intuitive.

— LOUNG UNG, AUTHOR AND HUMAN RIGHTS ACTIVIST

SHERYL SANDBERG

"The word 'female,' when inserted in front of something, is always with a note of surprise. Female COO, female pilot, female surgeon—as if the gender implies surprise, which it does. I am a female leader. One day there won't be female leaders. There will just be leaders."

S HERYL SANDBERG IS chief operating officer at Facebook. She oversees the firm's business operations including sales, marketing, business development, legal, human resources, public policy and communications. Prior to Facebook, Sheryl was vice president of Global Online Sales and Operations at Google, where she built and managed online sales for advertising and publishing and operations for consumer products worldwide. She was also instrumental in launching Google.org, Google's philanthropic arm. Sheryl previously served as chief of staff for the U.S. Treasury secretary during the Clinton administration, and began her career as an economist with the World Bank. She serves on the boards of Facebook, The Walt Disney Company, Women for Women International, V-Day, ONE, and chairs the board of Lean In. She is the author of *Lean In: Women, Work, and the Will to Lead,* a *New York Times* #1 Best Seller.

MARIANNE SCHNALL: Why do you think it is that we've not had a woman president so far?

SHERYL SANDBERG: I have a great story for you. There's a song that has all the names of the presidents, and so my kids were learning the names of all the presidents and my daughter, at four, looked at me, and her first question was, "Mommy, why are they all boys?"

I think women in leadership suffer from stereotyping, and when people expect a stereotype and are reminded of a stereotype, that actually makes the stereotype stronger. It's called stereotype threat, and it's why when women check off "Miss" or girls check off "Female" before taking a math test, the research shows they actually do worse. What has happened is that there aren't women in leadership roles, therefore people don't expect there to be women in leadership roles, therefore, there aren't women in leadership roles.

MS: What can we do to change that?

SS: It starts young. Girls are discouraged from leading at an early age. The word "bossy" is largely applied to girls, not boys. I think we need to expect and encourage our girls and women to lead and contribute. And I think we are so focused on supporting what we call "choice," that we don't mean real choice. When we say choice, we mean women get to choose to work or have families. We don't mean men choose to work or have families. Real choice would mean that people were choosing based on their interests and personal passions, not based on their gender.

MS: There is also the impact of how we treat women leaders. For example, some of the sexist commentary when Hillary was running, or some of the comments that are always made about women leaders like Nancy Pelosi. When women are in positions of power, or seen as confident or ambitious, they're often portrayed as unlikable.

SS: They are un-liked. As a woman gets more successful, she is less liked by people of both genders, and as a man gets more successful, he does not take a likability hit.

MS: Where is the entry for change? Is it in the media? Is it in our educational systems? Where can we fix some of these problems?

SS: It's the classic chicken-and-egg problem. We need more women leaders to show more women they can lead . . . and we need to show more women they can lead to get more women leaders. I think the first thing we need to do is decide that the status quo is not okay. When I say women have been 15 percent or 16 percent of the leadership in corporate America for ten years and it hasn't moved, people are astonished: "Really? It hasn't moved in ten years? We've stopped making progress?"

So the first thing is acknowledging there is a problem and deciding we want it to get better. In our society, we don't talk about gender, at all. I don't understand how you fix a problem if you can't acknowledge you have one.

MS: One of the things in particular that I think affects the political sphere—in terms of the dearth of women running for office—is the fact that it's such a hostile, mud-slinging experience where candidates are subjected to so much criticism. Do you think that's part of the reason that sometimes women are deterred from entering politics, because women are less likely to want to subject themselves to that?

SS: Yes, but also because women are less liked by running. It is all self-reinforcing, all of which we can change. I really believe we can change it. I think the dialogue on whether or not women can do it—can we have it all—is incredibly harmful. We need to recognize that we can't do it all, that we face trade-offs every single minute of the day. We have to stop beating ourselves up for not doing everything perfectly.

MS: What I think is so important about what you bring into the whole equation is the connection between a woman's personal and family life, just the realities of balancing that and how that impacts this whole conversation. How do you see the influence of gender roles? Some of this is not just specific to women, but it involves men changing their gender roles as well, yet we rarely talk about it.

SS: I know. I think that is a problem. We are stuck in our gender-specific roles and so it's just reinforcing. In my book, *Lean In,* I tell the story of my friend Sharon. She said that her daughter went to school, she was seven or something, and she was introducing her parents. She said, "This is Steve. He builds buildings and he loves to sing. This is Sharon," and she shows pictures of her parents, "She works full time. She wrote a book, and she never picks me up." Steve never picks her up! Sharon picks her up more than Steve, but that's what kids see.

I wrote a lot in my book about being identified as Facebook's female COO, and I actually did a Google search for "Facebook's male CEO" and there are no results, zero. I don't wake up in the morning and say, "What am I going to do today as Facebook's female COO?" But that is how I'm viewed by the world. I wrote at the end of my book, it's one of my favorite lines in the whole book, "One day there won't be 'female.'" The word "female," when inserted in front of something, is always with a note of surprise. Female COO, female pilot, female surgeon—as if the gender implies surprise, which it does. I am a female leader. One day there won't be female leaders. There will just be leaders. I personally think it's a numbers game. I basically think the system is broken and there are all kinds of institutional barriers, but if we can get enough women into jobs like yours and jobs like mine, that changes.

MS: There are a lot of generalizations out there that women are more collaborative and less confrontational. Do you agree with that? Why is this important? Not just as a fairness thing, but why do you think it's important that we make equality a priority, and what would women bring to the table that you think Washington and the world needs most now?

SS: There's been a lot written about what the world would be like with more women [leaders]. My view is that if all the players play, that creates more competition, and more records get broken. I just think we would perform better as a society. Plus, I want to live in a more equal world.

MS: You have worked in Washington as the chief of staff for the United States Treasury Department. What was that experience like, being a woman working in Washington?

SS: You know, I'm forty-three now. I was only thirty at the time I worked in Washington. At the time, the more senior people were men and the more junior people were women, but that was going to change as my generation progressed. And that, for me, has been the biggest disappointment: that it hasn't changed nearly as much as I hoped it would.

MS: Are you seeing progress? Certainly in this last election, it did seem like everybody was talking about women, and women did break some records in terms of representation. Do you think that something has happened and there's a shift?

SS: I think there has to be a shift, because you can't win elections just with Caucasian men anymore. You have to have minorities and women. The numbers just don't work anymore. So I think there will be a shift. But the women have to run in order to get elected. And right now, they are less inclined to do so.

MS: What generally are some of the most concrete and constructive changes that we can do as a culture, or a society, to improve things for women to become leaders in the political and corporate spheres?

SS: The concrete things are men need to do more childcare and house-work. We need to get to equality in the home. We cannot have equality in the office until we have equality in the home. It can't happen.

MS: Do you think there is also a problem about not only getting women into leadership positions, but once they are there, making sure women are emboldened to trust their own natural wisdom and instincts, so we're not just perpetuating old paradigms of power and leadership? Because I think sometimes part of the problem is that women try to do it in a way that's not authentic to them.

SS: I don't think it's that women try to do it in ways that are inauthentic. I think we don't have a basic construct of women in leadership. It goes against what we expect of women, which I think is the basis of the problem.

MS: I think we also need to encourage women to honor and value their own vision and thoughts, to make sure they know that they have something unique and valuable to offer the world. How did you do it? How did you tap into your own inner leader to give you the courage to follow your calling and speak out?

SS: I don't think I thought about it. I didn't think about gender very much at all. Now I think about it a lot, but I think that it was probably helpful not to think about gender.

MS: In terms of the type of leader that you are at Facebook, what have you learned being a manager of men and women? What ingredients do you try to instill in your own leadership in terms of managing your employees?

SS: I try to teach people about the likability penalty women pay for success, so when they hear, "Oh, this woman's doing a good job, but she's just not well liked by her peers," they have enough sense to question that and ask why. I talk to people about the value of talking about gender, because what's happening is women are not navigating through their careers or learning the ways they can stay in and lean in, and we have to change that. I think both male and female managers need to be able to talk to female employees about this. It's not easy. These are complicated things for people in companies to do, saying, "Are you thinking about having a child? We should talk about it." A lot of the legal advice everyone gets is to never mention it. Well, never mentioning it is not going to solve a problem. So I talk to people about being very explicit about it.

MS: There are also obviously policies that corporations and Washington could implement that could make it more family friendly—helpful policies that employers can do on their end, whether it's maternity leave, parental leave, or some other policy.

SS: I think all of those policies are really important. I think equal maternity and paternity leave are hugely important. How are we going to teach men to be equals if the average woman takes three months and the average man takes two weeks? People forget that there's a huge gap in our coverage.

MS: Do you feel hopeful that in your lifetime that we will have a woman president? Does that sound like something that is possible?

SS: I'm hopeful that Hillary's going to be that woman.

JESSICA VALENTI

"I think this conversation is important for everyone, because as much as we tend to focus on elite positions—like having Fortune 500 companies or the presidency or Congress—it's about leadership in our own lives. All these kinds of skills, limitations, and hurdles we're talking about are not just happening at the top levels, they're happening in everyday workplaces, as well."

J ESSICA VALENTI, CALLED one of the Top 100 Inspiring Women in the world by *The Guardian,* is the author of four books on feminism, politics, and culture. Her third book, *The Purity Myth: How America's Obsession with Virginity is Hurting Young Women,* won the 2010 Independent Publisher Book Award and was made into a documentary by the Media Education Foundation. She is also editor of the anthology *Yes Means Yes: Visions of Female Sexual Power and a World Without Rape,* which was named one of Publishers Weekly's Top 100 Books of 2009. Her latest book, *Why Have Kids?: A New Mom Explores the Truth About Parenting and Happiness,* was called a "brave and bracing critique of our unrealistic parenting ideals" by *Elle* magazine. Valenti founded Feministing.com, which *Columbia Journalism Review* called "head and shoulders above almost any writing on women's issues in mainstream media." Her writing has appeared in *Washington Post, The Nation, The Guardian* (UK), *The American Prospect, Ms. Magazine, Salon,* and *Bitch* magazine. She has won a Choice USA Generation Award and the 2011 Hillman Journalism Prize for her work with Feministing.

Valenti is a widely sought-after speaker who gives speeches at colleges, organizations, conferences and events across the country and abroad. She is also a frequent media commentator and has appeared on *The Colbert Report,* CNN, MSNBC, PBS, and *The Today Show*, among others. She received her Master's degree in Women's and Gender Studies from Rutgers University.

MARIANNE SCHNALL: You have a daughter. How would you explain to her the reasons why we haven't had a woman president?

JESSICA VALENTI: Wow, that's a hard one [*laughs*]. That's very complicated. I think that I would probably tell her that, unfortunately, we still live in a world where a lot of people think that women can't be as powerful as men, or that women aren't as good or as smart as men. And that that's not true and we're making some progress to change that and we're getting closer every day, but that we're not quite there yet. And that's why it's so important for us to do the work that we're doing and for her to think about feminism, as well, so that when she has children . . . I think I would probably try to put as optimistic a spin on it as I possibly could.

MS: Are you feeling optimistic? Do you feel like we're getting closer and that you might see a woman president in your lifetime?

JV: I do. I definitely think that we're going to see a woman president in my lifetime. I would be shocked [otherwise]. I would be sorely disappointed, but I would be shocked. I'm hoping that the next time around we'll have one.

MS: I know it's hard sometimes to answer these questions without making generalizations, but what qualities do you think women bring to positions of influence and leadership that the United States and the world most need now?

JV: I don't want to generalize. I don't know that women, as a broad category, have gender-specific leadership skills that men don't. I do think that women would be better off having a woman leader, if not just for the symbolism of it and how important it is for young girls to be able to see women in powerful positions. Obviously, the research kind of bears out that the more women you have in leadership positions, the parity continues to go up and the better women's issues do, so I think we have that to look forward to. But I don't know that I would say that there is any specific leadership quality that I think women could bring to the table that men couldn't. I mean, any woman who has to rise up in the ranks and get to the presidency has to experience a tremendous amount of sexism and hurdles and setbacks, and I imagine that is going to color the way she sees the world and the way sexism operates in the world, so I would hope that that influences the policy decisions, as well.

MS: In this last election we did hit some historic numbers, and yet it's obviously far from parity, there being 18 percent of women in Congress. What specific challenges do you think there are that keep women from entering and advancing through the political pipeline? What do you think we could do to change that?

JV: I think that there are so many things. I think if there was one big thing, it would be easy to answer and we could just get over it, but because it's kind of small oppressions along the way, it becomes more difficult to deal with. It starts with young girls are not taught to want to lead. Wanting to lead and wanting to be powerful and wanting to be in leadership positions are seen as negative qualities in women that are really crushed from an early age in our culture. Anyone you talk to in organizations that work to get more women into politics, they'll tell you that women don't run for office at the same levels that men do because they're taught to think that they're not qualified. So if a city council seat comes up and you ask a guy who has the same experience that a woman has, "Are you qualified?" he'll say, "Absolutely!" You talk to the woman and she'll say, "Well, no, I don't think so. I don't think I'm the right kind of person" or "I don't have the right kind of experience." So we have to start with building up confidence and just getting women to want to put their names in the hat, but there also needs to be a change in the media conversation, as well, around women leaders. If a woman runs for office, you can count how many times their outfits or their hair are mentioned or, as with Hillary Clinton, the way her voice sounds. The things that we focus on in this culture are completely different, so we also have to make sure that we're holding media accountable in the way that they're treating women leaders.

MS: I also think that sometimes the missing piece is talking about boys and men, because if men and boys are only seeing women in that stereotypical way or the way the media projects—or just focusing on how they look or not seeing them as leaders—we need to change gender pressures on men and boys, too, so they aren't oriented that way.

JV: Also, this idea that I think is really interesting that seems to be culturally pervasive, that women or people of color are in those positions because they're women or people of color. This is kind of back-lashing at affirmative action stuff where you constantly see people saying, "Oh, she's only in that position because she's a woman," or "Women are only going to vote for her because they're women," or "Obama got the black vote because he's black." Yet we never talk about white males as an identity, as well; it's considered the default. We have to find a way to make that more known and to introduce that into the conversation.

MS: With this last election, it feels like maybe things are starting to be more reflective, of both our electorate and our government, in terms of looking more like the face of America. What paradigms do you see emerging? Because it's not just the whole idea of including women, it's about diversity in general. So in terms of the conversation around intersectionality, how does that figure in to this larger picture?

JV: I think it factors in tremendously, and I think that's why you'll see so many feminists say it's not just about gender. It's not just about voting for someone because of their gender, either. It's about finding feminist candidates who understand issues of gender, who understand issues of race and class and sexism and homophobia, and you can bring that to the table so that they can change the conversation somewhat. It is for representation, but it's not just about representation, it's about structural change, as well.

MS: Obviously there are women of different races and classes who face very different limitations and are trying to survive and put food on the table and maybe don't see this conversation relating to their lives. Where do they fit into this conversation? How can this conversation be made to be more widely relevant?

JV: Well, you know, I think this conversation is important for everyone, because I think as much as we tend to focus on elite positions—like having Fortune 500 companies or the presidency or Congress—it's about leadership in our own lives. All these kinds of skills, limitations, and hurdles we're talking about are not just happening at the top levels, they're happening in everyday workplaces, as well. They're happening in schools. They're happening in the PTA. So I think we can do a better job of making sure that we do talk about that, that it's not just about elite positions and that it's not about trickle-down ideas, but about the ways these hurdles affect all of it.

MS: I remember when I interviewed Anna Deavere Smith that she kept stressing this point that she felt like there needs to be more women who, when they do reach positions of power and influence, feel that they have a responsibility to then go back and uplift other women. Do you think that's a message that's sometimes missing in this conversation?

JV: I do. I think that mentorship and generosity in our careers and in our experiences is often missing from the conversation. And it's not because women don't want to help other women. I think often it's because they have to do so much work to get where they are, that it's almost impossible to think about adding another thing on the pile of things they already have to do. So I think that can be a difficult task, but if we incorporate it as a seamless part of your everyday leadership, it becomes a little bit easier. And I did like what Sheryl Sandberg had to say about mentorship, that's it is not just approaching someone and saying, "Will you be my mentor?" and talking to them for an hour, once a week; it's about helping people out along the way and recognizing good work when you see it.

MS: You and I started back in the early days of the Internet when nobody really understood the impact the Internet could have, especially for women. Now people are saying that if the feminist movement had one central place it would be online. Is that how you view it as well?

JV: I definitely think the future of how we organize and where we're getting new ideas is certainly online. I think it doesn't mean that we need to give up on real-life action; I think that something very special happens when people talk to each other face to face and plan actions face to face. And what I wish I saw more of was the folks that do work online meeting up more in real life. You know, think about much how much has been accomplished online—the actions taken, the media created—with very little money, very little support. Imagine if we actually put some funding behind it, put some real kind of nine-to-five work behind it and had people meet up. I think it would be incredible.

MS: You and me both. In terms of the overall picture, there's always this misconception, and I never really quite understand where it comes from, that younger women are apathetic or they don't identify with feminism. You and I started out as young feminists and now we're both older, but you are still very much in touch with younger generations. What is your impression of younger women today?

JV: I think that more young women identify as feminists than probably ever before, largely because of the way that online activism operates. It used to be that if you called yourself a feminist in the seventies, it was because you sought out a feminist group; you came to it yourself. Now you're seeing people who are doing a Google search and coming upon feminism accidentally. Largely when you hear people say that, it's because they're not online, because they're not looking. Because they don't see young women coming to their meetings, they assume that young women aren't interested. And what I often tell them, they're like, "Well, young feminists are not coming to our meetings; they're not coming to our events," I say, "Well, are you [going] to their blogs? Are you in their comments section?" So I think it's a two-way street, and I think probably they would be very pleasantly surprised if they spent some time online.

MS: This is a conversation about leaders, so it's been very interesting in terms of thinking about, for example, Gloria Steinem. When you think about a feminist leader, you automatically think of Gloria—and you also were kind of the feminist "it" girl. Some people say that the reason we don't have more strength is because we don't have more visible faces as leaders. Do you think that that's true? Do you think that there is a need for more leaders in the feminist movement, or is that something that has become decentralized?

JV: I don't think we need—I'm against feminist iconography. I think it's only going to backfire, because feminism is such a nuanced thing, it's such a complicated topic and it's constantly moving and shifting and changing. I don't think that one person or two people or five people can totally represent the diversity of thought there. It's easy to fall into media traps like that, because the media loves to kind of coin someone like, "You are the feminist leader, and we want you in a magazine," and I think that can be alienating for some people, especially people who are really tired of seeing white, straight, middle class women constantly called leaders of a movement that they're working in, kind of anointed, out of nowhere. I just don't think it's useful anymore. I think what I really love about online feminism, and what we're seeing, is that it's become so democratized. And that it's not about one person or one organization, it's about all of us.

MS: There can often be a backlash that comes as a result of speaking out forcefully on an issue, which I know you have experienced. How do you deal with that when that happens? How do you brave through it and find your strength to speak out again?

JV: I feel like if I'm getting a lot of heat, especially misogynist hate or something like that, directed at me, it makes me feel like I'm probably

doing something right. You know, if you're making people feel uncomfortable it means that you're shaking core beliefs, which is what we're
supposed to be doing, which is what we want to do. So I just remember
that. And honestly, having a really wonderful community of feminists and
feminist friends around me makes it all worthwhile. So when something
bad happens, you can go to them and you have people that you trust and
people that care about you, so I think that makes it a lot easier.

MS: I know you wrote that great book *Why Have Kids?* It's very interesting to watch you become a mother. I have kids, too, and I know how much
it has transformed me, especially having daughters. Part of what's coming
out of Sheryl Sandberg's book is about balancing career and family and
how hard that is for women right now, which is just the truth of it. What
are your thoughts on that in terms of what we, as a society, can do? And
how may that be preventing women from becoming leaders and advancing
in the workplace, because of the challenges of balancing both?

JV: Well, I think part of the problem is that culturally we still tell women
that they need to be mothers, first and foremost, above all else, and if
you're not a mother first and if you don't put your identity as a mother
first, then you're doing it wrong, and I think that's scary to a lot of
women—no one wants to be thought of as a bad mother. And obviously
of what that means culturally: Being a mother first means staying at home.
It means not putting your kid in daycare. It means not taking a promotion.
And I just don't buy into that. I think that we need to change the way we
talk about motherhood. Like, yes, motherhood is certainly an important
part of my identity, but I'm a person first. I'm an individual first. And I
think if we can foster that, it will be helpful to parents, especially younger
women parents.

MS: Are you feeling hopeful about where we are now? It does seem that it's a little bit of two steps forward and one step back, but mostly do you feel like there's a shift happening?

JV: Yes. I do feel like there's a shift happening. I think we saw it in the presidential election, [in terms of] who came out for Obama. There was a Gallup Poll two days before the election in swing states and it showed that women in swing states, when asked what the number one most important issue was, they said abortion. So even though it wasn't necessarily being relayed publicly, I think women went into the voting booth and they were sick of it. I think they were sick of the Republican agenda on women. I think you saw it with Komen and Planned Parenthood—all the feminist online activism that's been happening—so I'm very optimistic.

MS: Man or woman, what do you think are the ingredients to successful leadership or the type of leader we most need now?

JV: I would say empathy and compassion are really things that we need in a lot of levels of government—the ability to put yourself in other people's shoes, no matter what their gender or identity.

MARIANNE WILLIAMSON

"American women are not holding up our part of the sky. But it's not because we don't care, so much as we're distracted. It's not because we're apathetic, so much as we're emotionally paralyzed. I've written about such things for many years, but now it's time to forge ahead and no longer be distracted, no longer be paralyzed. It's time to show up in a way we've never shown up before."

MARIANNE WILLIAMSON IS an internationally acclaimed spiritual author and lecturer. Six of her ten published books have been *New York Times* Best Sellers. Four of these have been #1 *New York Times* Best Sellers. A paragraph from *A Return to Love,* beginning "Our deepest fear is not that we are inadequate. Our deepest fear is that we are powerful beyond measure . . ." is considered an anthem for a contemporary generation of seekers. She has been a popular guest on television programs such as *The Oprah Winfrey Show, Larry King Live, Good Morning America,* and *Charlie Rose.* Williamson founded Project Angel Food, a meals-on-wheels program that serves homebound people with AIDS in the Los Angeles area. She also founded the Department of Peace Campaign, a grass roots campaign to establish a United States Department of Peace.

MARIANNE SCHNALL: Why do you think we haven't had a woman president so far?

MARIANNE WILLIAMSON: We haven't had a woman president yet for a multitude of reasons. More than anything else—and this is evidenced by the fact that we don't have anything near 50 percent representation in Congressional and state leadership, either—I think American women haven't yet developed, en masse, the emotional and psychological habits of power.

Politics in America is extraordinarily toxic, mean, even vicious. No man or woman goes into a political race, particularly a presidential one, without knowing in advance the personal price they're going to pay. Whether because we have cellular memories of being burned at the stake for speaking our minds, or the lingering paternalism and male chauvinism that still permeate parts of our political machinery, or the projections of suspicion onto any woman (by both men and women, I'm afraid) who really gets in there and claims leadership today, a woman needs a lot of muscle—spiritual as well as intellectual—to push through what needs to be pushed through in order to embark on a presidential campaign. She's going to have to be willing to not go along, in ways that are terrifying to a lot of women.

The good news is that I think we're on the brink of a tipping point, because enough women have run for office and won, enough women are empowered in other areas of the society, enough books have been written on the subject of female leadership, and enough social change has accumulated over the last few years. Also, it's obvious to enough people now that the old way is not working and that we need something radically new. I just hope that the woman who does break the barrier is offering something new, rather than just imitating how the guys have always done it.

MS: You recently organized a huge conference in California called Sister Giant, which featured the tagline "Women, Nonviolence, and Birthing a New American Politics." How would you describe your vision for a new American politics, and what role do you see women playing in that?

MW: American politics is a subject that gets a lot of attention, obviously. But it doesn't get very enlightened attention, at least not at this point in our history. There's very little heart in the current political conversation, or real wisdom or philosophical depth. But among many people I know, there's a yearning for that. People want the nation to transform in the same way they want their own lives to transform.

If you're interested in transforming your life, you can't just transform some things. You can't try to fix some things, but sweep other things under the rug because it's too hard to face them. And the same is true for a nation. America has a lot of dirty little secrets: our child poverty rate, at 23.1 percent, is second highest among thirty-five developed nations of the world (second only to Romania); our incarceration rate is higher than any nation in the world—we're 5 percent of the world's population, yet we incarcerate 25 percent of the world's prisoners. Citizens United, the National Defense Authorization Act—so many things that any reasonable person would consider at least an indirect threat to democracy, are staring us in the face as we speak. You can't change your life by just looking at the fun things, and you can't change your country by just looking at the fun things either.

I gave a talk at a university recently where several women students involved in social justice and human rights work were explaining what they want to do when they leave college. As they went around the table explaining what their plans were after they graduated, many of them said that they wanted to do "policy and/or advocacy work." I remember inwardly tilting my head, thinking how odd it was that women graduating from one of the best universities in the country—all of whom were really marvelous young women—wanted to go do policy and advocacy work, but not one said she wanted to be a senator or a congressman or a president. And in today's world, policy and advocacy work, in my mind, means we take our activism to a certain point but no further. In other words, we want passionately to lobby and persuade those in power, but for whatever reason we're not so comfortable with the idea of *becoming* those in power. And at a certain point, it's not enough to have the audacity of hope, or even the audacity of activism. We need the audacity to wield power.

I see a need to create a new political conversation—one that isn't so toxic, dysfunctional, and mean-spirited. I know there's no place for that within the current system, but the current system is boring to me. I think it's boring to a lot of people. But that's not to say that it's unimportant. This isn't about ignoring politics; it's about creating a new political conversation where conscience takes precedence over profit and humanitarian values trump economic ones. I know a lot of people think that's extremely naïve, but what I think is naïve is thinking we can continue to treat our fellow human beings and the planet on which we live in such a violent way as we do now, and expect the species to survive for another hundred years.

MS: Do you have a sense of what obstacles there are, either societal or self-imposed, that are preventing women from entering the political pipeline?

MW: When it comes to politics, women have an internal glass ceiling. We stand as good a chance as a man to win a political race, but women don't want to run at the same rate as men do. People point to the work-family balance issue, but I think it's much more than that. Many women don't have children, or have children who are no longer at home. There are some deeper psychological and emotional issues in play, like the fact that many of us feel like the embarrassment, humiliation, and personal demonization in politics are simply more than our hearts can take. What stops us is fear.

Who in their right mind would want to go into politics today? But that question is a serious conundrum, because as the French say, "If you don't do politics, politics will do you." With our own country moving every day in the direction of a plutocracy and facing global issues—from intractable violence to unsustainable poverty—that are turning our future probability vectors in ever more dire directions, no conscious person, socially or spiritually, can just sit this out. This is not a time in American history to go numb. And being awake and conscious for just an election or two won't cut it either. We need a sustained movement in the direction of a fundamental awakening of the heart—in politics as well as in everything else.

MS: It occurs to me when we are talking about the missing representation of women in politics that some of these qualities you say we need to inject into politics—such as caring and compassion and connection to our hearts—are often deemed as "feminine values" and are oftentimes more naturally represented by women. How do you see that inter-connection and the devaluing of the feminine, both literally and in this metaphysical way?

MW: There are feminine qualities in all people, and some men embody such forces as caring and compassion more profoundly than some women do. It takes more than a vagina to embody feminine values.

Which is not to say that women don't have an important role as carriers of those values into the world. Look at the nature kingdom: how the adult female in any advanced mammalian species so fiercely protects her young. The mama tiger, lion, bear and so forth—they show a fierce insistence on care and protection of the young. Even among the hyenas, the adult females encircle the cubs while they're feeding and will not let the adult males get anywhere near the food until the cubs have been fed. Truly the women of America could do better than the hyenas. And the fact that we don't do better than we do means we're not displaying the ultimate intention to survive. Seventeen thousand children starve on this planet every single day. That fact alone should blow any conscious person out of their chair. You know, my mother used to say that a woman's most important job is taking care of her children and her home. I laughed at that when I was younger, but I don't laugh at it anymore. I just realize now that every child on the planet is one of our children, and the Earth itself is our home.

When women think of power, we shouldn't think of it only for ourselves. We should be thinking about what we're going to do with power once we have it. Women should be standing up powerfully and passionately for the care and protection of children, as well as the care and protection of the earth itself. Women's voices should be front and center in protecting both our young and our habitat. That's the way it is in any species that survives.

MS: And part of this that's key is women having access to our own authentic voices and wisdom, and honoring and listening to our true inner voice. And yet there are so many messages and forces that, from girlhood on, try to get women to do the opposite of that. How do we get women to follow their true voices and instincts so that if we do get into positions of leadership, we do not just perpetuate old paradigms?

MW: If you're getting your guidance about who you are and what to do with your life only from the external world, then by definition you'll be led away from your authentic truth. Your authentic truth isn't in the material world. It's counterintuitive, but you have more power in the world when you know you're not of it.

A primary goal of the spiritual life is to learn to quiet the mind—through prayer and meditation, through spiritual practice—so that we can hear what in both Judaism and Christianity is called the small, still voice within. You stop whining so much about how the shallow voices of modernity do not love you when you remember who does. We become less emotionally attached to the approval of the world, once we access the deep level on which we don't approve of it either! There's a bigger game going on here than the worldly eye perceives. We're here to self-actualize individually and collectively, and the effort takes more than the intention to love—it takes the courage to act on it.

MS: I've also been heartened by seeing the trend of supportive men coming to understand that women's equality isn't just about equality or fairness, but realizing that the status of women is interconnected with so many other issues that are facing the planet that would serve all of humanity.

MW: To say that this is a conversation about women is not to say that it's a conversation against men! Men aren't holding us back anymore, so much as we hold ourselves back. And too often women hold each other back, unfortunately.

MS: Do you see the rising of women and feminine energy as part of the healing force coming to save the planet? Is that part of why the focus is on women?

MW: Yes, but the rising feminine doesn't mean much unless she's rising up through actual people. The goddess is asking for more than crystals and cut velvet scarves. She's asking for some fierceness and courage, too.

American women are not holding up our part of the sky. But it's not because we don't care, so much as we're distracted. It's not because we're apathetic, so much as we're emotionally paralyzed. I've written about such things for many years, but now it's time to forge ahead and no longer be distracted, no longer be paralyzed. It's time to show up in a way we've never shown up before.

MS: You have that very famous quote, "Our deepest fear is not that we are inadequate. Our deepest fear is that we are powerful beyond measure." How does that fit into this conversation?

MW: Martin Luther King, Jr., said, "Our lives begin to end on the day we stop talking about things that matter most." There is a perverse comfort zone to living a small life. For women, that zone has to do with the fact that we're less likely to be challenged, we're less likely to be criticized, we're less likely to be called angry or strident, if we simply go along and acquiesce to the prevailing patterns of thought and behavior. But as Krishnamurti said, "It is no measure of health to be well adjusted to a profoundly sick society." It's insane to let your children starve, to let your fellow man suffer needlessly, to allow the Earth to be raped when you could do something to help. Gandhi said that the problem with the world is that humanity is not in its right mind. That's still true, and the antidote to that is for enough of us to be in our right minds.

When we're in our right minds, we are hopeful. Because the arc of the moral universe does bend toward justice, nature does bend toward healing, and the heart does bend toward love. Our problem isn't that the universe isn't on our side; the problem is that too many of us are numb these days. Some of us need to stop whining. It's not like we're the first generation who faced serious challenges. But others rose to the occasion, and we need to, too.

MS: You often talk about turning love into a social and political force. That's something you don't normally hear candidates talking about, but what does that look like to you?

MW: We need more than new policies. We need a new worldview and a new bottom line. We need to replace economic values with humanitarian values as our ordering principle. What we're doing now is unsustainable and certainly undemocratic. If you have, as we have in the United States today, a situation where financial leverage determines political leverage, then only those with money get to wield political power. That automatically pushes aside the needs of children, because children have no financial leverage. That's why the women of the world must be their voice.

There is simply too much unnecessary suffering in our world. And we should see that as a national security risk, by the way. Given enough time, desperate people will tend to do desperate things. At a certain point you won't be able to build enough prisons or enough bombs to eradicate the effects of all that violence inside so many hearts.

The suffering of sentient beings matters, and it should be central to our political conversations. Right now, we have political and economic systems that practically guarantee the unnecessary suffering of millions of people—and then we just leave it to clergy and psychotherapists and doctors and charities (if not prisons) to clean up the mess. Give me a break. I'm all up for a conversation about personal responsibility, but we need societal responsibility as well.

MS: One of the things I feel always gets lost is the benefit of getting involved in creating positive change. It sounds very draining, and it's something you do for others, but what are the soul rewards? I think there's a piece that often goes missing about what it does for you and your own experience of life to get involved and give back and be a part of this hopeful movement we're talking about.

MW: What's "draining" is the life we're living now. We're living separated from our own deep humanity. We're living separated from our own vigor. We're living separated from the excitement that comes from being involved in the world. It's not as though life now is easy, and showing up for the world is hard. No—the way many of us are living now is diseased and dysfunctional, and showing up for the world is one of the ways we heal.

MELISSA ETHERIDGE

"Leadership in the future, whether it's male or female, I believe will start to come from a place of the idea of this great experiment called democracy . . . and to do that, we have to have it inside ourselves to know not to fear any diversity, but to be able to coexist with everything and anything, and that's where power and strength for communities and our country comes from."

I N FEBRUARY 2007, Melissa Etheridge celebrated a career milestone with a victory in the Best Song category at the Academy Awards for "I Need to Wake Up," written for the Al Gore documentary on global warming, *An Inconvenient Truth.* Over the course of her more than two decades as a performer and songwriter, she has shown herself to be an artist who has never allowed "inconvenient truths" to keep her down. Earlier in her recording career, Etheridge acknowledged her sexual orientation when it was considered less than prudent to do so. In October 2004, she was diagnosed with breast cancer, a health battle that, with her typical tenacity, she won. Despite losing her hair from chemotherapy, Etheridge appeared on the 2005 Grammy telecast to sing "Piece of My Heart" in tribute to Janis Joplin. By doing so, she gave hope to many women afflicted with the disease.

In 2011, Etheridge made her Broadway debut as St. Jimmy in Green Day's rock opera, *American Idiot,* and received her star on the Hollywood Walk of Fame. In 2012, she embarked on a worldwide tour, performing for sold-out crowds throughout Europe, Australia, and North America.

When not on tour, she records her syndicated Melissa Etheridge Radio Show for daily broadcast on stations throughout the United States and Canada. Her latest studio album, *4th Street Feeling,* debuted at number eighteen on the Billboard 200 chart.

MARIANNE SCHNALL: This book will touch on a variety of arenas—a woman president as a symbol, but also all sorts of themes connected to women's leadership and other areas. It was partially inspired by a conversation with my eight-year-old daughter, Lotus—we were talking about how there had been no woman presidents—and she was just astounded and she asked, "Why?"

MELISSA ETHERIDGE: She can't comprehend it.

MS: We've grown up with it, we've taken it for granted, it's just the way it is. But it got me thinking. What are some of your thoughts on why we haven't had a woman president?

ME: Well, it must be like when I was a child. I was a child in the sixties, and it was 1968 or 1969, and we were taking our first big family trip, and we went down to Florida from Kansas. On the way—in Georgia, I think it was—we stopped at a gas station to go to the bathroom, and I walked around the back and there were three bathrooms. It was WOMEN, MEN, and COLOREDS. I remember going, "Coloreds? *What?*" That concept was so ridiculous. But now, our children look at gay marriage—that's probably the last one; before that it would be women's rights. I remember telling my daughter that my mother used to work as a civil servant for the Army—she worked in computers, war games and scenarios, and she was a GS-15, the highest civilian rank you could get in the Army—and she was still paid half of what the guys who were working for her were paid. And my daughter's like, "Why did they stand for that?" That's why things like nursing and secretarial jobs don't pay as much, because those were the jobs that women were allowed to have. And we're just waking up. Our generation is in charge now. We're the ones. So in the sixties, it wasn't even okay to be a strong woman, and that beautiful movement we had in the seventies . . . I was a teenager, and it was women's lib, and in this liberation women were going to work and I didn't have to get married! It emancipated me as a teenager, as a woman. And that nugget of women is going to be in politics, and someday there's going to be—it was the prize—a woman president. There had never been one, and someday we will [have one].

I remember when Geraldine Ferraro in the eighties was chosen to be the vice-presidential running mate of Mondale, and that was huge. Huge. And we, here in California, the women who were elected as senators and these leaders who would come up . . . I remember Shirley Chisholm. My parents sat me down, and I remember listening to her speech at the Democratic National Convention. Those [women] were, as my friend Steven Spielberg always says, "Someone has to lie down on the barbed wire for everyone to go across." Mondale had to go down in flames so that my generation could experience and see and go, "This is what it looks like to have a woman running for the highest office." And they lay down on the barbed wire. And now it is totally conceivable, I would say highly probable, that Hillary Clinton is going to run for president and become the first female. I mean, I can see that; my children can see that. I wouldn't be going too far out on a limb, at all, to say that.

So we have—our generation, the women of the fifties and sixties and seventies—done our job. What we've done is to bring thought, because it's all about how we all perceive what's going on and the thought that a woman could be a leader. That if a woman leads us, we're not going to be overtaken by those evil forces out there because we'll be weak. That's the unspoken thing behind it: we will be perceived as weak. That's why Maggie Thatcher was elected as the first female prime minister of England, but she was the most conservative Iron Lady. She had to come from that, some would say "male," side of us to be elected. Now, can we actually stand up and say, "Okay, I feel safe, I feel protected, and I believe that a woman can comprehend what is best for us." It was always, "Well, she has babies. She's not going to go to war; because women have babies, they won't ever support war." Well, isn't that a good thing? [*laughs*] I think we have come to that point; we have changed the world in our thought to where, wait a minute—that might be a good thing. Let's try to get out of this now. I think we are tired of the business of war. That's the unspoken thing in all this [discussion about] a woman president.

MS: It's interesting, because I interviewed Sheryl Sandberg, and she was talking about this problem of the likability factor. She said that as a woman gets more successful, she's less liked by people of both genders—men and women—whereas as a man gets more successful, he doesn't take a likability hit. What can we do about this conundrum? It's a little bit of a catch-22.

ME: We have to like you, and you have to be able to kill someone [*laughs*]. Why would we like somebody who can actually do that? It says more about our own conundrum of how we're going to perceive who we are as a society, as people. And it's all changing so fast. Our children comprehend things on a level that took us our whole lifetime to get. So I actually look into the future and think, I can't even comprehend what's coming.

MS: It does feel like there's some kind of a shift happening, even in this last election, which was decided by a much more diverse electorate and the collective power of minority groups, including women. And of course we have reelected our first African American president. What will this mean for our country and our government to look more like America, which is, I guess, where we're headed?

ME: Right. It's the funny joke on America that we want to be perceived as one thing, and what we really are, and have always been, is this amazing diversity. This idea, this dream, that there's a land where anyone can come and become anything they dream. How do we hold the American dream? When you realize it's for everyone and it doesn't matter if someone else dreams it, you're still going to have enough. I don't care where you live now, there's a huge diversity of people. New York, L.A., the big cities—it's such a melting pot. It's happening everywhere. I go back to my hometown, [and] there are people looking for a life, and they're of all different colors and shapes and sizes and persuasions. And when we finally go, "Okay, I'm not going to be afraid of a person that's different from me, I'm not going to be afraid," we will become so amazingly powerful that we'll go, "Why didn't we do this before?"

MS: That's part of it—that this isn't necessarily about just equality. What are the benefits, do you think? Why is it important, for example, to have more women in leadership? Aside from a fairness thing, what does that mean?

ME: Because it's about balance. If you study history, look into history, or even are interested in history, you understand our ancient history and how before two thousand years ago we were a feminine-based culture. This idea that there's balance between male and female—we *have* to come to that. Not all the way, to where women rule and that's it, but understanding in each of us the male and female. These ideas that the woman can only do this and the man can only do that—constantly, every day, that's turned upside down on its head. So we can't play these roles anymore.

MS: Obviously society and the political process have a lot of obstacles, but the other piece of it is self-imposed obstacles from women themselves, because we are so indoctrinated by all of the forces that are out there, telling us to be like everybody else and not value our own voice or obsess about how we look, or whatever it is.

ME: Yeah, it's okay to want to be pretty. It's okay to wear a skirt and like your legs. I like the way women's legs look—it's fine. (Or not! I definitely always feel more comfortable in pants.) But one way is not right and the other wrong. I was that woman in the eighties who finally, I was in my twenties and, "Here I am, I'm a feminist!" and then it all went away—you know, Susan Faludi's *Backlash*. I remember reading that and saying, "Holy cow, this is exactly what's happening." There was a lot of that, "Well, they're just afraid of lesbians." They called them all lesbians, because, yes, there were lesbians who were leaders in women's rights. And yet it just tore the thing apart because they were afraid of their own. The straight women were like, "No, we can't." Then they had to be against lesbianism, and then all of a sudden you're screwed, you're the house divided. And it just fell apart. We're more afraid of being powerful than not having the power.

MS: What can we do to help women and girls to see themselves as change agents in the world? Or even you personally—where did you get the courage to find your authentic voice and your inner leader, to so boldly speak out and be your true self?

ME: You have to find it. The beautiful thing was, it was probably my relationship with my father that helped me the most. I find that a lot of our leaders have strong relationships with their fathers. The women who have that understand that "I can be strong and powerful, and I will still be supported by a male." When you have that, you feel that it's okay to be a woman *and* have that drive. And my father was a high school basketball coach, he was a teacher, he was a leader in the National Educational Association. He and my mother both were. He was a Republican and she was a Democrat. So I got both sides of politics, from both of them. And my mother worked, and she made more money than my father! She ran the finances, so I always had this really balanced feel in my home. So when you come from that and it's inside you, then you just are that. I remember when my first record was coming out and my record company said, "Well, what are you going to do about the 'gay' thing?" A guy at my record company finally said, "I don't want you to present yourself as something you're not"; then he said, "We don't need to be flag waving." That's what he said. And then a few years later, I did flag-wave. Yet everyone looked at me and thought, *There's no way she's going to, like, you know, show up with a guy and pretend like he's her boyfriend or something*. It's about walking in your truth. So as we raise our children, our young girls, show them by being an example. Show them that we can be balanced, that this is how it can be. And then their belief in it will be so strong that there will be no pushing it back, because they believe it that deeply. That's what brings about the change.

MS: I feel that having an African American president will help lead the way for a woman president, but I also think this rise of awareness and rights for LGBT issues, and the fact that we just elected Tammy Baldwin, who is the first openly gay politician to be elected to the United States Senate, as well as the first Wisconsin woman elected to the United States Senate, is not all in isolation. How do you see this as connected, as a general shift of all the paradigms?

ME: It's about the big balance. You can look at it as matriarchal and patriarchal. You can call it good and bad, light and dark. It's not only do we need the good to rise up, but we also need the "bad," the dark, the patriarchal.

It's not about going all one way. And once those who fear that comprehend that, and that fear fades, then all of these paradigms, from female president to not only what our government looks like, but what are the issues and how do we solve them—the solving, the answers, are going to be so amazingly different, because all the trouble goes away with a new understanding. Roe v. Wade, the right to an abortion, is going to become obsolete because women are going to understand their own reproductive power.

MS: Again, this has never been about women making better leaders than men—but in general, what do you think are the ingredients to successful leadership that the country, and the world, most need now, whether it's a woman or a man?

ME: Whether it's a woman or a man, it's understanding. It's a belief in oneself. In the last one hundred years, I believe it became a profession [to be] a politician. This was a profession you got into, and because of our capitalist society, it became something that you could make money at, which instantly corrupts it, right? Instantly. Because then our government becomes a corporation and a corporation's sole job is to just make more money. And . . . I think we see it starting to crumble. It's been crumbling. Our government—which is "of the people," which is representative of the people—is amazing. Our democracy and our whole Constitution is so incredible. To uphold it is an honor. We were raised in this country to believe that we were the best. That this was the country that was going to save the world. We were the leader of the free. And now we look around and we're kind of like, "Wait a minute [*laughs*]. We've got some problems here." And we understand that where that came from was the concept of freedom for everyone and a level playing field, and equality. So leadership in the future, whether it's male or female, I believe will start to come from the idea of this great experiment called democracy—that was based on

Native American principles [and on] the Greek, the ancient principles—and to do that, we have to have it inside ourselves to know not to fear any diversity, but to be able to coexist with everything and anything, and that's where power and strength for communities and our country comes from. The end.

MS: Even though you speak so well on all of these political and social themes, you are also an artist. How do you, as an artist and a musician, particularly a female musician, perceive the role and potential of art and music in terms of creating a culture and the messages we send our boys and girls and our men and women?

ME: That's always been its job. That's what it's always been doing. I'm so honored to be a musician, to be one of the artists of my time. I take it as a great responsibility. I take it as a chance to leave behind my legacy, and in the future, I hope these things come true that I believed in so dearly. I hope that I come from a long line of these artists who mirrored society and its changes, from John Lennon to Bob Dylan to Woody Guthrie. It goes all the way back to Billie Holiday and Bessie Smith and all these artists that . . . it wasn't about the money, it was about speaking the truth of what they saw around them. And that's the way that we have been able to capture historically; this is the way we saw it. I know the books say one thing, but there are recordings in the sixties that gave us that other side of the wars and civil rights and everything that we were going through. I'm honored to be a part of it.

MS: You've been a role model, because it's important for a girl to see an artist who has been able to be herself and speak her truth about it and not get herself all decked out in the high heels and makeup and sexy clothes. To me, there aren't enough female artists like you out there, especially when it comes to what girls see in terms of that culture.

ME: Well, every young girl or young woman I see at my shows, I'm just so grateful. It's my favorite thing when they come up and say, "You just really changed my life. You've given me a role model." I do take it as a great responsibility.

MS: You said that you foresee that we will see a woman president in your lifetime. What about . . . do you foresee a day when we will have a gay president?

ME: Yes, I do. I think that, again, once the duality, the polarities of black and white and "You're gay" or "You're straight," that's also going to become more in the mix . . . as I see in this younger generation. I think, you're in your twenties, you get your choices, and if you like this, too, that just widens your choice. It's doubled my choices [*laughs*], but I'm not going to draw my lines yet. There are always those who are one way or another, as I was and am. It's that beautiful middle that will change the world. It's like, yes, my life partner whom I chose is of the same sex, but it's again not something that defines me or puts me in a box. I am a woman, and that's just part of the wonderful, gorgeous makeup of me, one of many, many ingredients that go in. It's those definitions that we're [using to try] to keep everyone in these boxes, so we can all be safe, and it's like, "You know what? It's all out, and the diversity is there."

MS: So you feel hopeful?

ME: Oh yes, absolutely.

NICHOLAS KRISTOF

"I think that if we don't have gender diversity at the top of American politics and in corporate boards, then we're just going to get weaker decisions, and I think that's what we've been stuck with. And so I think that the great strength that women bring when they move into senior levels of politics is not that they're more nurturing, caring, maternal figures, but that they will bring a certain level of different perspective, a different way of thinking, and that is just really valuable for all of us. This is not something that is going to benefit the women of America; it's something that's going to benefit all of America."

NICHOLAS KRISTOF, a columnist for *The New York Times* since November 2001, is a two-time Pulitzer Prize winner who writes op-ed columns that appear twice a week. After graduating from Harvard College, he won a Rhodes Scholarship in 1981 to Magdalen College, Oxford, where he read law with first-class honors.

After joining *The New York Times* in 1984, initially covering economics, Kristof served as a correspondent in Los Angeles and as bureau chief in Hong Kong, Beijing, and Tokyo. In 2000, he covered the presidential campaign and authored the chapter on George W. Bush in the reference book *The Presidents*. Kristof also served as associate managing editor of *The New York Times,* responsible for Sunday editions. In 1990, Kristof and his wife, Sheryl WuDunn, became the first married couple to win a

Pulitzer Prize for their coverage of China's Tiananmen Square democracy movement. They are also coauthors of *Half the Sky: Turning Oppression into Opportunity for Women Worldwide,* a *New York Times* best-selling book about the challenges facing women around the globe. Kristof won a second Pulitzer in 2006, for what the judges called "his graphic, deeply reported columns that, at personal risk, focused attention on genocide in Darfur and that gave voice to the voiceless in other parts of the world." Kristof has taken a special interest in web journalism and was the first blogger on the *New York Times* website.

MARIANNE SCHNALL: What are the factors involved in why we've not had a woman president so far?

NICHOLAS KRISTOF: I think part of it goes back to the research from social psychology that shows that women can essentially be perceived as authoritative or as nice, but not as both. When people are picking politicians, they generally want somebody who is an authority figure and also somebody who's nice, and I think that we have been socialized to think that men can be both, but that it's harder for women to be both. So I think that is one reason why women haven't done as well in politics and in the corporate suite as in some other areas. Of course, these are attitudes that are absorbed by women, not quite as much as by men, but the gender gap on that is not as great as one would think.

I think there's also something to Sheryl Sandberg's point about women sometimes not leaning forward as aggressively as they might in zero-sum contests like politics. I think that is changing to some degree, but I also think that women may be, for whatever reason, better at governing than at the political process of getting into a position to govern.

MS: Yes, and the system itself isn't too woman friendly. Now, what you were saying about this catch-22 for women around gender roles is interesting, because I remember when I interviewed Gloria Steinem and she was talking about how what's needed is a redefining of gender roles for both men and women. That we also need to be educating men and boys in terms of their perception of gender roles in order to create this change. That for boys and men to see women as competent leaders and in positions of authority, on the flip side, they need to see themselves as nurturers and caretakers, so that we're not in these very defined roles all the time.

NK: Right. I think that changes over time. I mean, I remember when I was a kid, there was a popular kind of word puzzle that was going around. It involved a child in a car accident being taken to the hospital, and the father and the child were both injured, and the child is taken into surgery, and the surgeon says, "Oh my God, I can't operate; it's my child." And the puzzle was, how could this be, since the father was injured? Now it seems to be obvious [*laughs*]: the surgeon is the mother. But I remember people being completely baffled by how this could possibly be—is the surgeon speaking metaphorically? [*laughs*] And I think that there's reasonable evidence that these kinds of expectations change, not in one fell swoop as somebody becomes president, but bit by bit as women become mayors, become county chiefs, and probably become legislators as well, although I think it's more important that they become executives—whether it's a county executive, a mayor, or a governor—than [take on] a legislative role. We are beginning to see some progress at the political grassroots, but progress in politics hasn't nearly matched the progress that women made in so many educational roles and so many other social roles—education in particular.

MS: Why do you think that is? Why do you think that the political arena has been one of the last to have more women advancing?

NK: In education, for example, in terms of university presidents, I think there is a premium on people who can work well with faculty, who can play very well with others, who can manage to get what they want done by giving other people credit. And universities are also maybe the places in the country where attitudes are most enlightened—and even there, the progress has been relatively recent and more focused on top-end, more liberal universities, where women become university presidents one after the other, rather than in other arenas. I think that this really deep-rooted sense that you see in surveys that a woman can be either nice or an authority figure, but not both, is much less true among highly educated people in a university environment. It's more of an issue in politics, where you need the median voters' support to get elected, and that is going to be a lagging indicator.

MS: I feel like with Hillary's run, it was an interesting experiment about this whole conversation, and certainly you could see from some of the press coverage that she was caught in this double bind on some of the things that you're talking about in terms of being likable and also showing herself as a strong leader. What do you think were some of the most interesting observations from her candidacy? Was there anything that we can glean or learn, constructively, from what happened when she ran?

NK: Well, I think the pioneers blaze trails for the rest of society, and that's as true of the Oregon Trail as of the early female politicians. And it has become progressively easier for others to focus on issues, rather than on what the women are wearing, or whether they're being snappy, this kind of thing.

There is some fascinating research from India about women as local village chiefs, and this happened randomly due to the way the Indian Constitution was changed so you could really measure pretty effectively what the impact was of a woman becoming a village chief. The one result was that women actually seemed to do better in some respects. They were slightly less corrupt, probably because they weren't part of the deeply embedded networks. They cared more about water supply, probably because women were traditionally the people who were collecting water. Although the women seemed to actually do slightly better as village chiefs than men did, the villagers themselves—the first time they got a woman village chief—thought she was worse. But that was only true for the first time a woman became chief. A few years later, when you had a second round of women becoming village chiefs, people seemed to be kind of socialized to think that was fine, and there was no longer this prejudice against woman village chiefs. And in the same way, I think that it's just kind of an impossible task for those pioneers, but after a while, people get used to women in executive authority and worry less about the color of their dress or what they've done with their hair, and care more about their policies.

MS: Sometimes I feel like this all gets incorrectly framed as being just about equality, as a sort of fairness argument. As a man, why do you think having more women in leadership is important?

NK: I'm a little skeptical of the argument that women are inherently better leaders than men, which has been popular in some circles—that they're more consensual and this kind of thing. I do think that there is very solid evidence that more diverse groups come up with better decisions, and people who study decision making have typically found that the group that comes out with the most optimal results is not the group containing the most optimal individuals, but rather the most diverse individuals. I think that if we don't have gender diversity at the top of American politics and in corporate boards, then we're just going to get weaker decisions, and I think that's what we've been stuck with. And so I think that the great strength that women bring when they move into senior levels of politics is not that they're more nurturing, caring, maternal figures, but that they will bring a certain level of different perspective, a different way of thinking, and that is just really valuable for all of us. This is not something that is going to benefit the women of America; it's something that's going to benefit all of America.

MS: Now, you also have a global perspective. Where does the United States fit in in terms of women in positions of leadership and the status of women? Obviously, there are other countries that have already elected female heads of state.

NK: If you look at heads of government or heads of state, we're laggards. A lot of countries have been way, way ahead of us. I sort of question how good a measure that is. In South Asia, for example, you've had women heads of government in Bangladesh and Sri Lanka, in India and Pakistan, and it doesn't seem to me that it's really done much of anything for women in those countries. In *Half the Sky,* we tried to look at whether countries that had a female leader were doing better for girls' education in those countries, were doing better for maternal mortality in those countries. We found no correlation. In the Philippines, for example, in recent years they've had two male presidents and two female presidents, and it has been the two men who have been much better on reproductive health and creating access to birth control than the two women presidents. So I'm wary of thinking this is an issue of female solidarity and that women at the top are necessarily going to make things better for women at the bottom. It's especially true when you have the women who do become leaders, as in South Asia, who are typically coming from elite families—perhaps their father was president—and they're sometimes treated by the system as kind of honorary men.

But, having dissed those countries [*laughs*], I think they have in some ways made real strides. There's no question that the United States lags, not only in terms of not electing a female president, but if you just look at the number of female governors, female members of Congress, then we're well behind. Europe, especially northern Europe, I think, has really been the place where you have seen women kind of being normalized as leaders, and a substantial share in parliaments, in executive office, and I think it is making a real difference in their societies. Often the first woman to make progress in politics has been kind of an incredibly tough, macho figure and a conservative figure. It may be that voters, when they're suspicious of women politicians, are only willing to support somebody who is extremely against the type—and I'm thinking of Golda Meir, Margaret Thatcher, people like that. I think that in northern Europe, you see a situation where it's perfectly normal and routine to have a woman candidate for political office, including the top offices, and where there are enough women in meetings that nobody feels they have to be just incredibly tough with somebody because they don't happen to have a Y chromosome.

MS: You're known as one of the most prolific and passionate writers and advocates for women and girls worldwide, and yet you are, of course, a man. Why has this been a special area of interest for you?

NK: Well, I guess, for starters, I'm wary of the idea that only women should be writing about women's issues. If that's the case, then the issue is lost from the start. If it had been only blacks writing about civil-rights issues, it would never have gotten the kind of national attraction that it did. Likewise, gay rights really began to advance when you had more straight people saying that this is just intolerable. And so I think we have to see this as a major issue of human rights and justice and of making the system work that affects all of us, and that men need to be a part of, as well as women.

MS: Recently, I was telling my daughters about some of the things going on in the world that happen to girls and women, and certainly there have been some recent, very extreme cases of violent acts. But, having covered this for so many years, where do you see us in terms of where we are in the evolution of women's rights or the oppression of women worldwide? Is the situation improving? Do you see the rising of a backlash?

NK: I think that there's enormous progress under way. I think this is a war that we're winning, both abroad and at home. You look at the number of girls who are going to school, for example. Globally and traditionally, families have sent their sons but not their daughters. These days, in primary education around the world, there's essentially no longer a gender gap. There is in secondary school, but not primary school. And these kinds of issues that used to be just invisible are now actually getting on the agenda. The outrage over the gang rape in India recently was a sign of progress, because these are things that happen all the time and it's good that it got this kind of attention. Likewise, if you look at domestic violence, or at sexual violence in the United States—the numbers are not particularly reliable, but there's no reason to think that they're more unreliable now than they were before—every record we have shows that both domestic violence and rape are going down, quite sharply, over the last few decades. I think that's because attitudes are changing, and police—I mean, there's still a long way to go, but they are much more likely to treat somebody who was raped at a party, or by an acquaintance, more seriously than they would have twenty years ago. If you look at attitudes toward a husband beating up his wife, then it used to be that men and women are like that: "Well, he probably shouldn't do it, but what did she do?" In any case, it's not for outsiders to interfere, and you used to have national magazines that showed ads of husbands spanking their wives because they made a bad cup of coffee, this kind of a thing; it was sort of a joke. And nobody thinks today that it's a joke. So I think we are really seeing progress at home. I think that is mirrored abroad, and I just think we need to continue the momentum. Because there's still a long way to go.

MS: One of the things I was thinking about today was when I interviewed Eve Ensler a couple of years ago. We were talking about the rising of women, and she thought we were going to see somewhat of a global backlash. And I was reading an article in *The New York Times* a day or two ago talking about the case in India, saying that part of the rise in violence against women could possibly be attributed to the increase in women's freedoms that is causing tension. I couldn't help but also think about here in the United States, where even over the recent election there was this whole retro backlash against women's reproductive rights. Do you think that's possible? That as women are rising up in society, there might be a backlash as well?

NK: Yes, I think that is true. I think that backlash is real, is happening, that there are a lot of men who have been marginalized—that's true of India, that's true of the United States—and they feel resentful that there are women who are thriving and they aren't. So I think that is real and that's going to continue, but I think that at the end of the day, those folks are going to lose.

MS: Are you hopeful that we will see a woman president during your lifetime? Are there any women on the political horizon who you think would make good presidential candidates?

NK: Yeah, I think that we will see a woman president in my lifetime. I think it's really hard to predict. I would have been certain that we would see a woman president before we saw a black president, and, well, that happened. Politics is very difficult to predict as far as who it will be [is concerned]—whether it will be Hillary Clinton or somebody else—but I think that it will indeed happen. I think that there are already going to be increasing benefits for people who have a running mate who is a woman, and that then puts people in line. So, one way or the other, I think your daughter is going to see a woman president, and if she is interested in politics, I think that she will be judged, when the time comes, much more on her policies and less on her chromosomes than would be the case today.

GLORIA STEINEM

*"The deeper problem is that as children we are still raised mainly
by women, so we associate female authority with childhood. . . .
And I think we saw it in the response to Hillary in 2008 when
big, grown-up, otherwise adult television commentators were
saying things like, 'I cross my legs when I see her. She reminds
me of my first wife, standing outside alimony court.' People
who would not ever say such things, normally, were saying
them about Hillary, because, I would guess, deep down they felt
regressed by a powerful woman. The last time they saw one they
were six years old."*

GLORIA STEINEM IS a best-selling author, lecturer, editor, and feminist activist. She travels in the United States and other countries
as an organizer and lecturer and is a frequent media spokeswoman on
issues of equality. She is particularly interested in the shared origins of
sex and race caste systems, gender roles and child abuse as roots of violence, non-violent conflict resolution, the cultures of indigenous peoples,
and organizing across boundaries for peace and justice. In 1972 she co-
founded *Ms. Magazine*, which has become a landmark in both women's
rights and American journalism. She also co-founded the Women's Media
Center and the National Women's Political Caucus, a group that continues to work to advance the numbers of pro-equality women in elected
and appointed office at a national and state level. She now lives in New

York City and is currently at work on *Road to the Heart: America As if Everyone Mattered,* a book about her more than thirty years on the road as a feminist organizer.

MARIANNE SCHNALL: This book was partially inspired by my eight-year-old daughter, Lotus, who upon discovering recently that there had been no woman president, ever, asked this very simple, quizzical question of me. She just looked at me and went, "Why?" I actually found that simple, innocent question really hard to answer. And this book will be dealing with not just electing women to the presidency, which is symbolic, but overall themes around women and politics and leadership and power. Going back to that simple question, why do you think it is that we have not yet had a woman president?

GLORIA STEINEM: One reason is that women weren't citizens from 1776 through the constitutional amendment [in 1920]. We were possessions, like tables and chairs. So there was not the opportunity [for women] to own property, to have the right to one's own earnings, to have the right to your own children. You could be forcibly returned to a violent husband. You were property, literally, like a thing. And the laws of slavery were modeled on the laws affecting wives, so that takes care of the long time through the 1920s [*laughs*]. And since then, we have been overcoming legal barriers. For instance, women couldn't sit on juries, law schools didn't accept women, or accepted a small percentage of women when I was growing up. When I would have gone to law school, Harvard accepted no women and Columbia accepted 5 percent. So those are just symbolic areas, but they're illustrative, real, powerful barriers.

There are also what are called cultural barriers, but I'm not sure we should call them cultural, because it seems to me what affects men is called political and what affects women is called cultural. So the idea that only women could raise children, which is alive among men [*laughs*], meant that also when this wave of feminism began in the seventies and we began to try to elect women, there were two frequent questions of women candidates. One: If you don't have children, why not? And two: If you do have children, why aren't you home with them? When the National Women's Political Caucus began, which was the first organization devoted totally to appointing and electing women, the major way that women got into high political office was as widows. You married a man who was the governor or a senator. He died through no fault of yours [*laughs*], and only then were you allowed to take over the seat—the supposition being that you were carrying on your husband's work.

MS: I remember when I interviewed you at the Women's Media Center Awards in December 2011, and at that time you were saying, in regards to Hillary's presidential run, that you didn't think we were ready then for a woman president. Do you still feel that way?

GS: No. Thanks in large part to the many courageous women in politics, but especially Hillary because she was so visible in 2008. And since then, as secretary of state, I think she's helped to change people's expectations.

But as I was saying then, the deeper problem is that we are still raised as children, mainly by women, so we associate female authority with childhood. We, as women, have our own example to go by, so sometimes we change—although there are also women who don't think that female authority is appropriate to public life. But it's more likely to be men, and I think we saw it in the response to Hillary in 2008 when big, grown-up, otherwise adult television commentators were saying things like, "I cross my legs when I see her. She reminds me of my first wife, standing outside alimony court." People who would not ever say such things, normally, were saying them about Hillary, because, I would guess, deep down they felt regressed by a powerful woman. The last time they saw one they were six years old.

MS: What a conundrum for women, though. Because if women who are confident or ambitious or powerful or in positions of leadership are seen as unlikable, how can women be accepted and respected as leaders?

GS: You do it anyway. You just go forward, and you end up changing the image eventually, and you may take a lot of punishment along the way. But I do think that now we could elect a woman, including Hillary, as president, because of the bravery of a lot of women and especially Hillary. But Shirley Chisholm also took the WHITE MALE ONLY sign off of the White House door all by herself.

MS: So you do think that there's a real possibility? That would be very exciting.

GS: I do now. In 2008, I did not believe that a woman could win.

MS: I feel like this whole conversation gets reframed incorrectly sometimes as almost like a fairness thing, a men versus women conversation, that it's some type of competition. Why would electing a woman as president be important?

GS: It's important because we need the talent of the whole country, not just a small percentage of it. Once at Ms. Magazine we tried to figure out the talent pool from which we were choosing presidents. First you eliminated half the country, the females. Then you eliminated by class, race—because obviously Obama had not yet been elected. Anyway, we ended up with 6 percent. So it's important for the whole country that we are able to choose from *all* of our talent, otherwise we lower our standards.

Secondly, gender is still a social force, so it's still probably true, not always, but probably true that women are somewhat less likely to choose an aggressive solution and more likely to choose a conciliatory one. Not that a conciliatory one is always right, but it's just that it tends to be the least present in public life.

MS: I don't know if you saw the interview on ABC where Diane Sawyer was talking to a group of female members of the Senate. Two of the women, Susan Collins and Claire McCaskill, made statements that they felt women were by nature more collaborative and less confrontational.

GS: I think it's true. It's not by nature, but it's by culture. Because there is no such thing as gender; it's totally made up, but it's very powerful.

MS: Those do seem like qualities that would be needed in Washington. I don't know if you remember when I was considering doing this book, I emailed you and you said, "From a tactical point of view, your writing it would be good, because you know it's not about biology or a job for one woman, but making life better for all women, hence not about Sarah Palin or Margaret Thatcher, who was elected to be anti-union, not pro-women. That sometimes gets lost." That's the other side of the coin. Can you talk about that distinction?

GS: Well, people are people. We're not into biological determinism here, because that would be to abandon men, among other things. Men are human beings, too, but they're made to feel that they have to earn their masculinity and to sometimes get into an extreme cult of masculinity that requires control and violence. Cesar Chavez used to say, "We want to rescue the executioner from being the executioner, as well as the victim from being the victim."

MS: We were just talking about society only wanting to see women in feminine roles, and this notion that power and leadership is often seen as masculine. Sometimes I think we're talking not in literal gender terms, but conceptually, where sometimes feminine values like cooperation and care and empathy and compassion are seen as soft or weak, rather than part of the full circle of human qualities.

GS: But that's just because masculinity is perceived as superior, necessary, inevitable, conquering, winning—all those things.

MS: I had an interesting conversation when I interviewed Michael Kimmel. He said that it is really important to make sure that this conversation is not anti-men—that men not only lately are being there to support women, they understand why it would be helpful to the world to have more women in these positions, but also to free themselves.

GS: I've forgotten who said, "The woman a man most fears is the woman inside himself."

MS: I feel like Obama does have what you might call more "feminine" traits, in terms of being conciliatory and showing how important family is to him—

GS: I think we ought to forget about talking about masculine and feminine altogether; we should talk about humans.

MS: I actually think that's where we're headed. That's why I'm always talking about how feminism has to be about more of the human conversation.

GS: That is what it's about, and it kind of sets my teeth on edge when spirituality people talk about the "eternal feminine." Like we're giving in to the difference.

MS: I think a lot of this is the linguistics of things. While advocating for the fact that, of course, we do want equality for more women, but at the same time, being careful that it's not framed as women are perfect or better—all these things that have always been part of the misconceptions of the feminist movement.

GS: It is because culture is what it is, right now. Society is what it is. It's probable that walking around female for twenty years, or fifty years, in this culture has given someone a set of experiences that men don't necessarily have—in the same way that walking around as a black person or a Hispanic person or a gay person gives people a different set of experiences than a white, heterosexual person. Experience is everything. Somebody who has experienced something is more expert at it than the experts. We need politicians who look like the country.

MS: Which, after this last election, I feel like we're starting to make some progress. There are many other countries who obviously have already elected female heads of state, and the United States is ninetieth in the world in terms of women in national legislatures. What do these other countries know that we don't, and why is the United States lagging so far behind when we are so much more progressive and democratic in other areas?

GS: Well, I'm not sure we are so much progressive and democratic, because in economic division we're low down on the list, too. The division between rich and poor here is exceeded only by four other major countries, I think. There are a variety of reasons and they all function in different ways. One is there's more power in this country. It's still the dominant power in the world, so there's more competition for these jobs. One is that we are multi-racial, and racism always increases sexism because you have to maintain control of women and reproduction in order to maintain racial difference. So one-race countries, generally speaking, as the Scandinavian example, for instance, have slightly less motivation to remain sexist. Another is that we are big and decentralized, so social reform has to take place fifty times, whereas in France or Sweden or Finland it only takes place once in the national legislature. And the final one is the power of family, which is deep here, but is not as deep as in India, say, and many other countries. So because Nehru's family, the ruling family, was so strong or had such power, even a daughter was acceptable. Now if she had had a brother, he would have been Prime Minister, no doubt. But since Indira Gandhi didn't have a brother, even a woman was acceptable because of the power. The disaster of being a female was mitigated by the power of being in that family.

MS: That's really interesting. Are you feeling hopeful with the last election? Sometimes it feels crazy to be celebrating twenty women in the Senate. While it's a big milestone, it's still obviously so lacking. Are you feeling progress, like we are making a steady climb?

GS: I am, but it depends what we do. I feel hopeful, but I feel hopeful that you and I will act. It's not automatic. Nothing is automatic.

MS: What does that mean to the common person?

GS: It means recognizing that the voting booth is the only place on Earth in which everybody's equal—so, using it. We're still not doing so well in percentages of who votes.

MS: In terms of women running themselves, what do you think are some of the factors or obstacles—either societal or sometimes even self-imposed—that deter women from entering the political pipeline? And what can we do as a society to encourage more women to run?

GS: One is that politics is a rough game and that women are culturally taught to seek approval, not disapproval. So as Sheryl Sandberg points out, we have to lean in—lean in and not be dependent on being liked, as much as the culture has encouraged us to be. Money, of course, is a big barrier, a huge barrier. I've raised money for candidates, who, if I'm raising money for them, probably are all the same on the issues. But if I'm raising money for a man running for the Senate, someone will give me $1,000; if it's a woman, they'll give me $200 or $300. Not consciously, but unconsciously, as if women can get along on less or they're ashamed to give a man less. We have to name that and be conscious of giving women candidates as much as we would a male candidate. And we have to also, at the same time, do with less money, because we're more likely to be opposed to the Koch Brothers and some of the others, so we need to be really good at community organizing. It's a much more democratic message than just paying for TV ads.

Now we could do many other things to reform the electoral system, which would help everyone, especially women. For instance, radio and television stations have to have FCC licenses because they are essentially renting the public airwaves. There's no reason why the FCC couldn't require stations to, in return for a license, give a percentage of their time free to candidates. That would take a lot of the money out of the political contest.

MS: It does seem that there's a lot that could be done structurally. Do you think part of the issue is that not just women, but people in general, have gotten a little cynical about the political arena as a forum for effective change?

GS: A great deal of effort has been extended toward making us cynical. I remember during the Nixon administration when it was pretty clear that the Republicans benefited from a low voter turnout, because then it was older, richer, white voters, so they quite consciously depicted politics as dirty: "You wouldn't want to get involved. Your vote doesn't count." Neither of which is true. So we have to understand that that was a conscious campaign to keep us from voting. And it's still a conscious campaign to keep us from voting. I'm not saying everybody who believes that is giving in to the campaign—they believe that for their own independent reasons—but there's also a campaign to tell us that. It's not unlike saying to women, "Well, money is dirty and business is crooked. You wouldn't want to get involved." It's a way of keeping us out.

MS: In the movie *Miss Representation,* there was one thing that really stood out to me: Carolyn Heldman said that when children are seven years old, boys and girls say they want to become president in roughly the same numbers. By the time they're fifteen, however, the number of girls who say they'd like to be president drops off dramatically, as compared to the boys. What role do you think the media plays in all this?

GS: Well, of course, the media is the main purveyor of masculinity and femininity. And, as Carol Gilligan pointed out so brilliantly, when little girls are eleven and twelve, or perhaps even younger, the gender role comes down upon them. And the purpose of the gender role is to turn us toward having babies and taking care of them for nothing.

MS: I keep thinking back to Hillary's presidential bid, and I thought one of the most interesting times we've had in a while was during the race between Obama and Hillary. At one point there was this messy dialogue around race and gender.

GS: It was outrageous. It made me so angry for people to be told they have to choose between sex and race. It's, first of all, rendering most women in the world invisible who experience both sex and race or color. It's outrageous to present that choice. It's like saying which is more important, your legs or your arms? It's just awful.

MS: Yes, and I thought it was interesting that it felt a little generational, as though generally the older generation was supporting Hillary and the younger generation was supporting Obama.

GS: Yes, but that made perfect sense because for older women, including a lot of black women, who supported Hillary, this was their last chance to ever see a female president. For younger women, they would have many other chances, or some other chances.

MS: What women do you see on the political landscape right now that you think would make good future candidates?

GS: Well, I think Kirsten Gillibrand is outstanding—a whole person who leads a whole life and is an excellent senator. I think the same is true of Elizabeth Warren. The same is true of Maxine Waters, but because she came into politics earlier, because she's older, she probably will not be present in political life long enough to get the reward she deserves.

MS: I have to say out of all of the answers in the piece I did for CNN about what it would take to make a woman president, people were most intrigued by yours, which was about gender roles. You said, "Because we are raised by women and we associate women with childhood. . . . one of the most helpful things we can do long term is to make sure that kids have loving and nurturing male figures as well as female figures, and authoritative and expert female figures as well as male figures." From a cognitive place, we can all feel we absolutely need to do that, but what are some concrete ways as a society we can begin to support those shifts?

GS: Well, it's up to each person and everyone's situation is different, so I'm not trying to say that people have to do one thing. But we could understand that boys can be babysitters. We can, before we have children with someone, try to make sure that they want to be nurturing parents, if they're men. Sheryl Sandberg always says this: The single most important career decision you make is the partner you choose, supposing you want to have children.

MS: I think we are moving toward that. I also think that some of this is about appealing to women to value their visions and opinions, knowing that they actually have something to offer the world through their voices in leadership. How did you tap into your inner leader? What advice would you give on having the courage to honor your voice and to speak out and contribute your influence, even though sometimes society is pushing against that?

GS: Hang out with people who make you feel smart, not dumb. That's crucial. Because if they make you feel dumb, they're not supporting you and they're not helping you. It isn't that we're right or wrong. It doesn't have to do with being right all the time, but if you have consistency of support from people who value your opinion, it will help you to value your opinion. We're communal people. You can't do it by yourself.

MS: Do you feel hopeful that we will have a woman president?

GS: I feel hopeful, because I feel hopeful that you and I and the people reading this will act.

★ ★

WHAT DO YOU THINK NEEDS TO CHANGE IN ORDER TO GET MORE WOMEN INTO POLITICS AND ULTIMATELY THE PRESIDENCY?

★ ★

I think some of it, when it comes specifically to this type of political power, it's campaign finance reform, because I feel like women don't want to have to go out and raise those massive amounts of money that it now requires. They feel guilty. They feel responsible. They don't want to do it. So I think campaign finance reform is a huge part of women running for office. I also think the news media has to change. I mean, it is still shocking to me how many times you read an article and it comments on a woman's clothes and just her appearance—and women feel humiliated by that. It's just not something they want to have to go through. So I just think the news media really has to be mandated to only describe a female politician in the same exact way they would describe a male politician.

> —AMY RICHARDS, AUTHOR, COFOUNDER OF THIRD WAVE
> FOUNDATION

It's in the unladylike category to be talking about money and asking about money, but I think you won't become president of the United States if you don't get the money thing. You have to understand who has it. You have to convince them to give it to you. You have to feel that you're worthy of it.

> —CAROL JENKINS, MEDIA CONSULTANT, FOUNDING PRESIDENT OF
> WOMEN'S MEDIA CENTER

I think my prescription would be, we just need to get to that tipping point. So much research shows that generally, if you can get 33 percent of women in any one community—whether it's a corporate board or the op-ed pages—that you shift the social dynamic and you shift the way people perceive your leadership. And I think that what we're experiencing is that we're really approaching that tipping point with women, where unfortunately, Nancy and Hillary and others have been the ones who sort of laid the groundwork and dealt with all that backlash. And once we get a critical mass of women in political office and into very visible leadership positions, I think not only will it become normalized, but there will just be more styles of leadership for people to look at.

> —COURTNEY E. MARTIN, AUTHOR, BLOGGER, AND SPEAKER

I think that the number-one change is a change of perspective. It is people beginning to say, "Who is the most qualified person for the job?" and not looking at their friends or whom they are closest to, but looking at their qualifications.

—REPRESENTATIVE MARSHA BLACKBURN (R)

I think that as more women are running for office and running successfully, that we're seeing others do it, and that is a great motivator and is a great example and it challenges others to consider doing it. . . . Other women are saying, "You know what, maybe I could do that," and all of that is going to lead to women reaching new heights and ultimately someone running for the presidency and winning.

—REPRESENTATIVE CATHY McMORRIS RODGERS (R)

It's getting more women in the pipeline, in every area, toward power. That's in the pipeline toward power in the corporate world and changing the ethics there. It's toward getting women more power in politics, in the entertainment industry, you name it. . . . The pipeline is important, and getting women to run is important, and then funding is really absolutely crucial. And being there for the women politicians, if they act in a principled manner. Being there for them in a way that is really loud and clear. Not forgetting once they win. . . . We need to get on their mailing lists. We need to tweet and email and call and fax and use whatever means of communication—carrier pigeon, if necessary— when they have bills up that we approve of. We need to become less apathetic and more involved in legislation, or else we'll have legislation that will kill us.

—ROBIN MORGAN, AUTHOR, COFOUNDER OF
WOMEN'S MEDIA CENTER

ANITA HILL

"Take the tools and the skills and the resources of every kind that
you have, and go out, find something that you know is not fair,
is not just, and begin to change it. In whatever way you know, in
whatever way is appropriate for you, but don't ignore it. Don't
think it's somebody else's job to change it. Confront it in your
own way, and make it your job to make change."

THE YOUNGEST OF thirteen children from a farm in rural Oklahoma, Anita Hill received her JD from Yale Law School in 1980. She began her career in private practice in Washington, D.C. Before becoming a law professor, she worked at the U.S. Education Department and Equal Employment Opportunity Commission. In 1989, Hill became the first African American to be tenured at the University of Oklahoma College of Law, where she taught Contracts and Commercial Law. In 1991, she testified at the Senate confirmation hearings of Clarence Thomas, gaining national exposure when her allegations of sexual harassment were made public. Currently, at Brandeis University, she teaches civil rights courses. As counsel to Cohen Milstein, Hill advises on class-action workplace discrimination cases.

Hill is the subject of Freida Lee Mock's documentary *Anita,* which premiered in January 2013 at the Sundance Film Festival. Hill's latest book is *Reimagining Equality: Stories of Gender, Race, and Finding Home.* She has also written her biography, *Speaking Truth to Power,* and coedited with professor Emma Coleman Jordan *Race, Gender, and Power in America: The Legacy of the Hill-Thomas Hearings*. *Time, Newsweek, The New York Times, The Boston Globe,* and *Ms. Magazine* have published Hill's commentary, and she has appeared on many national television programs.

MARIANNE SCHNALL: What is your sense of why we have not yet had a woman president?

ANITA HILL: I think we've had, and we continued to have, this skewed concept of what leadership looks like, how it appears. Leadership in our minds, unfortunately, has a gender, and the gender is male. We see that not only in politics; we see it also in just about every kind of business and different aspects of our lives, even in environments where you are presumed to be very liberal and open to change. And there are all kinds of cultural factors. I always talk about cultural factors, because I think very often when you talk about politics, you'll hear people say if women could raise money or if they were going up through the ranks or . . . You hear all of these reasons why [electing a woman president] is not possible, [based] purely on money and, to some extent, on system, but I think we can't discount the role of culture in shaping our concept of what women can do.

MS: How do you see that? How do you view the role of culture in terms of this conversation?

AH: Let's say, for example, Hillary Clinton does ultimately run for president in this next election cycle. Even though she's been secretary of state, a world leader, you're going to have people questioning whether or not she has the [right] kind of toughness. They won't question her analyzing skills so much as they will her toughness, and her toughness is going to be defined by this male approach, muscular approach, to what it means to be tough. If you think back to the primary election where Hillary Clinton and Barack Obama were sort of neck and neck, at some point they were trading places, I guess. He was always ahead of her, but in terms of electoral-college votes . . . the moment we saw tears in her eyes—and not on her face; they were just in her eyes—came with all of the questions about whether or not she was tough, and whether or not she could be president if she was going to have that kind of emotional response. So it's clear to me that we have these ideas about what it takes to be the leader of the free world that have nothing to do with the qualities that we want to see in a leader, or even some of the qualities that we value in male leaders, like their ability to connect with the emotions that people experience, but they may become demerits for women.

MS: On the flip side of what you were saying about the pushback she got when she showed emotion, when she was perceived as tough, there were all these reverse comments and sexist novelty items like the "Hillary nut-cracker." It's like you can't win either way.

AH: There's no way you can possibly be both people that you're supposed to be, the way they're defining her, and there's no way that you could ever satisfy some people, because they just cannot conceptualize what a woman leader should be and could be.

MS: A lot of times this gets framed as a fairness or equality issue, but why is it important that we have more women there, aside from just basic parity for parity's sake? What do you think women would bring?

AH: They'll broaden the information that goes into decision making. I think people tend to connect with and bring into their own circles people who are

like them, so by bringing in one person, you are more likely to bring additional women voices into the decision-making process, and that's going
to be better for everyone if the perspective is broadened. I think we've got
so many complex issues that cannot be resolved by looking at them from
one perspective. And ultimately, allowing more women in will help make
better decisions if, in fact, those women are powerful and in tune with and
connected with other women's voices, and perhaps voices of people who
have been left out of the conversation, including people of color.

MS: By the way, that's part of what I'm hoping this book is also going to
speak to. It's not just about women specifically but about diversity in general, how we would all benefit. You referenced this last election. Do you
see a changing paradigm, both in our elected officials and in the way the
face in Washington is starting to look a little bit more like America? Do
you think the trend is heading in the right direction?

AH: I think you're starting to see it. Twenty women in the Senate is significant, but I do think that the tensions in the other direction, toward a more
conservative approach of who belongs in those roles, is real. I don't think
we can discount the fact that there are people who just are not concerned
about diversity and that they really are very much traditional and conservative. And not just in a political sense, in terms of the way they vote on
particular pieces of legislation, but conservative in terms of the desire to
see broader representation in our representative bodies. I think there are
some interesting things going on worldwide. I've sort of been following this
whole move in Europe to make sure that more women are on boards, and
I think it's all of these things that we see that start inching us forward, even
though they don't look like much at the time, but they move us toward
something different. Now, I also think that we've got a problem, and that is
popular culture that reinforces some of the negatives about women's roles.

MS: There's been a lot of talk, because women internalize that so much, that there are also psychological obstacles that women impose on themselves, by not naturally advocating for themselves in the workplace, or these studies that say that women have to be almost begged to run for office. Do you think that that's also a factor?

AH: Yes, but I don't know that women will need to be begged if they know that there's a system that's not rigged against them. So it's like a chicken-and-egg thing. I don't know that women would need to be begged if they thought that they were going into a process that was fair and that was going to treat them fairly. So what comes first? I'm not sure, but I think you're right that women are going to have to take risks to get engaged, and I think they can build opportunities for other women. But then you ask yourself—when you say to women, "Oh, you have to," I guess the new phrase is, "lean in"—how much risk are we willing to ask women to take without providing them with some kind of security that they're not just doing that for nothing? I'm not sure where the point is where we start saying yes, we want women to lean in, but on the other hand, we also want to assure them that there is a system where it's going to be worth their effort if they lean in.

MS: Exactly. It is a bit of a chicken-and-egg problem. You were also talking about women being willing to take those risks. I actually found myself getting a little emotional when I was watching the *MAKERS* documentary, when it gets to the part where it talks about your role in history. I can't think of many people who took as much of a high-profile risk as you did. You're a hero to many people, in terms of the courage that you had, especially back then, to speak out. How did you find your courage and strength to speak out?

AH: When you talk about people who do things that people perceive as really courageous, most of the time what motivates them is not the risk that they're looking at, of what might happen that would be really, really disastrous for them, but what's the importance of what it is you're trying to achieve? And I think for me, when I look at those things, I look at some of my role models . . . people like Rosa Parks, and Ada Lois Sipuel Fisher, who, as a twenty year old, sued to integrate the University of Oklahoma College of Law. And in the case of both of those women, I've read some of what they cared about and what was important to them, and I think what they were looking at was not the consequences of doing a thing as much as the consequences of not doing it. So for me, when I think about the hearing, what motivated me to do it was bigger than the consequences of doing it. I mean, I knew that I had important information about Clarence Thomas, what kind of judge he was going to be, because I knew about his own behavior that really said that he had no respect for the law and that he believed himself to be above the law. In the situation I'm talking about, it happened to be sexual harassment, which carried with it another kind of meaning, in that what it meant for me was that we're going to have some-body in a position of ultimate authority, as a member of a group of nine, but still having a role to play in deciding the rights of women and people of color, in cases of discrimination. And knowing that the law was going to be written by and shaped by someone with a disregard for it was what I was looking at. And that was the consequence, and I could have an impact on how that shaped and took place. That was really what motivated me— it just outweighed the consequences.

Now, I didn't know what all the consequences were [*laughs*], and maybe that helped, but I think that there's someplace in your conscience that says, *If I don't act, then I will have been a part of something that I don't want to live with*. I would have been moving away from something and turning my back on something. Then, on the other hand, you know that there are going to be negative consequences . . . and, for me, I felt that I had the personal resources to be able to deal with it—I had the family, I had my friends. I felt that I could weather whatever occurred as a result. And I don't know that I was all that logical in what I did, but that's why I did it. And then I tell people, "Then you pray a lot" [*laughs*]. I mean, you really do—you pray and you look to your family and you look to the people who love you and you have faith in God and you have faith in the people around you . . . and then you do what you know is best.

MS: There are so many lessons in your story, especially as we're talking about how women running for office, or just stepping out in any way, are sometimes subject to so many different forms of personal attack and scrutiny. Do you remember how you got through that? How did you not let that get to you? What did give you strength during that time?

AH: Well, so much of the scrutiny was just lies. It was just outright lies, and even on the part of some of the senators, some comments and statements that were made were just not true. So knowing that I knew the truth, that was very helpful, and knowing that the people around me knew the truth, that was also very helpful. I mean, some of the things that they ascribed to me were just so untrue and so unreal that it was disturbing, but it also took away some of the sting, because I knew it wasn't true and I knew that and I had enough people around me who knew who I was and what I am. So that's in part how I dealt with it. I wouldn't ever say that it didn't get to me, that it didn't hurt. And I will say I was reluctant, you know, there was stuff about "Oh, she couldn't give testimony against an important black man," the whole racial issue. That was not my biggest concern. My biggest concern was that the process was not interested in getting to the truth, and that was the only thing that was risky for me.

MS: I was looking at *MAKERS,* when they show that amazing footage of all the congresswomen marching to the Senate to demand that you be heard. Talk about the importance of having women in Congress! Do you remember how you felt about the fact that those women did come to your defense, and how important that was?

AH: Let's just put it in this way: seeing that they were willing to, by going over to the Senate, sort of step out of their "place," step out of what their defined roles as congresswomen were, and approach the Senate, which was clearly outside of protocol—had it not been for those women, there very likely would not have been a hearing. But if you look at the women who did go over —Patsy Mink, Eleanor Holmes Norton, and Patricia Schroeder—I mean, these were all pioneers in women's, gender, and racial issues. If you think about Patsy Mink with Title IX and Patricia Schroeder with the Violence Against Women Act and Eleanor Holmes Norton from the time she was in New York at the New York Human Rights Commission—all of these women were pioneers, and they just knew, certainly before I did, why the testimony was of significance. I mean, I thought it was significant for the issue that I am telling you about, the role that Clarence Thomas would go on to play on the court. I had no idea, really, that it was going to lead to a conversation about gender equality, more generally gender representation, and even specifically sexual harassment.

MS: That was really remarkable. And in fact, Eleanor Holmes Norton always says that your case sparked the Year of the Woman.

AH: Yes, it did. I mean, if you go back and you look at why some of these women who went into Congress ran—as a matter of fact, Barbara Boxer was in that group of women who went over to the Senate, and in the next few months she was elected to the Senate [laughs]. Again, it's all very interesting, but it also shows you—this is another point that I try to make— that if you think about what happened after the hearing, the conventional wisdom was that women would never come forward again after witnessing what the Judiciary Committee did with my testimony. It also shows you that women are incredibly brave, and once they understand that they have rights and are in the position to pursue them, they will. Because even though the conventional wisdom was that women would not come forward, women in fact doubled the rate of filing sexual harassment claims in the year following the hearing. So to me there are so many lessons from that episode in history that go from the political lessons to the lessons that have to do with women's rights and rights enforcement, and even into our relationships, our interpersonal relationships. The fact that women could now tell their families and friends about their experiences, it was a significant breakthrough for us, socially and culturally.

MS: Do you think since that time the situation has improved, specifically in terms of sexual harassment cases, in the workplace climate for women and as far as women's awareness of what their rights are is concerned, and also in terms of that courage to speak out?

AH: I think we've made some progress, and I hear from women from time to time and get thousands of letters from women who say, "I was having problems in the workplace, and after your hearing, things changed." Or that just the culture in the workplace has changed. Now, I am not naive enough to believe that there is no sexual harassment. It continues to exist. It continues to be a problem, and women continue to feel threatened in ways that keep us from coming forward. So, yes, we changed, but we have not resolved the issue.

MS: Do you think—and we talk about this whole need for more women in Washington—if more women had been there in the decision-making capacities, Clarence Thomas would have been confirmed?

AH: Well, you know, it was a very narrow margin. And it was interesting: there were two women in the Senate, and one voted to confirm and one voted against confirmation. Let's just say it this way: if the nine women who went over from Congress to the Senate had been in the Senate [*laughs*], then Clarence Thomas would not have been confirmed. So women's representation is important, but I guess that is to say, the kind of women who understand women's lives and women's perspectives and the significance of the issues we confront in the country in general [are important]. If those women are in, yes, I think they can change the climate, and it would have changed what happened in 1991.

MS: We were talking when we first started about this notion of having to appear tough to be a leader. I think that Barack Obama has redefined that a little bit, because he is not this tough-talking, macho guy. He talks a lot about how important his family is, he's very comfortable showing his emotion, so I think in some ways, he's been a different kind of leader. He tries to reach to both aisles and be more conciliatory, so I think he's done a lot in redefining how we see leaders, too.

AH: Well, I agree with you. But also, there is a certain kind of muscularity that he exhibits when it comes to drones, for example [*laughs*]. And so I think that's going to be an issue when it comes to a woman. Will women, for example, have to be more inclined to go to war to prove themselves as suitable military leaders? I mean, will you have to be, on a scale of hawkishness [*laughs*], a ten, as opposed to a male leader, who might be a seven?

MS: What do you think are the most important ingredients that we need in a leader today, male or female?

AH: I think that most important is the ability to connect with the problems of people who are not like you—who have been underserved by government historically, who don't enjoy the privileges that you do. And maybe my concept of what is important in leadership is shaped by the time. I am, of course, shaped by my history, and it's shaped by some of the issues that I deal with with my academic colleagues. I work in a school— a school for social policy—and we look at issues and ways to improve circumstances for people who are going to be left behind politically or economically in this country. And so the ability to connect with those people, really connect, and design policies that will include their well-being—with an understanding that as they go, so goes the rest of the country—I think that is important and may be the most critical characteristic of a leader today. Because so often those are the people who are not going to be represented by a lobbyist or a very important vocal donor, so those are the interests that can get lost. And I think those are the interests that maybe some leaders will take for granted—"Oh well, we have social safety nets for them"—without really considering what's going to be best. We could just assume, well, we have some things in place for them, but have not necessarily given any real thought to whether those things work and how they work and what the strategic goals for those programs are.

MS: Now, being on college campuses, you probably have a finger on the pulse of what's happening. There's a lot of talk that younger women are possibly a little bit apathetic or don't see themselves as feminists. What is your impression of both young women and young people today, because you are on a campus interacting with them all the time?

AH: You know, I see young women coming at these issues from all sides. Some of them come with a consciousness that, yes, these are important issues and want to address some. Some come at them when they're confronted with bias, and then they realize, "Oh, gosh, now I must be aware, because it's hitting *me*." And some just don't think that they're important in their lives. I don't think that's any different from women my age, honestly. I do think that they have a different way of dealing with these issues and addressing them, but you have to remember that for women of my generation, we were shaped by our times. I grew up watching movement take shape, on television, and they don't have that frame of reference, and so the way they react and they respond is going to be shaped by how they have seen issues come to the fore. And I don't think they've seen movement so much as they've seen sort of one-off situations. Like, for example, Sandra Fluke, the young woman who was denied the opportunity to testify about birth control. They see, for example, problems on campus with sexual assault, or they see what went on at Yale a couple of years ago, and at Amherst. They're not part of a movement; they're part of episodes. I think that we're just facing a different time and we have to realize that just as we are shaped by our times or what our times were when we were growing up, they are as well. It doesn't mean that they don't care or that they don't see the issues, but I do think that they have a different way of engaging with them.

MS: Obviously, you have so much wisdom to offer, and you're now working with your students. What do you try to instill in them as they go off into the world? What do you hope that they come away with, and generally, what would your words of wisdom or advice be to young women today?

AH: My advice would be, with the people whom I try to give something to, to take the tools and the skills and the resources of every kind that you have, and go out, find something that you know is not fair, is not just, and begin to change it. In whatever way you know, in whatever way is appropriate for you, but don't ignore it. Don't think it's somebody else's job to change it. Confront it in your own way, and make it your job to make change.

KIRSTEN GILLIBRAND

"My own experience in Congress is when women are on committees and at hearings, the nature of the discussion is different and the outcomes are better—we reach better solutions, better decisions are made. So I really want to create a nationwide call to action to get more women engaged. . . . To say, 'Women, we need you to be advocates, to be heard on the issues you care about, to be voting, to be running for office, to be part of decision-making.'"

U.S. SENATOR KIRSTEN Gillibrand was twice elected to the U.S. Senate, in just four years, with an overwhelming 63 percent of the vote in 2010, and a New York state record-breaking 72 percent in 2012. After first being elected to the House of Representatives in 2006, she was appointed to serve in the seat vacated by Secretary of State Hillary Clinton in January 2009. She is the mother of two young sons, Theo and Henry, ages nine and four.

In a short time, Gillibrand has made her presence felt in Washington. She helped lead the fight to repeal "Don't Ask, Don't Tell," worked tirelessly to successfully pass legislation to provide health care for the 9/11 first responders who are sick and dying from toxins at Ground Zero, and served as an architect in passing the STOCK Act, that for the first time makes it clearly illegal for members of Congress to profit from non-public information. *The New York Times* called her commitment to promoting transparency in Congress a "quiet touch of revolution," and The Sunlight Foundation, the leading advocacy organization dedicated to openness in government, praises Gillibrand as a "pioneer" for her work. Kirsten has been a leading voice for how to grow our economy, protect middle class families, strengthen our national security, end the war in Afghanistan, protect women's rights, and get women more engaged in the political process. She is the founder of Off the Sidelines, an initiative and website that offers encouragement and resources to help women make a difference in their communities and make their voices heard. *Newsweek* and *The Daily Beast* have twice named Gillibrand one of "150 Women Who Shake the World."

MARIANNE SCHNALL: Do you think you will see a woman president in your lifetime?

KIRSTEN GILLIBRAND: I think we will have a woman president, and I think her name will be Hillary Clinton. Her breadth of experience would make her the most well prepared president in history, and I am going to do everything I can do to support her if she decides to run in 2016.

MS: Do you think the American consciousness is ready for a woman president?

KG: Absolutely.

MS: What made you decide to launch the Off the Sidelines initiative?

KG: Well, it really occurred to me over the last few years that women are not sufficiently part of the decision-making fabric of this country—whether in Congress, state governments, corporate boardrooms, or corner suites, there are not enough women's voices being heard. So when we're actually trying to look at issues like the economy, solving these problems, I feel that if more women's voices were heard, if more women were part of decision-making, our outcomes would be better. And a lot of studies support that; a lot of studies show that when women are on corporate boards, companies do better. My own experience in Congress is when women are on committees and at hearings, the nature of the discussion is different and the outcomes are better—we reach better solutions, better decisions are made. So I really want to create a nationwide call to action to get more women engaged both in solving this economic crisis and entering political life and being heard on political issues.

So it's very much like the Rosie the Riveter campaign was during World War II. During that campaign, the problem was men were fighting the war and the war industries needed workers. And women rarely worked outside the home, so they had to have a call to action. So Rosie the Riveter was born and her sleeves are rolled up, she's got a kerchief on—the slogan was "We can do it!" My grandmother was a riveter, my great-aunt, my great-grandmother was a riveter—and they literally went to the arsenal and worked during World War II to make a difference and to help, to help the country.

So I feel like we need Rosie the Riveter of our generation. That campaign alone brought two million women into the work force within fourteen months, and by the end of the war, six million. So if we can have a similar call to action, to say, "Women, we need you to be advocates, to be heard on the issues you care about, to be voting, to be running for office, to be part of decision making." And on the economic side, if we are going to out-innovate, out-compete, and out-educate other countries, our competitors, we are only going to succeed if women are leading the way. And that's largely because women are now graduating with more than 50 percent of advanced degrees, more than 50 percent of college degrees, and women-owned and minority-owned businesses are the fastest growing sector within small businesses. So if we can address things like equal pay—women are earning 77 cents on the dollar—if we had equal pay in this country, you could raise the GDP by up to 9 percent. Because women-owned businesses are so fast growing, if they had the same access to capital—women start businesses with eight times less capital than men—we would see greater economic growth. With women's participation in the economy, in economic and political decision-making, we would have a better result. And we frankly just need women right now to be part of these decisions.

MS: One of the things that often happens is that these efforts to boost women's representation are wrongly misinterpreted as being somehow anti-male, which of course they aren't. Keeping that in mind, what qualities do you think women can bring to leadership that are most needed in the world right now?

KG: Well, I think a woman's perspective often will complement a male's perspective. In fact, oftentimes we see the problem differently, we see the solution differently, and so by bringing that perspective to the table, you will have a more holistic approach. For example, women are often very good listeners, often good consensus-builders, often able to compromise and reach across party lines in Congress, able to forge deals and reach better solutions. So I think by nature we are very good at consensus-building, but we also often seek political office for different reasons. Many women come to political life because they want to solve problems or address a certain issue that they care deeply about—less often are they coming to Washington for power of self-aggrandizement.

MS: Women today are faced with many challenges of balancing work and family, something I know you can relate to and frequently talk about.

Oftentimes as women, we think we need to hide the truth of our personal realities. Do you think we need to be talking more about those issues and challenges to inform policy and create change?

KG: We've had these women's economic empowerment roundtables all across the state—we had one in Syracuse, Rochester, Buffalo, New York City. But some of the feedback we got through those conferences is that there are some impediments for women entering the work force; for example, affordable daycare, good quality early childhood education. Mothers in particular often want to enter the work force, but don't have the childcare or the support they need to do so. So making sure employers know that when they provide childcare services, or when they make it easier for parents to work, they are increasing access to very good workers and to who's available for the work force. That it's a very pro-economy issue if you can provide affordable daycare. A lot of studies show that if you do that, if you provide it on site or make it accessible, that actually a lot of parents are more productive workers as a result. So there is a lot of upside to it. I have a number of pieces of legislation to address that problem, both on the affordability side and tax credit legislation, to double the tax credit for early childhood education. But then I also have a number of incentives for businesses and employers to create opportunities for on-site daycare or easily accessible daycare.

MS: When you said we needed a call to action, it does feel like we are at an important cusp of history and that the need for change is urgent.

KG: It is urgent—I mean, this is one of the toughest economic crises we have been in, certainly in my lifetime, and I believe if we are going to grow our economy and really create a competitive environment against other nations, we need women as part of that effort. We need women leading the way. I really think that until women are able to achieve their potential, America will not achieve hers.

MS: I recently interviewed Nancy Pelosi who, as the first female speaker of the House, also had a very interesting perspective on the hurdles that women face entering politics. When she was talking about it, she didn't call it a glass ceiling. She called it a "marble ceiling."

KG: Yeah, there are a lot of marbles in Washington [*laughs*].

MS: Entering the political arena can seem very intimidating—not just the extreme effort of running for office, but also oftentimes being one of very few women in the room. What advice or perspective can you offer on that?

KG: Well, I think the most important message for women is that they can do it. That this is something they can do. That you can find a way to balance a career and family— that there is a way that you can be part of the decision-making fabric of this country and still be a good mother. For a lot of women, that's the challenge: "Can I do both? Is it the right time in my family's life to take on these challenges?" And my call to action is very comprehensive. Do whatever you can do; it's a question of: Are you voting? Are you being heard? Are there issues that you care about that you could advocate for and let your representatives know how important they are to you? Would you ever consider running for office? Really making that request of women's participation across the board.

Many organizations have done studies, and one thing they've found is that women really need to be asked to participate, that they respond very well when they're asked to run for office. The studies also show that when women do run, they win—they do have the ability, they do have the tenacity, they do have the drive, they can raise the funds. So I think we need a call to action. We need to actually invite women to come to the table, both in corporate America and in political life, because we need their thoughts, views, and guidance on these very important decisions that our country is making.

MS: How does Off the Sidelines work in terms of helping arm women with the resources, tools, or inspiration that they need? How can they use this project in their lives?

KG: Well, right now it raises awareness. It actually [provides] the information about these structural problems in society that are impediments for women. A lot of young women, for example, don't know that on average a woman earns 77 cents on the dollar for the same work. They may not know that women start their small businesses with eight times less capital than men do. They may not realize that women only sit on 16 percent of Fortune 500 boards and make up only 4 percent of CEOs. And I think once you create that awareness of the challenge ahead of us and amplify that with the call to action to get involved, what my website does is allow them to get where they need to go. So, for example, we have links to how to vote if you are not registered, links to how to run for office, to some great campaign training programs around the country. It has links to if you want to pick candidates and support them, how to get involved in advocacy. We are trying to create a one-stop shop for empowerment, so that once you understand the issues and what the challenges are, you can go to make a difference.

MS: I saw on your site that you said, "getting off the sidelines is a state of mind." How would you describe that state of mind?

KG: It's basically an understanding that women's voices matter. That through our own advocacy, through our own participation, the country will be better off. And that the decisions that we will make in government and in companies will be better decisions because of women's participation.

MS: Where do your own passion and commitment come from? You need to have drive to do all that you do. What is your motivating force?

KG: Well, it's very born and bred in me. My grandmother really inspired me as a young girl—these were all things she taught me. She was a woman who came from very modest means, never went to college and was a secretary in the Albany State Legislature. She wanted to have a say in local political life on the issues that were being debated, and what priorities the people who represented her had. So what she did was she organized other women and she got them engaged and involved and working on campaigns with candidates that they valued. And she made a huge impact on the political landscape throughout her lifetime. Her passion for making sure women were heard and fighting for issues she cared about, and using the grassroots tools to amplify her voice, was very important to me. So I have great respect for public service; I also understand how important women's voices are and that they can make the difference. So throughout my whole life I have been involved in a lot of women's organizations that empower women; that do campaign training for women; that raise money for women. I think it's important that women are part of our decision-making in this country.

Now, the other thing that the [Off the Sidelines] website does that I think is important—you know, I had a significant role model in my life, my grandmother. And I also had many role models that inspired me like Hillary Clinton and other women who achieved great things in their lives.

What the website does is offer stories. And they are just stories from regular women about what got them off the sidelines, why they care about an issue, and what they're going to do about it. I am hoping that those stories will inspire other women, because oftentimes women need to see other women doing things as a guide or as a role model.

MS: So much of this is rooted in women knowing their power and valuing their true voice, something we often lose touch with early on. If you could go back and give one piece of advice to your younger woman and girl self, what would it be?

KG: To do public service. I think that when young people are asked to help others—through community activity, through cleaning up the neighborhood, through helping at a senior center, through being a candy striper at a local hospital—that opportunity to serve when you are young really creates a heart of service in people. And they understand how important advocacy is, and how important service is. So if I were to give my young self advice, I would encourage myself to do even more public service and community service.

MS: These days when people look at the world, it can feel very overwhelming, and it's very easy to feel disempowered as if there's nothing you can personally do that can make a difference. What encouragement, advice or inspiration would you offer to them?

KG: Well, one thing my grandmother always told me is that I could do anything I wanted as long as I didn't give up and just worked hard at it every day. There is nothing that you cannot do if you put your mind to it and really fight hard.

★ ★

WHEN YOU EMPOWER A GIRL

★ ★

It's not just rhetoric, it is a fact, that when you change a girl's life you affect her vision of herself and her immediate world and the world that she will have an impact on. . . . Statistics have shown that when you empower a girl, you don't just change that one girl's life, you change the whole family.

—Oprah Winfrey

Everyone is essentially brought up not to be a girl, right? I think from the time all of us—women, men, boys, and girls—are born, we're taught that the worst thing you can be is a girl. That to be a leader you should never be a "girl." To be a man, you should not be a "girl." To be a woman, you can't be a "girl." So it must be pretty powerful to be a girl if everyone's taught not to be one. What is it about being a girl that everyone's so scared of? I think everybody has a girl inside them—men and women have the qualities of intensity, emotion, wit, compassion, revolutionary zeal, originality, and heart. Some people have more girl, some people have less girl, but all of us have been taught to shut our girl down. If you look at girls themselves around the world, they are such a potent force for change and good—for questioning, for disrupting, and for resisting—and yet they are under siege in so many places. Everywhere. Whether they're being told that they should starve themselves to please the fashion setters, or whether they're being told to cover up or shut themselves down.

The more girls feel confident in themselves, the more they are able to express who they really are. I think we have to find situations where girls find their own voices. We have to help girls find activities that fulfill their deepest selves. If you live in a society that tells you your whole point is to be pretty and skinny, then you'll spend your days working to achieve that. But if you're brought up in a world that tells you that your point is to make the world better and to contribute and to transform consciousness, then you will go and work on achieving that.

—Eve Ensler

I'm raising two girls, and I say to them, "I need you to be strong and soft. You can be smart and beautiful. You can dress well and be a woman. You can be feminine! You can be all of these things, and even though you may think they sound contradictory, they're not." I think that's a really good thing we can teach young girls—that if you're twenty pounds overweight, you're not dumb, you're not not beautiful, you're not not strong. And the more we give each other examples of that, the more honest we are with each other, the little bit easier it is to use your voice and step out.

—MARIA SHRIVER

Girls and women face many challenges in achieving equality with men and boys. In education, access to justice, property rights, health services, politics, business—in almost every aspect of life, women are treated differently and often worse than men, and girls are often given fewer opportunities than boys.

As Elders [a group of global leaders who work together for peace and human rights], we are fully committed to the principle that all human beings are of equal worth. We highlight equality for girls and women, not just women's rights. That is important, as girls, especially adolescent girls, have been almost invisible in debates on equal rights. Yet it is in adolescence that events can have a huge effect on a girl's life.

—MARY ROBINSON, FIRST FEMALE PRESIDENT OF IRELAND

Girls—and this is proven time and time again—they do what they see, not what they're told . . . The more that you can expose them to examples of people doing—especially women, but equally expose them to men who are taking on child rearing and men who are leaving work at five o'clock and women who are doing the things that sort of defy stereotypes—then that exposure is going to become so valuable.

—AMY RICHARDS, AUTHOR, COFOUNDER OF
THIRD WAVE FOUNDATION

ELIZABETH LESSER

"It is not just getting a vagina in the White House; it's everyone, men and women, looking really deeply at our values—leadership values, at least, and social organizing-principle values—which came from the fact that only men were in the halls of power when the laws were being written, when the values were being determined. So it's not as easy as just getting a woman in the White House; it's also hoping and working to make sure that that woman, or the next woman, or the women she brings along with her, are also talking about our social values."

ELIZABETH LESSER IS the cofounder of Omega Institute, the United States' largest lifelong learning center, focusing on health, wellness, spirituality, creativity, and social change. She is the *New York Times* best-selling author of *Broken Open: How Difficult Times Can Help Us Grow* and *The Seeker's Guide: Making Your Life a Spiritual Adventure*. For more than thirty years, Lesser has worked with leading figures in the fields of healing—healing self and healing society. Her work at Omega has included leading the organization, developing its curricula, teaching, and writing the yearly Omega catalog, a reference book that describes the work of some of the most eminent thinkers and practitioners of our times.

For the past ten years, Lesser has spearheaded Omega's popular Women & Power conferences, renowned gatherings featuring women leaders, authors, activists, and artists from around the world. She is the founder of the Women's Leadership Center at Omega. In 2008, she helped Oprah Winfrey produce a ten-week online seminar based on Eckhart Tolle's book *A New Earth*. She is an ongoing host on Oprah's *Soul Series,* a weekly radio show on Sirius/XM.

MARIANNE SCHNALL: Why do you think we have not yet had a woman president?

ELIZABETH LESSER: Well, that's a multilayered question. I think it's embedded in the psychology of women, men, girls, boys, nations, organizations, and schools that what it takes to lead—and what it takes to lead something as important and large as a nation that has an economy and a military—is anathema to what we have told ourselves is appropriate and charming for a woman. It's so deep in our psyche. It's deeper than we know. No matter how liberated we are as individual women and how much work we've put into convincing ourselves of our inherent equality with men, we still don't even believe it ourselves. And how could we? It's embedded in every part of our culture. There's religion; there's art, the greatest authors, the greatest playwrights; there's the hero's journey. Every single mythology and area of human expertise is still, either consciously or unconsciously, pervaded by the idea that it is beautiful for a man to exert his ego, his will, and his leadership, and it is beautiful and charming for a woman to defer, to support, to nurture, and not to push her way and her will.

So, yes, it's amazing and promising that an African American overcame the stereotypes of having a smaller brain and all of the terrible, untrue things we've told each other about racial differences. It doesn't surprise me that that one fell before the stereotype of a woman not being a natural leader fell, because I think that's even more deeply in our subconscious. And from the very first myths and creation story—every creation story, or let's say most of the creation myths that still infuse our psyches: Christian, Jewish, Muslim, the Asian religions'—the creation stories still have man being created first and primary, and woman being, I would think, from an afterthought to an evil addition to the story. So that is my long, rambling answer.

MS: Given everything that you just said, are you feeling like we're moving in a direction where our consciousness, men's and women's, is ready to see a day when a woman will be president? Do you think you will see a woman president in your lifetime? And what will it take?

EL: It depends on how long I live [*laughs*]. The answer is yes. I am incredibly hopeful and, if not in my lifetime, soon we will see a woman president, so I do think we're ready. I do think these things happen, the way it did with Obama, in surprising moments. It is like, are we ready? Maybe. And then, all of a sudden, it happens because of a perfect storm of a particular person and a particular time. So absolutely this will happen, and that will be impressive and a time for celebration, but I will not rest. It will not be a time to say, "Whew, we made it. On to the next." It will be the very first of a continuing work in progress of women and men being seen as equally valid for leadership. And by that I mean it is not just getting a vagina in the White House; it's everyone, men and women, looking really deeply at our values—leadership values, at least, and social organizing-principle values— which came from the fact that only men were in the halls of power when the laws were being written, when the values were being determined. So it's not as easy as just getting a woman in the White House; it's also hoping and working to make sure that that woman, or the next woman, or the women she brings along with her, are also talking about our social values.

MS: Something I know you have explored through the Omega Women & Power conferences is this whole notion of changing the current paradigm of power. What is your vision of how that needs to change?

EL: It's been so interesting, the language that's caught on, this "lean in" from Sheryl Sandberg. It's fabulous. I love the metaphor of it, and I'm so pleased that her book is doing so well, but a glaring omission from the whole concept of leaning in is, what are we leaning in *to*? Why would I want to lean in so deeply, with so much fervor and time, to something that is at the root of so many of our problems? Why do I want to lean in to a workweek that is so crushing to family? Why should I encourage young women to lean in to a corporate structure where there's no maternity leave to speak of, no paternity leave to speak of? I am not just interested in women being paid as much as men; I'm also interested in [what they're being] paid for. What are we doing this for? If it's just to be equal in a system that is sort of akin to the Titanic, I don't want to lean in to the Titanic. I want to get the hell out of the Titanic and lean in to something of my own creation and encourage other people to lean out and rebuild. So that's the revolutionary in me. I realize that it's also critical that we lean in to the institutions we already have and make change from within. I'm not just throwing this whole message out, but I'm asking that as we lean in, we also try to create more humane structures that honor other aspects of life than money and power, and that we create systems that support the beauty of families and the Earth.

MS: I 100 percent agree with you on that, and I think there's a catch-22. On the one hand, in order to get into some of these positions of influence—to even make those changes and get more women in politics—Washington right now is such a dysfunctional place, and running for office is such a nightmarish, corrupt experience, that it's hard to convince people who may have those sensibilities to want to go through that machine. And yet it's the machine that's running things right now, so even to transform it . . .

EL: It's a real catch-22. And all of us will have our different roles, and they'll all be really important. That's why I'm not on the "let's trash Sheryl's message" [bandwagon], because there are some people who just point-blank are saying, "I'm not interested in leaning in to corporate America." I'm not being as revolutionary as that, but I do think that you can lean in and out at the same time. As Carla [Goldstein, cofounder of Omega Women's Leadership Center] was saying, "Let's just stand up and poke our head out from the trance of 'equality means getting exactly what men have,' when what men have is something that's taking us all down." You know, I know so many younger men, especially, who have taken seriously this call by their women to be more involved with their family, and they're finding it now just as impossible to stay within structures that don't really allow you to have a family. So I honor the people who are staying within the system and trying to make change from within, and sometimes that does require you to just fight like hell in the old style, just to get in there. But what usually happens, and we have history to teach us this, is that once you get in . . . you know, [it's like] Nietzsche says: "Be careful, when fighting monsters, you don't become one."

MS: When I interviewed Anita Hill, she said something about how she was concerned that women—because one of the things that may hold back our perception of having a woman in the White House is this notion that maybe she wouldn't be tough enough to deal with a military situation or war—might be more inclined to prove their toughness if they do get to that position, which I found actually interesting and a little bit concerning.

EL: Margaret Thatcher . . . that's the whole notion there that the first line of women presidents and women leaders will have to prove themselves and overprove themselves, and hopefully they'll get in and allow the next group of women to be a little more aligned with their true values, and the next. That may be true, but it will only be true if we constantly remind ourselves that this system we are trying like hell to get into was not created by us. And if you get these awful, sick feelings in your stomach about what it is you're perpetuating, pay attention to them. Listen to them. Don't let what happened to men happen to us, where it turns into heart attacks and it turns into a soul-crushing experience, where you emerge forty years later and you think, *Whoa, that was my life?* So we have the benefit of being strangers in a strange land, and strangers to a system are often the ones who feel the inhumanity of it the most. And so it behooves us to stay strange [*laughs*] and not to go all the way in so that we can't report back to the powers that be and say, "Guess what? We're here, and we're going to change it also." And that's why they don't want us in there, by the way. A strong woman is dangerous! A strong woman who stays attentive to her body, her feelings, her heart, is going to make real problems for the status quo.

MS: It feels like that's part of the catch-22 that women have, even the conversation that's coming up with Sheryl's book and the likability factor. If women are perceived as too soft or too emotional, they're penalized, but if they seem to be ambitious or strong, they take a likability hit. It does seem like you can't win whichever way you go.

EL: The only way you can win—and we can win and we are winning and we will win—is if . . . first of all, we want everyone to win, because this isn't about men losing and women winning. But the real way we can win is, as we do this leaning in and gaining our voice and toughening our aggression muscles, all of this is really important, but at the same time, we also have to try to keep our hearts open, our femaleness, and whether it's by nature or nurture doesn't even really matter anymore. Females do tend to be more attentive to others, with a more nurturing spirit, a longer view of what's helpful to multiple generations down the line. We have to stay attentive to those values that we have honed over millennia by being keepers of the family and keepers of the heart, so we can become more aggressive, more strategic, less concerned about whether people like us . . . and at the same time, we can stay centered in our feeling function, be proud to be emotional creatures, and hone the multi-intelligence that lives in every human being: intelligence of the heart, intelligence of the body, of the spirit—not just these mechanistic intelligences of rationality. We can lean in, lean out, and stand up, all at the same time.

MS: There was a recent article in *The New York Times* about women holding more power in the Senate, saying that having more women in the Senate is affecting the "tenor" of the climate there. There was this quote from this Republican senator, Rob Portman. He said of women in Washington, "I don't want to generalize, because this isn't true of all of them, but they tend to be interested in finding common ground, so I think it's going to have and is having a positive impact on the Senate." Beyond basic equality and fairness, why is it important to have more women represented or to have a woman president? Steering away from making big generalizations, what do you think women would bring to leadership?

EL: Well, it is generalizations, because obviously there are great differences among all groups, but some generalizations have actually been mapped now, especially in the corporate world. There are so many studies done about how there is a women's way of leadership that's different from men's. Again, I just want to reiterate, some men are more female-like in their leadership, and some women are more male-like, so it's not everyone, but you can generalize to say that women tend to be more inclusive, they tend to listen better, they tend to bring people to consensus, and they also tend to think outside of the box of priorities, because they've been strangers in the strange land, so they're not as acclimated to the priorities that have already been set. So they're not so much on autopilot. They tend to—and this is the same in corporate America as well—ask why. "Why have we been doing it like this the whole time?" And, "We do it a different way." They question the way things have always been done, because they haven't been doing them. And this is the same for all minorities. It's uncomfortable, but it's a good idea to get new thinking in. And women, whether we like it or not . . . [over] thousands of years—it doesn't matter if it's nature or nurture—have been trained to nurture the family. We're very intelligent people, like men, and our domain has been the family or elementary school, and we have learned deeply what it takes to care for other people. This has been our domain. Fortunately, we're being allowed now to be in many domains, but we have a collective wisdom in an area that is the most needed now. How do we care for each other? How do we care for our home, the Earth? We know something about this, because we've been doing it.

MS: All these studies say that in addition to the structural obstacles that are there, there may also be self-imposed obstacles that hold women back from wanting to run for office, or even negotiating for a raise or just generally advocating for themselves. Do you think that there are psychological factors that are holding women back from valuing their voice enough to want to pursue leadership positions?

EL: Absolutely, 100 percent yes. I could not agree more with Sheryl that [part of this] potent brew of social conditioning is that it's good to be demure, and that makes women second-guess their ability to raise their hand and say, "My way! Let's do it my way." So we've been conditioned that way, and some of that is deeply standing in our way, and we must work on it in order to get into positions of power. On the other hand, some of what keeps us from barging through obstacles is actually a great strength that this society does not honor. It's the value women have, which is: listen to other people, ask for directions, be vulnerable within relationships—meaning, bare your soul, tell your truth, admit your weakness. These are good qualities. I would hate to think that in our race to the top we would let go of some of our most stellar qualities, the very qualities that a new leader needs. This is our big challenge now: to be strong, resolute, not concerned if we're not liked, able to ask for what we want, able to believe that "I know as much as he knows" . . . I don't know if you've ever watched Brené Brown's TED talk, the most-watched TED talk. Now, TED is a bastion of masculine thinking, and TED values the brilliance of the mind and technology, but of all the talks that ever were on TED, it's this woman talking about the power of vulnerability. It's gotten something like nine or ten million hits. Something in the culture all over the world now knows that there is great power in being vulnerable in relationships, not being dominating, baring your weakness, saying, "I don't know, I am wrong, I am sorry." These are not very well-honed traits in the males of our species, and it is what we need, and women need to teach it, and it's a huge dilemma. How do we remain vulnerable as we race to the top? I don't have the answer, but I know it can be done—as long as we keep saying that it's important.

MS: With the launch and development of the Omega Women's Leadership Center, and also previously, through the conferences, you've been immersed in many of these themes. What have you learned about how to cultivate woman leaders and the whole notion of leadership? What stands out to you as being interesting or surprising or important?

EL: Well, it always surprises me the hunger women have. You can almost hear a collective sigh and collective shoulders dropping down from ears and a relaxation when you say things like, "Do you think your workweek is way too long and each day extends too long, so that this battle you're in every day is, how do I balance children and home with work?" It shocks me that these conversations aren't happening more, but it also touches me that there's a great hunger for something other than just power for power's sake, money for money's sake. Women seem right away to light up and say, "Oh my God, we've got to talk about this. This isn't being talked about. What do we want to create with our power?" And also, [there's] this kind of looking around guiltily, like, *Am I allowed to talk about this?* Is there really room in any conversation about leadership to talk about my health, my depression, my fears, my children, my marriage? Is there room in this conversation? Isn't that getting too personal? Isn't that mixing work and home life? And with the tiniest bit of encouragement—like, no, it's appropriate. It's valid. We've got to lead in this area. We've got to talk about childcare, maternity and paternity leave, shared jobs, priorities for governments. We've got to talk about this. We can't only talk about equal pay and gender parity in heads of corporations. We've got to talk about the why—there's a hunger in women if you get them alone in a room and give them props.

MS: From an evolutionary perspective, looking at where humanity is on a spiritual level with what's happening in the world and the paradigms that are changing, are you feeling optimistic, not just regarding women, but in general? Obviously, we are facing serious problems with the condition of the Earth, and with war and violence around the world, yet lately I do feel a little bit of a shift, a little bit of a rising of consciousness. Do you feel hopeful?

EL: I live and breathe in hope. I am just a lover of life and humans, and I think it's all a mysterious and glorious dance, even when it's really hard. But I don't presume to know what God really has in store for us. I think our modes of perception—our brains, our senses—they're very tiny and puny and inadequate to really know what's going on. So I try not to get myself all worked up and even ask that question. I feel like if I can stay full of joy and love and service and do it out of a sense of love and not out of a sense of fear and panic and hatred . . . if I can just stay faithful, then I think my work will be better. So if you ask, am I hopeful? Are we evolving? To be honest, I would have to say I don't know, but I think so, and I choose so. I choose to know that in my heart of hearts.

Well, we haven't had a woman president because we, women, have had to completely change the world in order to make a woman president happen. Since Abigail Adams asked John to "remember the ladies" in the United States Constitution and he mocked her—and women were not mentioned in the Constitution of the United States—we have been on a long, slow, and sometimes meandering but constant path toward greater equality and our fair share of the table. And now I passionately believe it's women's moment to achieve equality and our fair share of the table. But we have to do it. The people who are in power, who are mostly men, have no reason to step aside for us. We have everything we need now, but it's up to us to take that next step.

—GLORIA FELDT, AUTHOR AND FORMER PRESIDENT OF
  PLANNED PARENTHOOD

I think that we haven't had a woman president because I don't think that the vast majority of people trust women in conventional forms of leadership. I don't think that people want women telling them what to do. And, unfortunately, that's the role of what a president does, either symbolically or actually. I think that people don't want that because they resist it, and I think people don't want that because they fear it. They fear for the woman herself and they fear for themselves—that our country won't be as protected with a woman guiding it as they are with a man. And those are very outdated notions of protection and security, but I think that they are deeply embedded in many people.

—AMY RICHARDS, AUTHOR, COFOUNDER OF THIRD WAVE
  FOUNDATION

One of the reasons that we don't have a woman president is that we haven't had enough women in the pipeline. We haven't had enough women governors, we haven't had enough women mayors of major cities. And the second reason we haven't had a woman president is, it turns out, that it is extremely difficult to get women elected to executive offices; it's related to the purse. It's extremely difficult to get women elected to executive office, period, and the presidency being kind of the ultimate executive office. Then if we look at the two major things that voters think a president is supposed to deal with, war and the economy, those are the two issues that voters tend to have the most concerns about women on. Women candidates are running behind in terms of being perceived as being good on the economy. And it's not reinforced by our broader culture: We don't have that many women CEOs. We don't have that many women in manufacturing highlighted. So if you want jobs, if you want someone to compete in an international trade environment—in some of the ways people think, particularly in a global economy, that to compete internationally is to wage the war of the economy—that's very tough for women to be perceived as strong in that arena. Then the other aspect, of course, is military war. We haven't had that many women generals. We haven't had a women joint chiefs of staff. We haven't had a woman in charge of Iraq or Afghanistan. So in general, the pipeline is very, very thin and the cultural pipeline is very thin. The places that voters would have gotten accustomed to and believe in the leadership of women still remains. These two central areas are still very non-traditional areas for voters.

— CELINDA LAKE, POLLSTER AND DEMOCRATIC POLITICAL
  STRATEGIST

I think it's because in this country we still associate leadership with men. Even the term of the president, and the name of the president as commander in chief, evokes an image for people that is militaristic, that is male. And that was the big question about Hillary Clinton: Could she be the commander in chief? Could she be like a man? And if you're asking could a woman be like a man, then you might as well, in some ways, really have a man [laughs].

— CAROL GILLIGAN, PhD, AUTHOR AND PSYCHOLOGIST

KATHY NAJIMY

"I don't know a girl, a teenager or woman—no matter how smart, how feminist, how educated, how cool, how sequestered in the country, how raised by feminist parents—I don't know one who doesn't have at least three-quarters of her thought process sucked up by how fat or thin she is. So when you have a whole gender, when you have most of the female population, concentrating on something that ultimately means nothing, it usurps the time they might be dreaming of becoming ... perhaps ... the president of the United States. So you have fewer women who are up for it, fewer women armed with what it takes to overcome all this smothering of spirit, and, therefore, fewer female candidates to choose from. Maybe that's why we don't have a woman president."

KATHY NAJIMY IS an award-winning actress, writer, director, speaker, and activist. Her work includes memorable performances in more than twenty-five films and several TV projects, as well as on- and off-Broadway plays. Her films include *Sister Act, Sister Act 2, Hocus Pocus, Hope Floats,* Oscar winner *WALL-E, Soapdish, The Guilt Trip* with Barbra Streisand, *The Wedding Planner, The Fisher King,* and more. Her memorable TV roles include Showtime's *The Big C;* three seasons as Olive on *Veronica's Closet* with Kirstie Alley; CBS's *Numb3rs;* fourteen seasons as Peggy Hill on the Emmy Award–winning Fox hit *King of the*

Hill; Five, directed by Jennifer Aniston; *Desperate Housewives; Chicago Hope;* and more. Kathy starred on Broadway as Mae West in *Dirty Blonde* and won an Outer Critics Best Actress award.

With Mo Gaffney, Najimy starred in and wrote *The Kathy and Mo Show,* her long-running, multiaward-winning, off-Broadway feminist play that won an Obie Award and became two hit HBO specials. In 2005, Kathy was named Woman of the Year by *Ms. Magazine.* For her thirty-plus years of AIDS activism, she has been honored with the L.A. Shanti Founder Award, as well as the L.A. Gay & Lesbian Center's Distinguished Achievement. She is an enthusiastic supporter of women's and girls' rights, AIDS awareness, LGBT rights, animal rights, and reproductive rights. Kathy frequently travels around the country to keynote-speak on these issues.

MARIANNE SCHNALL: Why do you think we've never had a woman president?

KATHY NAJIMY: I think, even with the advances that we've made, which are considerable, there's been a lot of backlash as well. I believe that sexism and misogyny are as alive today in some places as they were twenty years ago. We know women are as smart as, if not smarter than, men, and as capable as, if not more capable than, men, and we actually had a woman running for president who was more qualified than the men running for president. But still, all the knowing doesn't affect the gut sexism that lives within. Across America and the world, there are still men and women who believe that women are second-class citizens, inferior, and that their sole purpose is birthing, mothering, wifing, and maybe . . . kindergarten teaching. It seems we are not ready to hand our beloved country over to someone who we really believe—not instinctually or authentically, but because we've been taught and conditioned to believe it—is not as qualified simply because she is a woman.

MS: Are you feeling hopeful? Do you foresee a woman president in your lifetime?

KN: Yes. In my opinion, I think Hillary Clinton is, at this moment in time, the most qualified person for president. She spent eight years in the White House, not just planning tea parties but affecting change and legislation and traveling the world, building foreign relations—accumulating experience. And for those reasons, I think she is supremely qualified to run this country. One of the only things keeping her out of the White House is our shared agreement that we will care more about her hairstyle and her pantsuit than we do about her experience, intelligence, and how fiercely qualified she is. I can't think of anybody who would be better for the position. But I also would not be surprised if the wave of fear washes over our country and she never gets the chance.

MS: I remember interviewing Sheryl Sandberg, and she was talking about the likability hit and the backlash that powerful women often experience—about how women who are openly ambitious or confident are often perceived as unattractive and unlikable, and how one deals with that conundrum in terms of a very intrinsic problem. I'm not sure what the simple answer to that is, other than seeing more women leaders and becoming comfortable with that.

KN: Well, wanting to have a likable president is human nature. I think if somebody got up there and they reflected all of my personal values but they seemed like the most unlikable person ever, I think I might be hesitant, because it's human nature. We gravitate toward things we like. So, man or woman, I don't think unlikable is going to be voted president. However, we know the reasons that Hillary Clinton is called unlikable are not issues of personality. She's actually hilarious—hilarious, smart, kind, fierce, committed, charming, perceptive, gracious, and a wonderful, supremely intelligent person. It's the sexist misconception of what she must really be like to have gotten where she is, and what she must be like to want to be—God forbid—a woman who runs America. Ambition and focus in women scare men, and I think they scare women. Perhaps because she is showing us full potential, and sometimes, someone living their full potential is threatening to folks; it brings up their own insecurities regarding lack of drive and ambition. We're taught from birth that an assertive, driven woman—a strong, successful, powerful woman—is somehow unattractive, unlikable.

It's why I have such a problem with the word "bitch." The reason I flinch when I hear the word bitch is because it is not usually about a woman who happened to be mean that day or said something wrong or hurt someone's feelings. It usually implicates an entire gender, and, in my experience, it's generally used sweepingly toward women who are successful, fierce, strong, in control, educated, who know what they want, thrive, and make no apologies for what they do well. So when someone says Oprah or Bella Abzug or Barbra Streisand or Hillary Clinton or Gloria Steinem is a bitch—what do all these women have in common? Their greatness! They're great, and they've grasped their birthright to be fully all they can be. So, to me, you're not just saying bitch when someone is mean or was nasty to you that day. You're saying, "You have no right to be who you are meant to be—to achieve, to fulfill your destiny gloriously."

MS: Do you feel like things are improving, from your vantage point? Where is the entry for change? Does the media have a role in this? Is it the way that girls or women are portrayed?

KN: I think it's a perfect storm of sexism and misogyny. It's girls being taught at every turn that their looks are their value. The first thing people say to a girl is a comment about her appearance—what she's wearing and how she looks. Honestly, there is nothing wrong with compliments or looking good. I like to look nice and wear fun clothes. I compliment people on their shirt or shiny hair. I think, *Good for you!* Shiny hair and nice earrings! I'm not against women or men looking great. But it becomes a problem when the praise of girls is almost exclusively directed at their appearance, their bodies, and their makeup, when it seems to be the only value we put on them. When the first and only praise directed at my daughter (since she was a toddler!) was, "You are so pretty!" how can that help but stick as being the most valuable thing about you? I always try to add with a smile, "And smart!" We learn from birth that prettiness, thinness, and being attractive to boys are the prize, the golden ring, the purpose and value of our life. And from that comes insecurity, addictions, eating disorders, and a warped disregard for all else women and girls have to offer.

So the low self-esteem, the track to failure and settling, spans all the way from objectification to more obvious marginalization. How girls get treated in class, how they are encouraged or not encouraged, the lack of opportunities they get in school from kindergarten to college, how their parents treat them, how much sexual and physical abuse they endure, the kinds of jobs they're groomed to be attracted to, the lack of role models and examples that they do or do not have, the kinds of employment they do or do not land—all of these things play a role.

The key to success and fulfillment is self-esteem—self-esteem, confidence, and a healthy body image. I don't know a girl, a teenager or woman—no matter how smart, how feminist, how educated, how cool, how sequestered in the country, how raised by feminist parents—I don't know one who doesn't have at least three-quarters of her thought process sucked up by how fat or thin she is. So when you have a whole gender, when you have most of the female population, concentrating on something that ultimately means nothing, it usurps the time they might be dreaming of becoming . . . perhaps . . . the president of the United States. So you have fewer women who are up for it, fewer women armed with what it takes to overcome all this smothering of spirit, and, therefore, fewer female candidates to choose from. Maybe that's why we don't have a woman president.

And the media? Unbelievable! Where do I start? Let's talk about Michelle Obama in the media. If I hear one more fucking thing about a goddamn short-sleeved dress, I might crack! The constant headline in the news about this amazing woman is her sleeves? How refreshing it might be to maybe have just 1 percent of the media focus on the programs she's dedicated to, the important change she's trying to implement, the causes she has championed and worked hard for. How about we see as much of that put into print as we do pages and pages about who made her damn dress?

Are the media partly culpable for their portrayal of women and its effect on girls' and women's low self-esteem and therefore lack of success? I say yes. From salacious music videos to pornographic billboards solidifying that your value is your sex; to one-dimensional, diminishing roles for women; to body and appearance scrutiny; to lack of scope and truth in portraying women's history; to magazines, newspapers, news shows, and TV shows that demean, insult, and exclude women; to music that promotes violence and abuse against women as hip and relevant; to the lack of adventurous, intelligent, and proud girl characters in our children's TV programming; to oppressive stories in animated films and fairy-tale books; to the consistent message that the goal is being desired and swept away by the prince; to the notion that the golden ring (literally) is finding someone to marry and support physically and emotionally so that then your husband can thrive and therefore take care of you. What you are left with is a bunch of capable and fierce but unencouraged—or excluded, misguided, and marginalized—girls and women.

So, what's the reason there aren't more women in high-achievement jobs, as well as in the political arena? Well, it's because of everything. Has it progressed? Yes, of course. Look, Hillary Clinton was running for president. There are more women CEOs, [more women] serving in public office, as well as more women making the choice to mother. We passed Title IX. All of these things are steps forward. But it's important to get a clear view of where we were, where we still are, and why.

I have a sixteen-year-old daughter, which makes all of this triply important for me. So important. So profound and scary. As I near midlife, thinking about Samia and her generation and her kids' generation and you and your daughters, Marianne, I am heartened. And progress is apparent in the fact that there are more women in the House and Senate than ever in history, because of the women's movement and millions of women all over the world. Women like Susan B. Anthony, Rosa Parks, Margaret Sanger, Sojourner Truth, Elizabeth Cady Stanton, Gloria Steinem, Bella Abzug, Marie Wilson, Eve Ensler, you, Rosario Dawson, Sandra Fluke, Lena Dunham, Naomi Wolf, Glenn Close, Jane Fonda, Madeleine Albright, Nancy Pelosi—and the scores of women here and all over the world still with us and not, encouraging us to live in our rightful power. Yes, it *is* getting better. It is getting better, and at the same time, honestly, it is so glaringly obvious why there already *isn't* a woman president that you could just stick your finger out and touch it.

MS: How do you feel, being in the entertainment industry, in terms of the role that the entertainment industry and media play in how women and girls are portrayed, and how that affects the consciousness of not just girls, but also the boys who maybe see them that way?

KN: I say it all the time: We aren't all just born sexist, racist, and homophobic. It is taught, and it is taught in so many different arenas and in so many ways—and a lot of it, especially now, is from the Internet. My daughter talks about boys' ideas of how girls look because of the porn they see on the Internet, and so many girls are obsessed with comparing themselves and how they look. Self-harm and eating disorders are rampant. One out of every six eleven-year-old girls is on a diet or has body issues. Girls are pressured to shave and pluck and obsess and wear clothes that maybe aren't authentic to their taste . . . because of easily accessible pornographic images in the media and on the Internet. And by porn, I don't mean erotica meant for adults. I don't even mean strictly *porn* porn, because porn can be a car commercial, an ice cream commercial, or a poster ad for jeans. It's all porn. We get assaulted every single day by billboards, magazines, television shows, and films telling us there is one way to be. And usually the quest to conform takes up our time and, all too often, our lives.

It's complicated, because I believe in sexy. I believe in freedom to love yourself and your body—to celebrate sexuality and wear makeup, hair, and clothes you choose to wear. There is freedom and fun in the creativity. What scares me is the driving force in girls' wanting to look one unattainable, acceptable way. That's what I'm looking at. What is the force, the fire, that's propelling them to act or dress like that, and what is the force that is creating in boys the want for all girls to look like the fictitious "women" in porn? Turn on a video game—it's rare to find a popular boys' video game where there's not a girl in a torn-up bikini being shot at. There's one popular video game out currently where you get extra points if you kill the prostitute. You'll likely find unapologetic rape. (Fun! Rape in video games! One hundred points!) Who's surprised?

Nobody's surprised that girls aren't achieving all that they are able to achieve. Sexism is real. And when girls are thinking that their biggest value and their worth—what's most important and most valid about them— is how they look, that's what they spend the most time thinking about and doing. And when boys are taught their birthright is taking action and adventure and making things happen and succeeding . . . then that's the road they're going to take. We aren't born with self-doubt, low self-esteem, eating disorders, self-hatred, pleasing, rape, molestation, violence against women—nope, we're not born with it. We're spoon-fed it.

In Hollywood, it's the same thing. I think the sexism in Hollywood affects women equally, but in a different way. Women all over the world are affected—from punitive, abusive religious traditions that don't allow work or education to someone making seventy cents to a man's dollar to being sexually harassed by a boss. For actors and actresses, there's age-ism, public opinion, and appearance. Weight restriction and conformity is legendary for women in TV, film, and music. Most are pressured (by many means) and forced to try to attain one virtually unattainable size. And in the quest, in the trying, we breed self-hate, eating disorders, addictions, and even death.

And then there is ageism. There's an obvious age ceiling at which certain actresses can get work, usually at around thirty-five or forty. There are a few exceptions: Helen Mirren gets a job, Susan Sarandon might get a job, and Meryl Streep might get a job. But on the whole, I'm talking about out of 100 percent of working female actors, there's probably 10 percent of leading women who get meaningful acting work after forty. The rest don't look right, because they don't look young. So you've got all these mature male actors still working who are playing leading men—and not only leading men with great story lines of triumph and mystery and success, but they are all still sex symbols! As the roles get less and less interesting and available for women after thirty-five, the men keep going, while the women keep getting replaced.

MS: You've obviously been advocating for women's issues for such a long time. Some of this feels like a tough slog, but ultimately, where are we now? Are you feeling frustrated? Are you feeling hopeful?

KN: It's so funny, Marianne, because in the minutiae of it, it seems that we are over our heads in this same kind of trouble and bullshit that we always have seen—when you know the amount of girls and women being battered and molested, when you look at the statistics, when you see what's happening politically and see reproductive rights sliding backward, it feels like we are right in the middle of the sinking, like we always have been. So I don't want to sugarcoat it and say that on all issues I'm feeling optimistic. Some I'm feeling just dreadful about. But at the same time, in a day you go through so many phases of being grateful, worried . . . and then hopeful! I'm so grateful for the steps that we've made going forward. We now have V-Day and One Billion Rising. That's great. That's a huge, crazy, Olympic leap forward—that was amazing! We have Roe v. Wade. We have Eve Ensler and her *Vagina Monologues,* we have Feminist.com, we have you and this book, and we have Gloria Steinem exuding her gloriousness. We have revolutionaries and visionaries in other countries devoted to abolishing rape, female genital mutilation, and other insidious rituals. We have some brilliant films and realistic, positive woman TV shows; women show-runners, directors, and writers . . . and we have the undeniable hope of the possibilities of our strong, smart, wonderful daughters! We celebrate the scores of young girls who are speaking up and creating! The gay rights movement, marriage equality, all the pro-choice and anti–violence against women legislation that's being passed. We have Hillary in the position she's in right now, and we have more women in Congress and the House than ever. Yes, there's a really great "moving forward" that I'm so happy for I could cry, and I am heartened and grateful. All of it is wonderful! And at the same time, given the more tactile, day-to-day, minute-by-minute reality that every three minutes a woman will be raped—some days I feel like I want to rip off my skin and jump. Because I know how hard it is to fight for one inch of freedom and choice. My heart breaks because of what's still happening to women and girls all over the world . . . every three minutes.

MS: You have always been such a bold, fearless personality—speaking out whether it's in your art or in your activism. Was that something that you always had naturally, or did you have to cultivate it in yourself?

KN: I think it occurred to me, finally, that the people I was trying to please and the results of being inauthentic and playing small weren't ultimately fulfilling. . . I'm kind and fair, and I believe in justice and fairness within an inch of my being, but the nice, pleasing part is just boring to me. And it's a waste of time. I feel like you can be kind, just, and fair without having to worry about if every single person likes you. You come to a point in life where you just go, "It's none of my business what people think of me. It's my business how I act, and am I acting in a way that I respect? Am I living in my skin? Am I as afraid to be as strong as I am to be liked?" Life is too short. Plus, I have a daughter. I want to mirror strength and goodness. You have to be willing to let go of some of the other things to move toward your authentic self.

WHY IS IT IMPORTANT TO HAVE MORE WOMEN'S VOICES REPRESENTED IN WASHINGTON AND OTHER LEADERSHIP POSITIONS?

Well, I think first off, independent of difference, if you're wasting half your talent, if you're not using half of your talent, if you're tying one hand behind your back, then you have a problem. And in today's tough world, where America's really struggling, I think, to maintain its leadership in the world, you cannot afford to waste half your talent. Secondly, I think as a country and a culture we are very strong about equality for women, equality for girls. We can't have true equality for girls if they never see themselves in penultimate leadership positions. And it isn't just a question of not seeing a woman as president. Not seeing a woman as chief of staff in the military. Not seeing a woman as the leading general or leader of any of the major branches of the military. Not seeing a woman governor in their state, ever. Not seeing a woman head of a major company in their state. Not seeing a woman mayor of the major city in their state. This really curtails. This really influences how they see themselves, so it has a profound impact on what girls think is possible for themselves . . . and in what, I think, is the core anchor principle of our culture and our country.

—CELINDA LAKE, POLLSTER AND DEMOCRATIC POLITICAL
   STRATEGIST

I think that the system won't work until there is more equality with women, people of color, and different sexual orientations having positions of power. It's just not going to work. The democracy that we're looking for will not work until everyone is included.

—CAROL JENKINS, MEDIA CONSULTANT, FOUNDING PRESIDENT
   OF WOMEN'S MEDIA CENTER

There are a gillion equity reasons, but I can just tell you from the very narrow perch that I sit on, which is in the arena of women's health, the classic example was the debate over healthcare and whether or not maternity benefits would be covered by health insurance. We have members of the United States Senate arguing against it, because they were never going to need maternity benefits.

It's as fundamental as that. Perhaps the most unique thing about women is that we reproduce. We have children. It is sort of an essential part of humanity [laughs] and yet, when you don't have women in the room making fundamental decisions about women's health and reproduction, then all the joys and challenges that happen once you do have children—childcare and healthcare for kids, and education—it's critical that you have women debating these policies and representing that point-of-view.

—CECILE RICHARDS, PRESIDENT OF PLANNED PARENTHOOD

It's huge. Just in the same way as African Americans rejoiced at there being a person of color in the White House. What does it mean when you see an African American president stepping off of Air Force One, over and over again on television? Slowly our perceptions of who is and should be a leader begins to change.

—RACHEL SIMMONS, AUTHOR, COFOUNDER OF
GIRLS LEADERSHIP INSTITUTE

The stats are showing over and over again in the corporate world that until you have at least 30 percent women on a board or in high level management, the conversation does not change. When you break over that 30 percent point, there is introduction of different ways of thinking about the corporation and in the corporation because there is strength in numbers.

—JODY WILLIAMS, NOBEL PEACE LAUREATE

Oh, it is so important. We are a better nation when the people who represent us are true representatives of who we are. If we have people who represent us who don't share our values or don't share our adventures or our backgrounds and they don't understand us, then we're a poorer nation for it. I think women represent such an important part of our society.

—REPRESENTATIVE ILEANA ROS-LEHTINEN (R)

ELEANOR HOLMES NORTON

"I don't even think of my life in terms of obstacles. You know, the fact that I was born in a city that had no democratic government—I mean, we had no local government, no democracy. Or that I was a black child that went to segregated schools, because the D.C. schools were segregated until the '54 decision. Or that I was a woman. I have never considered any of those things to be obstacles [laughs]. They're the things that give you fight. I just think if you sit down and count the obstacles, you're counting yourself out."

REPRESENTATIVE ELEANOR HOLMES Norton was elected in 1990 and is now in her twelfth term as the representative for the District of Columbia. Named by President Jimmy Carter as the first woman to chair the Equal Employment Opportunity Commission, she came to Congress as a national figure who had been a civil rights and feminist leader. Delegate Norton serves on the House Oversight and Government Reform Committee Subcommittee on Federal Workforce, U.S. Postal Service and the Census, and the Subcommittee on Energy Policy, Health Care and Entitlements. She also serves as the ranking member of the Transportation and Infrastructure Committee Subcommittee on Economic Development, Public Buildings, and Emergency Management, and is on the Subcommittee on Water Resources and Environment and the Subcommittee on Aviation.

MARIANNE SCHNALL: Why do you think we've not, as of yet, had a woman president?

ELEANOR HOLMES NORTON: Many people thought we would have had a woman president who comes from our majority group—there are more women than men in the country—before we had a black president who comes from a minority group. But we didn't. Presidential aspirations are far more linked to the person than to any other factor. For example, while the Republicans have tended to put forward candidates based almost on succession, Democratic presidents have popped out of nowhere. There's no longer a question about whether a woman could be president, because Hillary Clinton's run surely put that to rest. I had thought that the first woman president was likely to be someone from the military who had exceptional leadership experience, because the military gives you leadership responsibility that many people would respect, but I have put that aside. If you asked that question ten years ago, I think you would have answers about all kinds of preparatory things; I no longer think that's the case. Women are here at the top—not in nearly enough numbers—but at the top of business, of politics . . . I think it just takes the right woman to get up and choose to run.

MS: Do you feel like you will see a woman president in your lifetime?

EHN: Surely. I mean, I think the next president should be a woman. I don't see why not. I hope that Hillary Clinton's run has inspired women to understand that you do not need to have had her successive positions in order to run, but you need the kind of track record that will make people vote for you. I think men are prepared to vote for a woman to be president, especially considering the mess men have made of this country.

MS: I feel hopeful about that, too. Do you think that, in terms of being a milestone for women and the world, having a woman in the Oval Office would have the same impact that electing Barack Obama was for African American people? How symbolic do you think it would be to have a woman as president?

EHN: Look, the symbolism of the first black president really is a case unto itself. Here we have a minority group that began as slaves in this country, and then moved to being a hated minority, discriminated against until very recent history. That's a case by itself, so we can't look at women on the same grid. I began to wonder why it took women 150 years or so to get the right to vote. They slept with men who voted, yet most men came out against them having even the vote. When pressed, women know what to do. We saw that in the last election when they thought they might lose contraception and abortion. But when not pressed, women simply do what needs to be done. For example, there's no excuse for women [not to go] into the workforce in about equal numbers of men, or else the standard of living would collapse. There's no excuse for a country of this size and power and economy not to have educational childcare. We don't have any more than we had twenty years ago. But why is that? It's because women have not demanded it. You would think, though, that with the hardships that women endure they would have done so at least on childcare for their kids while they mandatorily go into the workforce. Women also were very quick to get behind a woman to be president. It's just that she had a formidable opponent. Imagine some other opponent, who was not as unusual and attractive. That's why I say this really goes to the moment in time. It goes to the person, and to pull all those together is very difficult. Barack Obama did it. It was not the moment in time, but it was the person. Nobody guessed it. Most people doubted it. Nobody would doubt if we had a half dozen candidates running next time and three of them were women. No one would doubt that the time has come. Certainly if we had three women—women of general appeal, whether Republican or Democrat, I think the country is more than ready.

MS: Just in general, in terms of in Washington, if more women were represented in our government, what changes do you think we would expect to see? This isn't just a question of equality and fairness. Why is this important?

EHN: We better not over-emphasize that, because what tends to happen, if you take some absolutely pure women's issues—let's leave aside the controversial ones like abortion—but take a pure issue like the Paycheck Fairness Act. I was an original co-sponsor of that bill. This is a bill that simply updates the Equal Pay Act, which was the first of the great civil rights acts. It was passed before the 1964 Act and the 1965 Act that of course brought about the civil rights revolution. And it's a bill that would simply update the Equal Pay Act in ways that are not very radical. That bill didn't have a single Republican woman co-sponsor, not a single woman on that side of the aisle to vote for it. I don't think that has always been the case. Even since I've been in Congress, I have seen Republican women who would have embraced that bill. But in a Congress that is as polarized as this one, there is not a dime's worth of difference between Republican men and Republican women. For example, we just passed one of the most popular pieces of legislation, the Violence Against Women Act. There were no Republican women sponsors of that bill. So I'm not going to sit here and tell you that all we need are some women and women will see results. It is important to note, I was amazed to note, the statistics—something like three times as many Democratic women got elected as Republican women. That's just overwhelming. Ask yourself why—because Republican women don't run on women's issues, so why should women go out of their way to vote for them? Women who do vote for them, vote for them on other issues.

MS: That's such an important point. I think it was Gloria Steinem who said to me that it's not about biology, it's about issues.

EHN: If you can't even embrace all-American issues like the Violence Against Women Act and the Equal Pay Act—and by the way the Equal Pay Act is everybody's favorite issue to gather around—if you can't embrace that, then you can't say that no matter what the party, all we need is a woman.

MS: This election was historic in terms of women being represented; however, still only 18 percent of Congress is women. I remember interviewing Nancy Pelosi who called it not just a glass ceiling, but a marble ceiling. In general, do you think there are specific obstacles in the political arena? What can we do to encourage more women into politics?

EHN: I really think there are obstacles. A very young woman who runs better watch out, because if she has children, if she's married—she's really got to have an understanding so that her family life does not crash. Men apparently do that. Women still disproportionately take on the household and the children's responsibilities . . . I know that Blanche Lincoln, who was a colleague of mine in the House, got pregnant, left the House because she learned she was going to have twins, and I'll be darned if she didn't come back, with twins, and become a Senator. That's a terrific role model.

MS: Right now, many women may feel discouraged to pursue politics as a career, also based on some of the cynicism and almost dysfunction they see in government today. What would you say?

EHN: I would say it's a clarion call for women.

MS: Why did you decide to pursue this yourself? What are the rewards of doing this as a career?

EHN: There are some rewards, but to be part of a legislative body, you've got to want to work with other people. You have to want to stand against those—rather strongly against those—who oppose you, then the rewards are small but all the sweeter when something happens that you want to happen. But unlike in real life, there is no reward such as "this is exactly the bill I wanted." It's not going to be your bill and only your bill. And women, I'm told, have a capacity to make compromises . . . that may be just the work for them, being a member of Congress. You have to learn how to fashion a compromise, one that does not forego principles in order to reach agreement. It seems to me that women are pretty good at that. I don't want to attach any of these characteristics to gender, but to the extent that you can, it does seem to me that this is a place ready-made for women.

MS: I remember seeing Diane Sawyer interviewing all of these women in Congress a few months ago, and they were saying that if more women had been in the room during the fiscal cliff conversations, this would have been settled. Do you think that is true?

EHN: No, not entirely. We're far too polarized today for a simple change of the gender of the actors to be all-healing. But, I do note that virtually the only Republicans willing to seek compromise consistently in the last Congress were two women: Susan Collins and Olympia Snowe, who has retired.

MS: What can we do to get more women in Washington? Do you have any sense of what it will take?

EHN: I do think women need to do a better job of pushing other women to run, for high office or for any office. Men are certainly not going to do that. I shouldn't say that, because the fact is that the parties do look for people who can help them win an election. I cannot explain, therefore, why there were so few Republican women even running, relative to Democratic women. Or maybe they were running and just didn't make it through. When you look at this House, the difference is startling, and it seems to me that that's where Republicans have an opportunity. I think somebody's got to take that opportunity, or else we're not going to break these stalemates.

MS: Not only are women obviously a minority in Washington, but black women are even more so. Do you think diversity in general is improving?

EHN: Of course it is. For example, a third of the black caucus is women, and if a third of the Congress were women, we'd be a whole lot better off. Women who want to lead the Congressional Black Caucus don't have any problem. It may be a tradition of greater equality because you couldn't do anything else. Greater equality because everybody must work—whether you were working in the fields, as slaves, or whether women worked in other women's homes, they worked. That's such a strong tradition of both women and men working in the black community that they bring that tradition with them to Congress.

MS: Today there's been this move, especially for younger feminists, toward this concept of intersectionality in feminism—that it's now about the greater diversity, the intersections of class and gender and sexuality, and all of these classifications that society uses to divide us. It's about the need for greater diversity, so that even having Barack Obama in office is a good, positive step toward getting a woman president there because it is about moving away from the non-diversity that we've seen. Do you think you're seeing more of that?

EHN: That's true. Hispanics supported Barack Obama because he's for affordable healthcare, but I'm sure they recognize fully that this will ease the way for other people of color to become president. It makes no sense for them not to support him if he supported their issues. But women, on diversity, the problem with that is the whole society is so compartmental- ized, whether it's on TV or . . . even Twitter and Facebook tend to line people up with their close friends. And that's terrific, but your friends tend to be like you. So the intersectionality is explicitly important and I think probably harder to reach today than it might have been before all of these special interests that we've all been put in began to define who we were.

MS: It's funny, because I just happen to have in front of me an interview I recently did with psychologist Carol Gilligan, and she had this quote: "The rule of older white men is patriarchal—it's not democratic. This election is the key, and why the Republicans didn't anticipate the outcome, is they didn't see women, people of color, young people—these are all the catego- ries that are dis-empowered in a patriarchal view. That's what the fight is about. It goes to the core of what I see as feminism, which is the movement to free democracy from patriarchy." Do you have any thoughts on that?

EHN: Yeah, I certainly agree with that. I tend to be more political—using the 2010 election as an example. They didn't think that these groups would come out [to vote]. They looked at the poor economy—as far as women and people of color were concerned, it was still poor. And I think that Romney even [admitted] that he was so late to concede because after the 2010 election, when the Republicans won the House, their pre-election models said that particularly people of color, but also women, wouldn't bother to vote, but their base of white men and to a lesser extent white married women, those people vote. Republicans underestimated how deeply people of color felt. And remember, all these groups had been attacked. Women had been attacked in the worst way, as to their reproductive health; Hispanics were maligned in the Republican primary; and blacks would just be on the back of some bus if you would have listened to some Republicans. So part of what happened in the last presidential election may not be repeated according to whether we are able to continue to motivate people to vote. Because it's true that the base of the Democratic Party is less likely to vote than the base of the Republican Party. So if you don't have Barack Obama on the ballot and you don't have flame-throwing retrograde Republicans on the other side, you have to ask yourself, will you get the same response from women and people of color? And our job is to make sure we do and not to assume that we've crossed the river and it's always going to happen.

MS: You have always seemed to have this innate sense of self and this courage to know your calling and to be pretty fearless about just speaking out for what you believe in. Was that something that came naturally to you or that you had to learn or develop? Where does that come from in you?

EHN: I had a head start being the oldest of three girls. And I've only come to this understanding, certainly a long time after I was grown, after this played out in my life . . . I think that gave me a head start. But remember, I went to law school when very few women or blacks went, so I've got to think that that had something to do with it. But I have to tell you that reinforcement whenever I did something good had a lot to do with it. Reinforcement for having good grades, for achieving things large and small, had a great deal to do with it. I wonder if we reward girls as easily as we do boys.

MS: On the flip side, what limiting obstacles did you face that you had to overcome and how did you overcome them?

EHN: I have no idea. I don't even think of my life in terms of obstacles. You know, the fact that I was born in a city that had no democratic govern-ment—I mean, we had no local government, no democracy. Or that I was a black child that went to segregated schools, because the D.C. schools were segregated until the '54 decision. Or that I was a woman. I have never con-sidered any of those things to be obstacles [*laughs*]. They're the things that give you fight. I just think if you sit down and count the obstacles, you're counting yourself out. I didn't think I had any obstacles. I just had to do it.

MS: That's a great answer. President Carter appointed you to serve as the first woman to chair the U.S. Equal Opportunity Employment Commission. How significant was that at the time?

EHN: At the time, it was [significant], but if you look at it today, nobody even takes a whimper at it. At the time, it was very significant. Not only because it was the Equal Opportunity Employment Commission, but because there were so few women in high positions in government. I recall no cabinet officials in that administration; there may have been women cabinet officials, but I can't remember who they were. This agency is not a cabinet agency, but it was a very high profile agency at a time when women didn't have anything approaching equality. It mattered to me, largely because I had wanted to be a civil rights attorney all my life and because I had been in the streets protesting to get precisely this commission without even a dream that I would one day lead it.

MS: If you had the ear of all the women and girls today, what's the mes-sage you think is most important that you would want them to hear?

EHN: I would just say, "Your time has come, your time has come,"—that's what I would say. "Just grab it."

MS: What does that look like, "your time has come"? What does that mean?

EHN: It means the bases are cleared. You can step up onto them. That's what I would say, not that there are still a thousand things for women to do before they can become elected officials or anything else.

MS: Are you feeling optimistic?

EHN: Oh sure, because I have studied history. It does take a long time, if you're as impatient as I am, for the obvious to happen. I could not afford to be pessimistic. When I was young, I couldn't understand why people weren't in the streets protesting racial segregation. Now I understand. I came to consciousness when it was possible to get into the streets, and even then, it took a woman sitting down and risking everything on a bus in, of all places, Montgomery, Alabama, to strike the spark that led to the non-violent civil rights movement.

★ ★

AS YOU REACH UP, PLEASE REACH OUT

★ ★

I think that it is very important for women to help each other. It is hard to be the only woman in the room. Having a support system is very important. When I was in office, I had a group of women foreign ministers that were my friends throughout the world, and my little saying is that there's a special place in hell for women who don't help each other. So I think there has to be the sense that once you have climbed the ladder of success, that you don't push it away from the building—you are only strengthened if there are more women.

—MADELEINE ALBRIGHT, FIRST FEMALE U.S. SECRETARY OF STATE

I'm probably the only person that's going to say this: I have trouble with some of the events that I go to that congratulate women, give them opportunities to network, leverage the power that they have, to have more power. I feel they could do more and I feel they need to do more, because what we're asking disenfranchised women to do is a lot more with fewer resources. I would like women in power in this country to do a lot more than they're doing to help others. It doesn't make me feel that great to go to events which are just about "them" getting more resources to climb . . . I would say to women, "As you reach up, please reach out."

—ANNA DEAVERE SMITH

I always think it's important for communities to join forces . . . You know, you hear everybody talk about the importance of being a part of a network, a part of knowing that there are women out there who are thinking like you and moving like you and organizing like you, and who understand what you're going through . . . Ram Dass talks about the illusion of aloneness, and I think that's what we all sometimes fall into, as women, as people of color, as educators, as organizers—this illusion that we're trying to do this all alone or that we'll never make a difference. Coming together is what allows us to keep moving forward.

—KERRY WASHINGTON

Sisters: talk to each other, be connected and informed, form women's circles, share your stories, work together, and take risks. Together we are invincible.

—ISABEL ALLENDE

I advocate that every woman be a part of a circle and a circle that meets at least once a month, or if you can't do that, once every two months or every four months. But you have to have a circle, a group of women—smart, wise, can-do women—who are in the world doing their work, and you need to meet with them as often as you can, so that they can see what you're doing and who you are, and you can see the same. And you can talk to each other about the world and about your lives in a circle of trust and safety. It's crucial. It is crucial for our psychological health and our spiritual growth. It's essential.

—ALICE WALKER

Be a sister—reach out to other women, ask for help when you need it. Women are very inclined to isolate ourselves and to feel like we have to solve our own problems alone, but we don't. Have the courage to put the issues out on the table if we see an injustice, if we see something that needs to be fixed. Have the courage to put it out there, because almost always, there will be other people who have that point of view, too, but they haven't had the courage to talk about it . . . Because there's great joy in joining together with other people to make something big happen. Huge joy. Even to make something small happen. But it's the joining together that gives you the joy.

—GLORIA FELDT, AUTHOR AND FORMER PRESIDENT OF
PLANNED PARENTHOOD

MARIE WILSON

"The first thing I thought about after I had worked on The White House Project for a few years was this: how are we going to get women to trust themselves, and how are we going to get the world to trust women? But how women can trust themselves, Marianne, I know now: we start to form groups. This is what The White House Project trained everybody to do, which is get a circle around you. And I say this in every speech: all women need about five women who really see them—who will give them good feedback, tell them the truth, and who will encourage them and give them courage to trust themselves and trust those values that are different. Because it's hard, when the world keeps shoving this other stuff at you, to really trust that the way you see the world is okay. So you have to have that. I think every woman needs that. I need that, don't you?"

MARIE WILSON HAS created and led women's organizations for almost forty years. She is founder and president emerita of The White House Project, creator of Take Our Daughters to Work Day, and author of *Closing the Leadership Gap: Why Women Can and Must Help Run the World.*

In 1998, Wilson founded The White House Project to build a truly representative democracy where women lead alongside men in all sectors. For fourteen years, The White House Project educated and trained thousands of women in how to run for office and changed how women in politics were represented in popular culture and the media. Wilson is an honorary founder of the Ms. Foundation for Women, where she was president for nearly two decades and where she pioneered a microenterprise for low-income women.

Wilson has been profiled in *The New York Times* "Public Lives" column and *O, The Oprah Magazine,* and she has appeared on *The Today Show, Good Morning America,* CNN, National Public Radio and other national programs. She has received several honorary doctorates. Wilson has five children and ten grandchildren. She lives in New York City.

MARIANNE SCHNALL: Why do you think it is that we've not had a woman president so far?

MARIE WILSON: In the most general terms, it has to do with the deeply unchanged culture in America, which has not changed since women entered the work force. The role of wife and mother is still the primary role that women have been in and that women are seen in. Even the First Lady is often seen as the Madonna, you know, if she tries to take on something, as Hillary found out and Michelle Obama has learned from. It's why Kathleen Hall Jamieson told us when we started our work, Marianne, that you have to change the conversation around women and around the presidency, as well.

But there are the questions that have to do with where our presidents come from: they come from the governors and we don't have enough female governors; they come from Congress and we don't have enough women in Congress. We don't have enough women in power for it to be normal for women to be president. The primary thing we are dealing with,

I think, is the culture's perception of where women belong. While slowly changing, it is still [prevalent] all over the country, keeping women out of leadership and in their roles.

So it's a cultural issue that I think people have a hard time grasping. And I think some of it is that there's a denial that women haven't achieved upper positions. People do think that we just haven't had a woman president because one hasn't come along. It eludes Americans—they think that women are in the pipelines, that women are everywhere. If you ask people how many women actually are in a governorship, for example, they would think they're half the governors of this country, because there's such a denial that we as Americans don't put women in power. There's this assumption that women are already there. So I think it's some of culture and some of this, "Well, they just haven't come along." It's very frustrating, but it's the same thing that happens with women at the CEO level, with women on the boards, because America is really in denial about the lack of women who are in the pipelines or any of these top leadership positions in the country. I swear, it's one of the big things that holds us back.

MS: The other more general question is, what do you think it will take to make a woman president?

MW: Well, having said all that, I think if Hillary ran today, she might win. I think it's interesting. I think what has changed is you've had women in the secretary of state role that is so visible and you've had Hillary particularly doing so well in this last four years. I think it will be a wild and fervent "we want change" kind of move—and that's not anything speaking but my gut. I think there's a real possibility, quite frankly, that Hillary Clinton will run in four years and that she will win.

MS: What special qualities do you think a woman president would bring to the table that the world most needs now?

MW: There's been a lot of research on that in terms of what women bring, but what we know is, by and large, their on-the-ground approach to war and peace. Also, women have a real propensity for collaboration and when they're in government—if you look at the legislature anywhere else—we know from research that women are more apt to work across the aisle, which is desperately needed right now.

   Plus, women have the experience of the private world, which is getting more and more important because you need to have people who understand what goes on with children right now, people who understand poverty and its effect on children and education. And women have that experience—education is women's top issue. Women understand the value of education. They have more compassion for the poorest people in this country, who happen to be women, right? That is going to be a real issue. And women have recently brought things to the table that we are now dealing with, with Elizabeth Warren and other women who called attention to the issues we are having in our economy long before the men would pay attention. Women are still calling out those issues. But I think the polls have shifted— you can't pick up a poll lately without seeing that women do a better job on so many issues and are trusted by the American people now on almost every issue that is a part of the presidency, at the same level as a man.

MS: What are some of the factors that you think deter women from entering the political pipeline in the first place?

MW: Well, there's a big deterrent in terms of how you have to raise money. And now it's even worse, because of the Supreme Court decision. First of all, we learned at The White House Project that because it's not normal to see women in power and leadership—and certainly in governorships, et cetera—that they again are not as comfortable saying, "I can do that." Therefore, we need to train women. I've been saying lately that maybe we should train every woman to run when she's in high school. I do believe that. Because if women are trained, then they will run because they want the experience. There are lots of ways to make women more visible.

There's even neuroscience now, telling us that 80 percent of our brains are gendered, and what women bring—because of the way the brain is structured—is this affinity to see the bigger picture and to ask more questions, and men tend to go straight to the solution. We can see what's happened with not having both perspectives, and I think right now women's perspective of looking at the whole picture before you make the decision is really important. We can always get guys in there who will say, "Now is the time to move," but we can't get as many guys in there who have the kind of brain that says, "Wait a minute, I want to see every way this will play itself out." We are seeing actually in the board meetings—the more women who get on boards—the guys on the board say the women get in there and they're not just interested in being right, they're trying to help with what the right thing is to do. So these attributes that rest both in what we now know about our brains and that come from being in the private world—because women have had to think long term, they've had to look at all of the factors in order to be in leadership at all—those are now coming to the fore.

I got tickled when the *Harvard Business Review,* about a month ago, these guys that have been studying leadership for years, came out with this "astounding" thing—ha!—and they published it in the *HBR,* on sixteen of the most important characteristics of leadership. They were talking about company presidents and how women are better, and they're like, "Look at this! Why aren't we putting women in?" When you get somebody like Warren Buffett standing up all the time and saying we're never going to make it if we don't use all our resources, particularly those of women.

You've got thought leaders now talking about this. So you know you've got research, you've got thought leaders. And now you've got two or three television programs on at once! We worked like mad to get *Commander in Chief* for six weeks! Now you have the *Veep* program. There are all these visualizations of women in leadership now—these make a difference. I like to watch all these programs that show women in these tough roles—as spies or detectives or even the president—because I see when other people watch them it shapes what they can't see in their own community. So I know you're right about your timing of this book, because I think this is moving in the right direction. And most important of all, because we've had these secretaries of state, because there are women in leadership positions in other countries, because we now know that wars are not going to be won the way we've been fighting them, we are looking for some of the ways that women are liable to deal with . . . with not blowing our world up, let's put it that way.

MS: Now it's funny, because I remember when I had first decided to do this book, and I had gotten an email from Gloria and she made the point that she thought I could do it because I understood that from a tactical point of view, it's not about biology, but about the issues. For example, it's not just about electing any woman, but a woman who actually represents pro-women principles and causes. How do you feel about the whole conundrum of having women in politics who aren't progressive when it comes to women's issues?

MW: Yes, it has to be that you get the right values. You have to have women who support those issues that allow other women to lead and bring other women along—issues that raise women out of poverty, make sure that women are safe and able to control their reproduction, and to have access to childcare. You have to have women who want full lives and lead in both the public and the private world for women and men, or you'll never change things.

MS: The other part of the issue is how can we help women learn to trust and value and use their natural wisdom and instincts so they're not just perpetuating the old paradigms of power and leadership? How can we embody the "feminine" qualities that we bring to the table, which often-times are not associated with being powerful?

MW: Well, that's the issue, isn't it? That's the first thing I thought about after I had worked on The White House Project for a few years was this: how are we going to get women to trust themselves, and how are we going to get the world to trust women? But how women can trust themselves, Marianne, I know now: we start to form groups. This is what The White House Project trained everybody to do, which is get a circle around you. And I say this in every speech: all women need about five women who really see them—who will give them good feedback, tell them the truth, and who will encourage them and give them courage to trust themselves and trust those values that are different. Because it's hard, when the world keeps shoving this other stuff at you, to really trust that the way you see the world is okay. So you have to have that. I think every woman needs that. I need that, don't you?

MS: Absolutely! You made that comment about starting leadership training for girls in high school; I remember in the film *Miss Representation* when Caroline Heldman made this point: "When children are seven years old, boys and girls say they want to become president in roughly the same num-bers. By the time they're fifteen however, the number of girls who say they would like to be president drops off dramatically, as compared to boys." Why do you think that happens and what can we do to change that trend?

MW: Well, that's what Take Our Daughters to Work Day and *Mother Daughter Revolution* were about. The more powerful women get, the more the world intervenes at pre-adolescence to say, "Guess what? You are going to be judged by your body." I'm looking at my feisty eight-year-old granddaughter and seeing how much the world is coming in on this confident, brilliant little girl—about her hair, about how she looks. And that is actually still at the very top right now, because if you look at adult women, they're wearing little skirts like little girls. I kind of disagree with some of the stuff that's been written and done lately about girls, because girls are not mean—they mean to have power. But when the country, the culture, the people around them keep talking about how you get power one way, which is to be a good girl—to look good and to be good—then it's hard to keep the idea that you could be a tough little president. That's the stuff they worked on for years at the Ms. Foundation: How do you keep girls strong and healthy? How do you sustain girls' resilience? And frankly, the more power women get, the more it starts coming at them. I think that's starting to change. But I think we have to remember that culture keeps coming back at you and pushing it in the other direction.

The good news is to remember that little boys want something different. We have grown men now actually doing different kinds of jobs, wanting to be parents. A recent poll showed that 63 percent of working men and women who have children under eighteen would trade more income for more time to be with their families.

MS: When I did that CNN article about what will it take to make a woman president, out of all the reflections that were shared in that piece, the one that people were intrigued by the most was what Gloria Steinem said: "In the last election I supported Hillary Clinton, because I thought she was simply the most experienced, but I felt it was too soon for a woman to win and that may still be the case, even though she transformed people's ideals.

Because we are raised by women, and so we associate women with childhood. Men especially may feel regressed when they see a powerful woman. The last time they saw one they were eight. So one of the most hopeful things we can do in the long term, is to make sure that kids have loving and nurturing male figures, as well as female figures, and authoritative and expert female figures, as well as male figures."

MW: Well, I think that's what's happening. You do see more men in these roles now. I read an interesting interview about men who are college educated, and they're starting to take caregiver jobs because of the economy, and they're saying things like, "Wow, you get paid to have good, meaningful work." I do think that when we value the work that has been largely unpaid and underpaid—mothering, domestic workers, caring for young and old—then the role of women will not just be the role of mother. It will start to have more value. And, yeah, Gloria's right—the last time you saw a powerful woman was when you were eight years old. The most powerful woman in your life is a mother. Elizabeth Debold—who was first author on our book *Mother Daughter Revolution: From Good Girls to Great Women*—talks eloquently about how boys are immediately cut off from the person who they are most dependent on: their mother. It takes a "superhero" to cut off the person who is nurturing you and be told not to be like her. It's so tough on little boys.

MS: There's this recent clip—Hillary was just recently interviewed by somebody who asked her "which designers of clothes do you prefer?" and she just looked at him dead in the face and said, "Would you ever ask a man that question?" It's so amazing that even as secretary of state that women are subjected to that. Women seem to have to walk that line between being too girly or too masculine, because women who are ambitious and powerful and speak their minds are often portrayed as "bitches" or anti-male—all these negative, unattractive things that are still associated with powerful women oftentimes holds women back because there is that backlash.

MW: That was the original backlash. At The White House Project we decided to work with, how can you be tough and caring? How can you bring yourself to the table? We did tons of research on that—we did it across party, we did it in focus groups, we worked on it like mad. And it really surprised me that what you're saying was true. But I'm just saying, I think we've come some place and that Hillary helped us get there. Because women don't want to be put in either of those categories. You look at somebody like Janet Napolitano. She comes across as tough. But people love her! Men and women love her. So there are some people who have done a good job of that. I think there's more flexibility for that now.

MS: Going back to Hillary's run—you would have thought there would have been momentum from that, to move women farther along, and yet I think at one point last year the number of women in Congress actually went down. Does that concern you? Do you see progress being made that's tangible?

MW: Oh, for God's sake, yes, but it didn't have to do with Hillary. It has to do with all kinds of things. When The White House Project started going into states and training women to even run for the positions that lead Congress, people were like, "We have a training program that trains twenty women." Come on. We are so far behind. That's why The White House Project trained 100 at a time. We can't do it unless we have tons of women running. Now we have more women running than we've ever had this year, right? So that's good. But you can't get there without having numbers of women put in the pipeline. The problem with women is, again, how much money it takes and we have no childcare. We've trained enough women to hear all of their objections. They don't like the climate. They don't like what's going on in politics. It's gotten even worse in terms of its lack of cooperative work and ability to get things done. Women don't want to waste their time. I think that's a huge problem right now, when you've got these kind of races, with this division and the nastiness that's going on. That really makes it hard. And when you don't see enough women there and you know that you're going to have to deal with these issues, because they do come up when there aren't enough women. It is a hostile climate. And we haven't had a national childcare period in forty years. What do you do with your freakin' children? It's so outrageous.

MS: You're such a wealth of knowledge and wisdom on this. I remember seeing the statistics in *Miss Representation,* and this was also in your book, about how we are ninetieth in the world in terms of women in national legislatures. Obviously, there are many other countries who have already elected female heads of state. What do they know that we don't? How is it possible that we're supposed to be the most progressive nation and yet here we are lagging so far behind?

MW: Well, first of all, they don't have winner-take-all elections. In most of the countries that have elected women leaders, women in power are parliamentary, so they run as part of a party and if they win, the women that are up there get to go in. Winner-take-all elections are deadly. And second, they're willing to establish quotas. Because we are living the big lie that this is a meritocracy. The biggest lie in America is that America is a fair country, that it's a meritocracy, that our institutions are meritocracies—they are not! So quotas are seen as affirmative action! That's why we are so far down, because these countries have quotas. Women are also so scared of quotas in this country. White men are a quota, really! That's what it comes down to. And so, the reasons are the winner-take-all elections and the fact that we won't establish quotas. That's how those women got in.

MS: How symbolic would it be to have a woman as president? What would that milestone mean for women and the world? Is it similar in the way that electing Barack Obama was?

MW: Yes. We did focus groups before we ever started The White House Project with all kinds of women and they would say, "Oh my God, having a woman president would change my life every day, because seeing somebody like that, at that level, particularly someone who represents and shares our values—someone who is moving other women along and is connected to women and is not trying to be man enough for the job—that will change how we see women as CEOs, that will change how we see women in daily life. I would feel more respected every day." And I think that's the bottom line: it would bring a great deal of what women in this country are seeking, which is real respect, because we don't really respect mothers, right?

MS: I know you've written books on all this, but if you had a magic wand, are there things that you would want to see immediately changed to make it a more realistic possibility? Are there things that we could be doing right now?

MW: There are things that we could be doing right now, but the most important thing is that we could actually change the way we do money and politics. If we could change the money, I think we could change things fairly soon. Because women would run. Get a real movement around national childcare, change the money in politics, and I think one of the things we could do is to change the way we do our voting to really make every vote count, like the FairVote organization, founded by Rob Richie. You have instant run-off and other ways that you count votes, so it isn't just winner-take-all elections. There are things that could be done to give outsiders a better chance. You can vote one, two, three—priority voting. Those are big ways to change. If you really started to say the way you run for office in this country is not about money. You can't raise money. You get so much money from the government or whatever and quotas would do it right away. Admitting that we're not a meritocracy and we are eager to have diversity and that we believe in research would help, and then we could say diversity means better government, and so we are going to make sure that we get a diverse government. There are ways it could happen.

★ ★

WOMEN OF POWER

★ ★

Get over the feeling that the two words don't go together—women and power. The fact is, if we don't put the two together and don't understand how power changes complexion in the hands of women, then we're not going to make it.

— JANE FONDA

It is all about women taking their power and asserting it. And that sort of goes back to the original question, why do we not have a woman president? It's because if women actually made it their mission to make that happen, they could. So I think power is something you have to take and use. It's just not given to you. I've been an organizer my entire life. The only thing you get is what you fight for and nothing more. I come out of an activist tradition and just believe that, and every day we have to push forward. Don't be patient and don't wait for someone to ask you and don't think everyone's going to like you, because if you're not pissing someone off, you're probably not doing your job! And that's how change happens, because people are bold and audacious . . . We've just got to be willing to make more people uncomfortable and push for the power that we deserve. I think it's happening, and I feel enormously hopeful.

— CECILE RICHARDS, PRESIDENT OF PLANNED PARENTHOOD

I believe if women believe that they can be free, that they can have a voice, that they can do whatever they want, and that they have the right and the mandate to fight for it, anything can happen. But part of it is breaking through our own sense of limitation and our fear that if we step forward, people won't like us. And I think that's the main thing we really have to break through—our own sense of limitations, what's been programmed into us, because that programming is very powerful.

— EVE ENSLER

I think the world is really hungering for women of power.

— ALICE WALKER

I am amazed by the strength of women. And the more they are being put down, the stronger they are. Women's strength just never ceases to amaze me and to inspire me.

—DIANE VON FURSTENBERG

Women resist embracing power because we have that old narrative in our heads that power means having power over, and that's a very negative connotation. And it's for good reason, because women have been discriminated against, women have been beaten and raped, and power over us has been very unpleasant. So there's a good reason for that. There's also a risk in changing any power relationship . . . You may risk losing your spouse. You may risk losing the love of people in your family who are important to you if you change yourself. But the risk of not making that change, in my view, is greater than the risk of making it. The risk of not making that change means that we will be stuck forever in this world where we are struggling just to have a fair shot!

If we shift how we're thinking about power from that old-fashioned, patriarchal, hierarchical, traditional power over to the expansive, innovative, infinite power to, it just changes everything. And it allows women who have been resisting taking powerful positions to take those positions. It frees us from the old strictures that have been in our minds. It's like, "Who wants to be one of those old, white, male politicians?" Right? That's what a lot of young women say: "I don't see myself in that picture." Well, change the picture. It's your picture. It's your turn. Put yourself in the picture, because the people who make the laws are the people who decide how you're going to be able to live. You have a vested interest in this.

—GLORIA FELDT, AUTHOR AND FORMER PRESIDENT OF PLANNED PARENTHOOD

KAY BAILEY HUTCHISON

"I do think that women are uniquely qualified for leadership. And I think that it is very rewarding to make a difference—to do something that you know makes a difference in quality of life is the reward. There's a lot that's hard about public service, there's no question about it. But it's very rewarding to have an impact, and I really think that is something that women should step up to the plate and do."

K AY BAILEY HUTCHISON is a regarded businesswoman and public servant with more than forty years of experience in the public and private sectors. She represents clients in banking, energy, transportation, telecommunications, and public policy.

Hutchison spent more than two decades as a public servant. In January 2013, she stepped down from her seat in the United States Senate. As a U.S. senator, she served in the Senate leadership, having first been elected vice chairman of the Republican Conference and later elected chairman of the Republican Policy Committee, the fourth-highest ranking Republican senator. Hutchison served as the ranking member on the Senate Committee on Commerce, Science and Transportation and the Appropriations Subcommittee for Commerce, Justice, and Science. She was also the chairman of the Military Construction Appropriations Subcommittee and served on the Defense Appropriations Subcommittee. In addition, the senator served as chairman of the Board of Visitors at the U.S. Military

Academy at West Point. She is the author of several books celebrating women who have broken barriers, including *American Heroines: The Spirited Women Who Shaped Our Country, Leading Ladies: American Trailblazers,* and her most recent book, *Unflinching Courage: Pioneering Women Who Shaped Texas.*

MARIANNE SCHNALL: Why do you think we've not yet had a woman president? What do you think it will take to make that happen?

KAY BAILEY HUTCHISON: I think that from my experience, early on, women running for elective office had to prove that they could do a job— that they could be effective, that they could represent the populace of whatever their district was—and there was a proving ground. I know when I was first running, everyone assumed that I would be weak, that all women were liberal, and I would say I was conservative, but then I would end up being weak and not voting for what I said that I believed in. And I think now that we have had women serve, be effective, have the same résumés and experience that men have—I think we're on the cusp of having a woman president, I do. And I think that Barack Obama had experience, and he had the guts to try, even before it was clear that he would be a serious contender. I mean, when you think that he challenged Hillary Clinton, that was pretty bold, and yet he took that chance, and we've got to have the woman who will take a chance and have the experience to show credibility and move on.

MS: There are certain pressures and stereotypes around women leaders that I've been hearing a lot in my interviews. On one hand, you can't appear to be too soft, because you have to appear like you're tough enough to handle certain situations that you might be confronted by in that position, but on the other side, sometimes there's also negativity that comes from women being perceived as too tough or too ambitious or powerful. As a woman leader yourself, were you aware of this? Did you feel like you could just be yourself? Did you feel the weight of some of these stereotypes and pressures, and do you think it's getting better or easier in terms of the public perception of women as leaders?

KBH: Oh, yes. I've gone from it being a disadvantage to, in reelection to the Senate, it being sort of a neutral. And then today, I think women have an advantage. So, yes, I think it's changing and, yes, in the early stages I think you had to show toughness. But today I think you can be yourself. People want what women have the advantage in, and that is integrity and honesty and sincerity and their willingness to listen as well as act. So I think that it was an obstacle to overcome just what your demeanor was, but now I think you can be yourself. I think we have some women who are tough, and some who are more soft on the outside, but firm. And I think you can kind of be what you are.

MS: That's certainly good to hear. With this last election there was a lot of talk about how history-making it was—in the sense that we do have this record number of women—and yet it's obviously far from parity. Why do you think there still is that lack of equal representation in Washington, and what do you think we can do to change that?

KBH: Well, it's going to happen naturally, because I believe that now women have the credentials, they have the stepping-stone experience, and I think that it's equalizing out. You know, maybe it's not quite there yet, but now it's just getting the candidates to come forward. And I think more and more are, as we see. When I came to the Senate, there were seven, then nine, and then it just grew and grew, and I think it's going to continue to grow and grow, because I really do think now it's an advantage. I think it's women believing that it's their time and they're ready. So I think every year it's going to get better.

MS: Sometimes this gets framed as just equality for equality's sake, but why is it important that we have women's voices represented in Washington and in leadership?

KBH: It's important because in a legislative body, you need the variety of life experiences. And I learned this when I was in the state Legislature and when I was in the Senate. In the state Legislature, I passed a bill for the fair treatment of rape victims. And when we got the bill to the floor, the men weren't against it, they had just never had the experience of the unfairness of the judicial system for rape victims. And we then passed a law that became the model in America, because every state was lacking in fair treatment. There was a different standard. And our law became a model. When I got to the Senate, I teamed with Barbara Mikulski for the Hutchison/ Mikulski bill that was The Homemaker IRA, and it was because of an experience I had: I was single, I started an IRA; I got married and couldn't contribute the same amount to my IRA. They allowed $250 for a spouse, which is, I mean, you might as well not do it. And yet you could put aside $2,500 if you had a job. And I said, no way is it [fair]—women who work inside the home should have the same retirement opportunities that women who work outside the home have. Nobody was against it—it was just that they never thought of it before. They'd never had the experience. So in a legislative body, you need the variety of experience to be able to represent the variety of the people.

MS: That's such an important point that often gets lost, because sometimes this is viewed as a women's issue, when it really is something that affects families and the whole of humanity. Your name has come up, not only as one of the most admired women leaders, but even as somebody who could have been a potential presidential candidate. Is that something that you envision, or have ever envisioned, for yourself as a possible path?

KBH: Oh, I had, in the past. But when George Bush was elected from Texas, for two terms, I felt like there would probably not be an opportunity for another Texan right after that, so my time was just not the right time. And now I've got twelve-year-old children and I'm not thinking about it at all. But there was a time when I did, and I would like to have had that opportunity, but president Bush was elected. And I even thought if he didn't run a second time, that would still be an option, but he did, so that was that.

MS: Do you think we will see a woman president in your lifetime? Do you feel optimistic about that?

KBH: Yes, I do. I think we will. I think we've got the women in the pipeline now, in both parties, frankly.

MS: Many women may feel discouraged to pursue this as a career, because it does look pretty daunting—both just the experience of running and from some of the dysfunction they see in Washington today, it can seem very challenging. What would you say to them? You had a very long and successful career—why should women consider this and what are the special rewards or fulfillment that comes from a career in public service?

KBH: I do think that women are uniquely qualified for leadership. And I think that it is very rewarding to make a difference—to do something that you know makes a difference in quality of life *is* the reward. There's a lot that's hard about public service, there's no question about it. But it's very rewarding to have an impact, and I really think that is something that women should step up to the plate and do, if they can financially, and if it's right for their family and their time. I just hope we have more and more.

MS: I've spoken to quite a few congresswomen for this project. What I really love to hear about is the bonding that goes on between the women in Washington, regardless of their political affiliation. What was your experience like working with the other women that were there, and did you have a sense of feeling like a minority or was that something that didn't really affect your experience?

KBH: When you are such a small part out of 100, when you're seven or nine, there's an adjustment on the other senators' part and on your part. And I would say that because you are an equal and you have an equal vote and you're part of the same committees and everything is done on seniority, there's no discrimination at all, but you tend to gravitate to the people with whom you have the most in common. And the women certainly had great relationships and we'd have bipartisan dinners together on a routine basis, and that was fun. But I think in the actual functioning of the Senate, that your vote is the same. And now we've got women committee chairs and we have for quite a few years, and when you're the committee chairman or you're the ranking member, your power is the same as the male person with whom you're dealing.

MS: I've been very moved by the fact that you've written all these books, including your most recent book, that are meant to celebrate the accomplishments of women that inspire you. I'm very aware, even in my girls' education, of the lack of focus on women's history or women historical figures in general. Did you feel that there was a real need to spotlight women like this? What was your motivation behind doing these projects?

KBH: The motivation was to show girls that women have had obstacles in America from the beginning, but they've overcome the obstacles and have paved the way for the following generations to excel and fulfill their potential. And I felt like the biographies are written about our Founding Fathers, but you don't find much about Abigail Adams and the Founding Mothers, who did so much. I wanted the record to show the women who broke the barriers and how far we've come. And in my books, I've highlighted the women who broke the barriers, but also the contemporary women. In my first one, it was so much fun, because in the areas where I profiled a barrier-breaking woman, I could interview the women still breaking barriers in the same field. So Amelia Earhart in aviation—I interviewed Sally Ride, the first woman in space. And I profiled Margaret Chase Smith and then interviewed Madeleine Albright and Sandra Day O'Connor and Condoleezza Rice. So we all have stood on the shoulders of those who came before. And that's why I think we have the women senators and governors and CEOs in business. I think a lot of it is seeing that progression in the way that it's done and that there's so much potential. If you're just willing to hang in there and be tough and follow your dreams with commitment and courage, you can do anything.

MS: I think that's so important, this idea of just admitting that sometimes there are obstacles, or barriers, and that no matter what your story is, there are things that you have to transcend. On your journey, were there limiting obstacles that you faced that you had to overcome?

KBH: Oh, yeah [*laughs*]. My first office was in 1972 when I was elected to the Texas Legislature, and I was the first Republican woman elected to the

Texas Legislature, ever, so I had to prove myself. I had to overcome the obstacles just to get elected, and that process was hard. And it was tough, but I hung in there and took that first step. Then there was no statewide elected Republican in Texas when I ran for state treasurer; there had been a governor and a senator, but never a lieutenant governor or an attorney general or a state treasurer. And I ran anyway, and won. And so that was another barrier. So, you know, all those barriers, and now no one thinks that it's unusual that there are a number of Republican women in the state legislature. And we have statewide office holders and it's no big deal. That's what I want: for it to be no big deal.

MS: In the course of these interviews, people sometimes raise the remarkable fact that it was not too long ago that women did not even have the right to vote, which still seems sort of mind blowing. Where do you feel we are in terms of the status of women here in the United States and around the world?

KBH: Oh, I think that America is the greatest place in the world to be a woman. I think we've had the respect from the beginning. We saw it in Alexis de Tocqueville's America that the respect that women had, even back in the early 1800s, was there. Women were dealt with as equals. Their opinions were listened to, which he observed was different from the European women that he had been around. So we've had the respect from the beginning. We didn't have the vote, which is hard to believe now, but our women had built on the respect, on the capability. They were running businesses, they were becoming a part of government. I think that maybe it was too slow, but it was a continuing progression forward. And I think that we are now accepted as equals; I think we have the capability to be judged on merit and without discrimination.

MS: What words of encouragement or advice would you want to offer a young woman thinking about running for office or pursuing a career in public service today?

KBH: My advice is to get enough experience before you get into politics, as opposed to running too young and before you know what you really believe. Know what you care about and have a firm political philosophy. You just have to have experience in the real world to be effective in representing people, because you need to understand the economics, you need to understand what role government should have and what it shouldn't have. And if you experience the regulatory arena, if you have seen a problem in education that you care about, or the building of urban areas— whatever your issue is, it should come from experience in the real world.

NOTE TO READERS

The expanded ebook edition of *What Will It Take to Make a Woman President* includes nineteen additional interviews with the following notable names: Amy Richards, Carol Gilligan, Carol Jenkins, Cathy McMorris Rodgers, Cecile Richards, Celinda Lake, Courtney E. Martin, Diane von Fürstenberg, Eleanor Smeal, Gloria Feldt, Ileana Ros-Lehtinen, Jody Williams, Julie Zeilinger, Marsha Blackburn, Mary Matalin, Rachel Simmons, Robin Morgan, Sandra Fluke, and Stephanie Schriock. Visit womanpresidentbook.com for details on the ebook and other updates, resources, and information.

ACKNOWLEDGMENTS

IF ONE OF the lessons to come out of this book is that women need support systems to succeed, this book is a testimony to that. I simply could not have done this work without my team. First off, there was my wonderful literary agent, Tracy Brown, who not only was the one who encouraged me to do this book, but mentored me through the process and became my biggest advocate—and allowed me to bounce everything off him—constantly offering me helpful and thoughtful feedback, advice, and suggestions. More than that, he is just a very special person, warm and smart and so caring—I am so thankful to have had his guidance for this book and beyond.

I also have to thank my tireless transcriber Helene Rodgville—not only did she transcribe nearly fifty interviews in less than six months (often after a hard day's work herself), she would frequently share her personal reflections and reactions to the interviews with me. Since Helene was often the first person to hear these interviews (she also had the unique privilege of hearing the audio and their voices), it was so gratifying to know she was enjoying the interviews and being affected by them.

And I must extend special thanks to Angela Joshi for her enormous contribution to this project from beginning to end. Angela was the editor on my first book, *Daring to Be Ourselves*, and she did such a great job on that project and was such a joy to work with that I knew I wanted to work with her again on this book. She did the first pass on editing the transcripts of the interviews, improving them with her insightful comments, clarifications, questions, or tweaks. Angela is a brilliant editor and such a good-hearted and insightful person and I always love working with her.

The next person I have to thank is my husband Tom Kay—not only did he constantly provide ideas, feedback, and suggestions, but his support in helping take care of our children made this book possible. Whether it was his taking the kids to get frozen yogurt after school as I awaited a call from a congresswoman or delivering yet another tape to the post office to be sent to the transcriber, he helped me as much as he was able. He is not only my soul mate but also a very loving and involved father to our two daughters.

I also want to deeply thank and express appreciation for the whole team at Seal Press—especially Krista Lyons, who believed in this book from the start, and Laura Mazer, who picked up this project midway through and served as the book's master steward and editor and whose encouragement and valuable feedback were vital. I have such enormous respect and admiration for the work Seal does and it was the perfect home for this project.

And a special thank you to the amazing people who granted interviews to me for this book. I am so humbled by the support I received from so many influential and inspiring people doing such incredible and important work in the world. All the people I interviewed seemed to care so much about this theme and the book's objective—and so many of the people I interviewed offered suggestions, contacts, or just generally cheered me on, which really meant the world to me. Their belief and support in this project sustained me as I became bleary-eyed towards the end when I would often do two to three interviews a day.

I also have to thank my wonderful parents, Carol and Norman Schnall—their support and enrichment has shaped and nurtured me in so many important and meaningful ways. My mother's story is inspiring in itself—she was one of the few female executives in a male-dominated industry and has served as a role model to me. As for my father, I was so blessed that he never made me feel like there was *anything* I could not do, quite the contrary he always encouraged and supported me. In addition, I want to thank my multi-talented, generous hearted, beautiful brother, Eric Schnall. He knows me better than anyone and has always been there for me. I am so happy to have him as my brother and friend.

And I must express my love and thanks to all my women friends—I am so blessed to have such extraordinary women in my life—all the love, laughter, encouragement, and advice I receive from you all continues to nourish, strengthen, and sustain me. And I also want to thank three exceptional women, all forces of nature, who have served as such important mentors and personal inspirations to me: Eve Ensler, Pat Mitchell, and Gloria Steinem.

Lastly, I want to thank my personal inspiration for this project, my extraordinary daughters, Jazmin and Lotus. I feel so grateful and proud to be your mother and love you so much. This book is dedicated to you and all the magnificent girls on this planet: May you deeply know and feel your worth, value your unique and important voice and vision, and believe in your heart that you can do and be anything—but also know that it is less about what you *do* and more about *being* fearlessly, gloriously all that you already are.

ABOUT THE AUTHOR

MARIANNE SCHNALL IS the founder and executive director of Feminist. com, a leading women's website and nonprofit organization, and the cofounder of EcoMall. com, one of the oldest environmental websites promoting earth-friendly living.

She is also a widely published writer and interviewer. Schnall's work has appeared in publications such as *O, The Oprah Magazine, Glamour, In Style, The Huffington Post,* Women's Media Center, CNN. com, *Ms. Magazine,* EW.com, and *Psychology Today*. She is a regular contributor to WAMC's nationally syndicated show *51% The Women's Perspective,* which is carried nationally on NPR, ABC, and Armed Forces Radio stations. She is also the author of *Daring to Be Ourselves: Influential Women Share Insights on Courage, Happiness, and Finding Your Own Voice* based on her interviews with a diversity of well known women.

A graduate of Cornell University, she also consults regularly with nonprofits and activists on optimizing their online impact. Visit her at marianneschnall.com.

SELECTED TITLES FROM SEAL PRESS

★ ★

No Excuses: 9 Ways Women Can Change How We Think about Power, by Gloria Feldt. $18.00, 978-1-58005-388-4. From the boardroom to the bedroom, public office to personal relationships, feminist icon Gloria Feldt offers women the tools they need to walk through the doors of opportunity and achieve parity with men.

A Thousand Sisters: My Journey into the Worst Place on Earth to Be a Woman, by Lisa Shannon, foreword by Zainab Salbi. $16.95, 978-1-58005-359-4. Through her inspiring story of turning what started as a solo 30-mile run to raise money for Congolese women into a national organization, Run for Congo Women, Lisa Shannon sounds a deeply moving call to action for each person to find in them the thing that brings meaning to a wounded world.

Full Frontal Feminism: A Young Woman's Guide to Why Feminism Matters, by Jessica Valenti. $15.95, 978-1-58005-201-6. A sassy and in-your-face look at contemporary feminism for women of all ages.

Beyond Belief: The Secret Lives of Women in Extreme Religions, edited by Cami Ostman and Susan Tive. $16.00, 978-1-58005-442-3. The rarely told perspectives of women from more than ten different religions showcase the difficulties of navigating women's roles in these strict (and sometimes radical) faiths.

A Little F'd Up: Why Feminism Is Not a Dirty Word, by Julie Zeilinger. $16.00, 978-1-58005-371-6. A wry, witty overview of feminism's past and present from the creator of FBomb, the popular feminist blog for young people.

Fast Times in Palestine: A Love Affair with a Homeless Homeland, by Pamela Olson. $16.00, 978-1-58005-482-9. A powerful, deeply moving account of the time Pamela Olson spent in Palestine—both the daily events that are universal to us all (house parties, concerts, barbecues, and weddings) as well as the violence, trauma, and political tensions that are particular to the country.

Find Seal Press Online
www.SealPress.com
www.Facebook.com/SealPress
Twitter: @SealPress